Mean Streets

Mean Streets

HOMELESSNESS, PUBLIC SPACE,
AND THE LIMITS OF CAPITAL

DON MITCHELL

THE UNIVERSITY OF GEORGIA PRESS
Athens

© 2020 by the University of Georgia Press
Athens, Georgia 30602
www.ugapress.org
All rights reserved
Set in 10/12.5 Minion 3 by Kaelin Chappell Broaddus

Most University of Georgia Press titles are
available from popular e-book vendors.

Printed digitally

Library of Congress Cataloging-in-Publication Data

Names: Mitchell, Don, 1961– author.
Title: Mean streets : homelessness, public space, and the limits of capital / Don Mitchell.
Description: Athens : The University of Georgia Press, [2020] | Series: Geographies of
    justice and social transformation; 47 | Includes bibliographical references and index.
Identifiers: LCCN 2019032948 | ISBN 9780820356891 (hardback) | ISBN 9780820356907
    (paperback) | ISBN 9780820356914 (ebook)
Subjects: LCSH: Homelessness—United States. | Public spaces—United States. | Urban
    policy—United States.
Classification: LCC HV4505 .M58 2020 | DDC 362.5/920973—dc23
LC record available at https://lccn.loc.gov/2019032948

CONTENTS

PREFACE

Mean Streets is the culmination of thirty years of researching and thinking about homelessness and public space in the American city. It brings together as a single, sustained argument a theory of the social and economic logic behind the historical development, evolution, and especially persistence of homelessness in the contemporary city—and how that persistence is fundamentally related to the way capital works in the urban built environment, and thus to the structure, function, meaning, use, and governance of urban public space. Yet while I argue that the problem of homelessness is at the root of many cities' ongoing efforts at public space management, these efforts, and especially their effects, extend well beyond the lives of homeless people (as important as those lives are in and of themselves). In a word, the problem of homelessness in the American city is the problem of the American city: what it is, who it is for, what it does, and why it matters. And the problem of the American city is epitomized in public space.

A generation of research has shown that the "publicness" in public space is hardly self-evident. But digging into *that* question is not the point of this book.[1] Rather, I take for granted that publicly accessible spaces of some sort, spaces within which public actions are possible, and spaces in which varied publics form, are both necessary to and a problem for capitalism (as a fully *social* system), and most particularly for the circulation and accumulation of capital (as a specific mode of historically evolved and determinant economic practice).* Public spaces are necessary to capitalism and capital circulation for a number of reasons, not only because (obviously) commonly accessible spaces for the movement of goods, people, information, and so forth are necessary if capitalist production and social reproduction (including the reproduction of the cap-

---

*All these key terms here get worked out in the pages that follow. But to avoid misinterpretation, let me right away define "determinant" or "to determine." I mean these in the sense developed by Raymond Williams. To determine is to set limits and exert pressure, and thus a determinant process is one that limits what is possible and puts on pressure to move in a particular direction. "Determine," then, is not a mechanical term but a dialectical one that always requires deep historical analyses to discover what the limits are (and how they are set) and the nature of the pressure exerted. See Williams, *Marxism and Literature*.

italist workforce) are to occur—that is, if there is going to be an economy at all. They are also necessary if there is going to be society at all. Humans are ineluctably social. We *must* share: ideas, companionship, pleasures, distrust and disgust, things, *space*. While Margaret Thatcher may have believed that there is no such thing as society, only individuals and families, no one else does. But, of course, *how* we share—how we meet and even live in common—is a fully historical and social question, not a natural result of our ineluctable or innate needs, just as the boundary between public and private is fully historical and social (privacy—the ability to absent oneself or one's family from the exposure of publicity—is just as ineluctable as is the need to be public).*

This is why public space is a problem for capitalism even as it is a necessity. For neither capitalism (again as a fully social system) nor the demands of capital circulation and accumulation can ever fully determine public space's production, use, or meaning. These are always struggled over. Indeed, what public space is, and what it becomes, is, as I argue throughout *Mean Streets*, both a result and an essential ingredient in *class* struggle within capitalism. That struggle and the spaces and practices that result in turn structure just what capitalism is—and what the patterns of capital circulation and accumulation in the built environment, as well as the modes of sociability possible, not only are, but can be. The problem of public space is thus a problem of the *limits* to capital: the limits of what it is possible for capital to do, socially and economically, as well as the limits to what capitalism can be as a system that organizes our social reproduction and whatever well-being (or not) that may entail. Quite obviously, capitalists want and need to shape public space in their own interests (to support smooth accumulation of more capital, to allow for the easy circulation of goods, to promote consumption so that the value in all that is produced can be "realized" and returned back to their hands, and sometimes just to provide space for their own pleasure, because they too must be social, somehow), but they do not always get their way. Public space *is* a class struggle. And in this struggle, while the capitalist class may not always get what it needs or wants, it *must*, broadly, get quite a lot of it, if capitalism is to not reach *its* limit.†

To determine is to set limits and exert pressures (see the first footnote), and

* Public spaces play many roles in the capitalist city (including, perhaps especially, strongly affecting property values), and many of these will be discussed in the pages that follow, but these roles are not *necessary* (in the sense used above) to capitalism and capital circulation, as the functions of providing space for movement and sociability are.

† In both some of my phrasing here and the invocation of the limits to capital, I am, of course, invoking the work on capital circulation in the built environment (and indeed much else) by David Harvey, which, as the following chapters will amply evidence, has been deeply influential. Equally influential has been Harvey's distinction between capital, as a political economic process with a central and necessary, if historically determined and evolving, logic, and capitalism, as a total social system rooted in and determined by that political economic process. Harvey, *Limits to Capital* and *Seventeen Contradictions*.

in this sense public space—and class struggle in and over it—determines (or, rather, is a determinant of) the nature of capitalism. It defines capitalism's limits. Yet class struggle has many facets, and so in this book I also show that homelessness *is* (also) class struggle, and one that determines what capitalism is and how capital circulates and accumulates. Homelessness too sets limits and exerts pressures. One of the things capital produces (ever more efficiently, it seems), as it circulates in and out of factories and other value-producing arenas, in and out of the built environment of the city and countryside, in and out of capitalists' and workers' hands, is homelessness. It has always done so: as chapter 1 shows, homelessness was there right at capitalism's birth and made it possible. While the shape and structure of homelessness, its precise role in social divisions of labor, and its status as a particular kind of problem for society have shifted and transformed historically and geographically over capitalism's long history, its *necessity* to capitalism as a social system reliant on the circulation and accumulation of capital has never disappeared. Nor can it ever disappear. Without homelessness there will be no capitalism.*

But what does it mean to say that homelessness *is* class struggle? Part 1 of *Mean Streets* seeks to answer that question—and to show that *how* it is class struggle is highly determinant not only of what public space is (and thus what the limits to capitalism in the city are) but also of the nature of social life for those who are conventionally housed, an argument more fully developed in part 2. In short, however, to say that homelessness is class struggle is to make a few basic points. First, homeless people compose a class in capitalism, and we forget that to our analytical and political peril. The nature and specific role of this class in capitalism, like the nature of homelessness itself, are historically and geographically variable. Second, and *therefore*, homelessness is *not* an attribute of individuals (as we too often think of it) but is rather a condition of society. Third, and perhaps counterintuitively (but nonetheless fully logically), homelessness is *not* a status of shelterlessness, at least not foundationally, but is rather both an effect and a determinant of the circulation of capital and the divisions of labor it requires. Shelterlessness (or houselessness, as many homeless activists and their advocates now call it) is an epiphenomenal form of deeper structural processes, for, as we will see, homeless people have historically, and not infrequently, been sheltered and even housed. Indeed, in the current moment the majority of homeless people in the United States have regular access to shelter, as crappy as it may be. In fact, at this epiphenomenal level, homelessness is precisely a *form* of sheltering in capitalism, just as much as are suburban

---

* This is not at all to say that overthrowing capitalism will automatically solve the problem of houselessness among some portion of the population—it did not in any of the state socialist societies that emerged after the Russian Revolution—but rather that homelessness plays an inescapable, foundational, and necessary role in capitalism; it is neither contingent nor epiphenomenal, but constitutive.

tract homes, tiny studios and bedsits, or luxury condos in towering skyscrapers. These deeper structural processes are (at the risk of repetition but also to foreshadow a main argument of the book) the dynamics of capital circulation and accumulation that require impoverishment of a significant, and growing, number of people in order to function at all, and an *ever* growing number of impoverished people to function well. And finally, given that homeless people form a class, defined not by their attributes but by their structural position in society, and that this structural position is determined by and necessary to the circulation and accumulation of capital, homelessness is class struggle not only because people indeed fight over what it is and what it means, but especially because the capitalist class (and *its* advocates) knows exactly what would be at stake if homelessness were to be abolished: its own successful reproduction as a class.

These are strong claims, but I think the pages that follow bear them out. Even so, it is probably worth making as clear as possible what these pages do and do *not* do. They do not focus on homeless people—*Mean Streets* is not a book about "the homeless"—though they do show to some degree what it means to survive right at the limits of capital. I do not focus on homeless people both because there already exist plenty of excellent ethnographic accounts of homeless people by scholars far better at undertaking such work than I could ever be,[2] as well as a growing library of excellent memoires, autobiographies, and oral histories by homeless people themselves,[3] and because my point is precisely to show homelessness is a *structural* condition of capitalist society. This is important politically.

If we constantly define homelessness as a set of individual attributes (usually such things as mental illness and substance abuse problems, sometimes such things as poor education or vulnerability to—or being victims of—abuse, every once in a while to the status of not having a permanent place to live), we might be able to intervene in people's lives, which of course can be vitally important,* but we will never be able to address the *fact* of homelessness in capitalism, much less its actual causes. We will never be able to create a politics adequate to the task of winning the class war that is homelessness. So this is not a book about "the homeless"—you will find precious little here about the lives of homeless people (though you will find much too much about their deaths, for the class war of homelessness is a deadly war)—and it is not (directly) a book about "homelessness" as a housing question (though you will find plenty on how the dynamics of housing is deeply entwined with the production of homelessness through capital circulation and accumulation).

In *Mean Streets*, I seek rather to develop an analysis that provides a basis, or at least an orientation, for political struggle. But yet another thing the book is *not*, then, is a book of false political optimism. History does not permit this. And

---

*Though also quite fraught. So deep is our sense that homelessness is a problem of individuals with severe problems, like alcoholism of mental illness, that even *housing* programs, like Housing First, are explicitly designed and sold to policy makers as *treatment* programs.

if nothing else, *Mean Streets* is a historical account. Or more accurately, I have written it as a historical geography of the present, an attempt to describe and explain the present landscape of capitalism, as seen through the conjoined struggles over homelessness and public space, as that landscape has evolved out of the past. I may not present a politically optimistic analysis, but neither do I present a politically naïve one, that is, an analysis rooted in an ontology of pure immanence as are so many works that seek, for example, to celebrate the commons as the antidote to capitalism. Such works tend to be not just historically ignorant (of, for example, just what the commons *has been* and therefore what it *is* and *can be*),[4] but especially, militantly *antihistorical*. In other words, my goal at every turn, even when speaking of the most current issues, has been to root my analysis in its historical and geographical context—that is, not just to root it in some idealist immanence, but to root it in reality as it has historically evolved.

For this reason *Mean Streets* ranges widely, from early "anti-homeless laws" in Bern, Switzerland, in the late fifteenth century to an appeals court chamber in Portland, Oregon, in the late summer of 2018. Some chapters, like chapters 2 and 3, which examine ways in which homelessness becomes an *overt* class struggle (it is usually covert), are deeply historical, but nonetheless vital for understanding the present moment. Others, like chapter 4 and all of part 2, do not dig as deeply back in time (stretching only into the 1990s) but are nonetheless historical in approach and method, always seeking to explain what happened, why it happened the way it did, and therefore what it meant at the time and what it means now. Only in this way can we begin to draw a complete and especially a logical picture of what homelessness is and of how public space is both necessary to and a problem for capitalism, and especially of the vitally important relationship between these two—the structural nature of homelessness and the problematic necessity of public space—in shaping capitalism as a fully social system, and the circulation and accumulation of capital as a specific mode of historically evolved and determinant economic practice.

And yet in all of part 2 of the book, homelessness (as such) is not the main focus, though public space is. This is because, I argue, the struggles over the relationship between homelessness and public space within capitalism are decisive for what public space is and how it is regulated and policed for society as a whole, the majority of which is housed. This decisiveness is not simple but in fact highly complex, historically, geographically, and in social practice. Obviously public space is governed differently for different classes (as much as the ideology of publicness, especially in America, might assert otherwise), and homeless people are at the blunt end of the club of law, to say nothing of the police, far more frequently than are the housed. But so too are people of color at the blunt end more than white people, and working-class people more than middle- or upper-class people. One of the tasks of both parts of the book is to examine this club of law—how it is wielded, and against whom, not forgetting those times when it might be wrapped in velvet. To do so I take seriously E. P. Thompson's injunction that law saturates all of social practice, that it never "keeps politely to a level," but is "at *every* bloody level," and, perhaps, especially that "it afford[s] an arena for class struggle, within which alternative notions of law [are] fought out."[5] Law saturates this book, from the first page to the last—it is on *every* bloody page—and the degree to which it is an arena for class struggle should become obvious. And it is precisely this that provides the rationale for part 2. If I have done my job well, then the way in which mean streets—streets that are *legally* mean—have metastasized (as I put it) matters for how the class struggle will unfold in the future. If the commonality of the forces shaping public space—and thus the nature of social life—can be recognized, then maybe the commonality of struggles (rather than their intra-class distinctions) can be too. I do not provide a clear map of these commonalities, but I do provide a basis on which one can begin to be drawn. One of these bases is the court of law.

That is why the recent decision in Portland to strike down (for now) Boise, Idaho's, anti-camping ordinance (chapter 1) is every bit as important as is the Supreme Court's 2003 decision to ban people like Kevin Hicks—primarily young black men—from many city streets altogether (chapter 6). It is why Denver's attempt to outlaw street speaking by "footloose" Industrial Workers of the World members (the homeless of their day) (chapter 2) is every bit as vital for understanding the limits of capital as is Minneapolis's attempt in 2006 to ban all "strangers" from the city's alleyways (chapters 4 and 7) or Las Vegas's attempt the same year to prohibit the sharing of food with poor people in public spaces (chapter 4). And it is why recent attempts across urban America to create highly regulated and controlled, nearly imprisoning, official homeless encampments (when they cannot abolish them altogether) (chapter 3) are every bit as vital to structuring a social life and form of political engagement suitable to contemporary capitalism's reproduction (chapter 5) as is the more general social process of inducing social acceptance for what can fairly be called a form of socially authoritarian governance of public space through the steady cultivation of public paranoia (chapter 7).

□ □ □

As has been indicated, *Mean Streets* is divided into two parts.* Part 1 begins by laying out two rather contrasting moments in recent homelessness history in the United States: on the one hand, the assertion by the Obama administration's Department of Justice, in a case working its way through the courts, that Boi-

* Some readers will find that many of the arguments, examples, and analyses are familiar. As I have said, this book is a culmination of thirty years of research and thinking. More immediately, *Mean Streets* is based on a series of essays I have written over the past two decades (see the acknowledgments), but in each case I have rewritten them to cut redundancies, to update as necessary, and, especially, to push forward a single, if multistrand, argument. I trust not only that there is a coherent logic to what follows, but also that the total is considerably more than the sum of its parts.

se's anti-camping ordinance was a form of cruel and unusual punishment (a position with which a federal Appeals Court recently agreed); and on the other hand, the brutal killing of Charly Keunang, known as Africa, a black homeless man living on the streets of LA's Skid Row. These two contrasting cases define the scope of the class struggle that *is* homelessness at the moment. But to see how requires four things. First, it requires a deep (if nonetheless still too abbreviated) history of homelessness from its roots in the birth of European capitalism to its present manifestation in the United States. Second, and in relation to this historical geography, it requires a theory of how capital circulates in and through the built environment of cities and countryside. Third, it requires an examination of how these first two—the historical geography of homelessness and the patterns of the circulation of capital—shape and are shaped by public space. Finally, then, it requires an understanding of why and how law (at every bloody level), regulation, and policing of public space come together to *determine* how the class war that is homelessness unfolds in the contemporary city.

Chapter 1 lays out this historical geography and theorization. Chapters 2 through 4 then deepen and exemplify the analysis, both historically and empirically. Chapter 2 reaches back to the early twentieth century and examines a moment of overt class war centered on footloose IWWs seeking to gain control of Denver's city streets so they could gain control over central parts of the Intermountain West's political economy. Pushing the history of homeless people's organizing both back (to the 1870s) and forward (into the present), chapter 3 examines the importance of homeless people *occupying* space, particularly in homeless encampments, to press their demands—and also just to live—and city authorities' often violent response to the homeless organizing and visibility that results. Chapter 4 is largely contemporary and examines how, but also and especially why, cities have increasingly sought to criminalize survival altogether. So ends part 1.

As is typical when working with deeply historical work and working through historical methods, many of the theoretical threads woven together in chapter 1 come slightly undone under the tugging forces of real historical processes, and so before turning to part 2, I offer a brief theoretical (but still historically and empirically inflected) interlude focusing particularly on the political economy of public space in the city.* The point is to revisit, revise, and extend the theoretical arguments about the circulation and accumulation of capital in the built environment first broached in chapter 1 as well as to set up the book's turn more specifically to questions of public space *itself* in part 2. The goal is to better under-

---

*Some readers might yearn for this fuller theoretical argument to come earlier, but I think otherwise. The theoretical arguments made in the interlude become explicable precisely because of the "tugging forces of real historical processes." That is to say, the first four chapters of the book together paint a picture of the historical geography of homelessness that will then allow readers to better *see* the broader, more general theoretical arguments made in the interlude.

stand how what has beset homeless people as they have been the targets on one front of the larger class war of which they are a part is coming for everyone else too, if, however, with decidedly uneven effects, including the very important effect that some large number of people *also* benefit from strategies *primarily* designed to benefit a quite narrow set of class interests (namely, the interest of circulating and accumulating capital in the built environment). Or, to put all this more simply, if what defines the streets in part 1 is a decided *meanness* (a meanness that is not mere spite, but especially a *strategy*), then part 2 shows that this meanness is *metastasizing*. It has metastasized right through the body of the city but is, perhaps, most malignant in urban public spaces.

Working through a series of court cases, seemingly unrelated to capitalism as a fully social system (much less capital circulation in the built environment as a particular political-economic process), chapter 5 examines how laws of public space, and especially those regulating protest in it, are helping to construct a kind of subject—or more accurately for capitalist democracies, a kind of citizen—most appropriate to the demands of capitalist production and reproduction: what Marx called the "purely atomic" individual. Chapter 5 concludes by returning to the question of homeless people in public space, but the main point of the chapter is precisely to move beyond only issues of homelessness to better understand how struggles over law are class struggles that are dialectically entwined—as they are with the production of homelessness—with the very reproduction of capitalism in the city. A focus on law continues in chapter 6, which examines the curious case of Kevin Hicks, arrested for trying to bring diapers to his baby and spend time with his girlfriend, who lived in a Richmond, Virginia, public housing project. Through this case, property—what it is, how it functions—has been significantly reworked. In the process a key solution to the *problem* of public space in the contemporary city has been offered, a solution that seeks to recognize the necessity of commonly accessible space while ensuring that such accessibility is on highly regimented terms. In a world where de jure *apartheid* (itself a solution to the problem of public space) is no longer socially possible, the strange case of Kevin Hicks show how it is created *de facto* anyway. Chapter 7 serves as something of a conclusion. Focusing on the rising importance of the policing of trespass law as it relates to publicly accessible space (a matter also central to chapter 6) and rooting the analysis in an argument about the productive importance of induced paranoia as a governance strategy, the chapter returns to an argument implicit in part 1, explicit in the interlude, and central to the analysis (if largely behind the scenes) in part 2: an argument about how homelessness as class struggle and mean streets metastasized are two aspects of a more general struggle over the production of *abstract space*—space abstracted out of its particularity and made fully commensurable; that is, the true space of capitalism—in the capitalist city. If capitalism has a goal, an end, then it is the full abstraction of space, the complete remaking of space into commensurable or exchangeable space, the total reduction of space into *only* a commodity—a commodity that embodies value that expands, circulates, and is "realized," allowing for ever more accumulation.

And that's where we end: right at the limits of capital (and capitalism). As Henri Lefebvre long ago recognized, if space becomes *fully* abstract, capitalism cannot survive.[6] It cannot survive because, in fact, capitalism requires difference. And so, as Lefebvre also argued, it is *only* the class struggle (broadly defined to include innumerable other forms of otherness) that keeps abstract space from "papering over" the world. In other words, homelessness (as class struggle and class war) is both a necessity and a problem for capitalism in a way it never fully intends (or can control): *homelessness* itself constructs difference, or more accurately differentiated space, and thus saves capitalism from itself. *It* is what we must pin our political and social hopes on if we want to ensure that mean streets—another name for abstract space—do not *completely* metastasize and kill us all.

Mean Streets

PART 1

Homelessness as Class War

First and foremost, homelessness must be seen as a component, an extreme reflection, of general social, economic, and political patterns, not as an isolated problem, separate and apart.

—Peter Marcuse, "Neutralizing Homelessness" (1988)

CHAPTER 1

Boise, "Africa," and the Limits to Capital

Instead, the question asked by [Los Angeles Police] Chief Beck and by much of
the media was smaller. Meaner. "What did *this* man do to deserve to die?"

—Jeff Sharlet, "The Invisible Man" (2015)

In what at the time seemed a remarkable move, the U.S. Department of Justice under the Obama administration determined that anti-camping ordinances
in American cities, which targeted homeless people, were cruel. In August 2015
the department filed a "Statement of Interest" in a lawsuit in Boise, Idaho, supporting homeless people who claimed that the city's policy of citing and sometimes arresting them for sleeping in public violated the Eighth Amendment's
ban on "cruel and unusual punishment." In a press release announcing its action, the department suggested that "it should not be controversial that punishing conduct that is a universal and unavoidable consequence of being human"—
sleeping—"violates the Eighth Amendment. . . . Sleeping is a life-sustaining
activity—i.e. it must occur at some time and in some place. If a person literally has nowhere else to go, then enforcement of the anti-camping ordinance
against that person criminalizes her for being homeless."[1] Though fairly limited
in its scope, the department's Statement of Interest was important. It clearly announced, for the first time, that the U.S. government understood bans on sleeping and camping, at least in some circumstances, to be unconstitutional. (While
they are cruel, however, it stretches credulity to suggest they are unusual: such
bans now cover more than 35 percent of American cities.)[2] The statement read
like it could have been written by the lawyers at the National Law Center on
Homelessness and Poverty (NLCHP) or any number of advocates and critical
scholars who have been making just this case for thirty years.[3] The department's
intervention was a real victory in a very long struggle by homeless people and
their advocates and should be understood as such. It's important to get the state
on your side.

But it was only a small victory in a minor skirmish of a much larger war that continues, it seems, to go the other way. This part of the book examines just why, more than thirty years into the so-called crisis of homelessness in advanced capitalist cities, that is the case. Why is there a never-ending war on homeless people? What's at stake? Can, under current circumstances, the little victories represented by such acts as the Department of Justice's filing be built on to bring about a reversal in this war? In other words, the point of this book is to understand the *structural* (rather than the social-psychological or putatively cultural) forces shaping urban homelessness and its management, structural forces that are deeply rooted in the continually restructuring political economy of the city and particularly its public spaces. By focusing on the logics of capital circulation and accumulation, urban homelessness, social and political reactions to it, and attempts to regulate it all become explicable.

Mean Streets

Debates over how to manage homelessness and homeless people, and the political firestorms that inevitably accompany these debates, seem never to go away. The Department of Justice's intervention received little press coverage, but what it did receive was drowned out by much louder voices intent on vilifying homeless people as a root of all that is wrong with American cities. All that summer long, New York's tabloid press had been on a warpath against homeless people, publishing incendiary story after incendiary story about how the homeless were (once again) destroying New York's quality of life, illustrated most sensationally by a *New York Post* cover photo of a disheveled man with a blanket draped over his shoulders, urinating in a street, with the giant headline superimposed: "20 years of cleaning up New York City PISSED AWAY."[4] By the end of August former mayor Rudolph Giuliani weighed in, complaining about what he perceived as a declining quality of life in his Upper East Side neighborhood. "Do you know when people lived on the streets and didn't use bathrooms inside?" he asked. "It's called the Dark Ages." It was time, he said, for New York to return to the strategies his administration pioneered, which he summarized like this: "You chase 'em and you chase 'em and you chase 'em and either they get the treatment they need or you chase 'em out of the city."[5] Meanwhile, across the country, San Francisco mayor Ed Lee announced in mid-August that all the homeless people in his city "were going to have to leave" before the Super Bowl was held there the following February. He did not say how this was going to be accomplished, but the same article in which he was quoted also pointed out that it was a "contentious debate" in the city—the most expensive housing market in the country—as to whether it was worth it to "even bother trying" to find shelter for homeless people.*

* It will likely surprise no one to learn that Mayor Lee did not succeed in making homeless people leave the city, but he did manage to make life for many of them even more miserable than it had been

There might be a debate as to whether to find housing for homeless people, but there does not seem to be much of a debate at all—just a continuing firestorm—about whether to criminalize them, the Department of Justice's legal opinions notwithstanding. According to the NLCHP, the number of cities with citywide bans on camping in public places increased 60 percent between 2011 and 2014, while bans on sleeping in cars increased 119 percent over the same period. According to a 2010 study, 74 percent of sixteen hundred homeless people interviewed knew of no safe or legal place they could sleep in the town or city in which they resided. Nor was it easy for homeless people just to *be* in a city (much less eke out a living): already covering many more cities than the kind of camping ordinances the Department of Justice was interested in, anti-loitering ordinances (35 percent increase), sit-lie laws that ban sitting or lying down in public (43 percent increase), and anti-begging laws (25 percent increase) also expanded significantly. Nine percent of American cities make it a crime to share food in public with homeless people.*

Nor has intense enforcement of petty laws against homeless people—so called "quality-of-life" or "broken-windows" policing—abated, as homeless people are disproportionately cited for jaywalking, littering, talking back to police officers, refusing to move along, loitering, and more. Such citations often carry stiff fines that homeless people cannot afford, and when they do not pay them the citations are converted to arrest warrants. Los Angeles's Skid Row is paradigmatic. Pioneered in his first stint as police chief in New York City under Giuliani, William Bratton took "zero-tolerance" policing with him to Los Angeles's Skid Row (the largest concentration of homeless people in the United States) when he became chief of that city's police in 2002. Called the Safer Streets Initiative, Bratton's Los Angeles zero-tolerance policies outlasted his tenure (which ended in 2009), and the results are as shocking as they are typical of the state of homelessness in America. Over four months alone in 2006–2007 (the height of Bratton's reign), police arrested more than five thousand people on Skid Row;

---

in his attempts to sweep them into invisibility. See Sarah Nir, "San Francisco Firefighters Become Unintended Safety Net for the Homeless," *New York Times*, August 26, 2015, and the photo essay by Robert Gumpert, introduced by Rebecca Solnit, "Division Street."

*Over the 2011–2014 period, citywide bans on sleeping in public showed no increase, and bans on sleeping in particular places decreased by 34 percent. This is largely due to the fact that sleeping bans have frequently been thrown out as unconstitutional. Cities are replacing sleeping bans with camping bans. A 2016 report by NLCHP shows that cities' efforts to criminalize homelessness have continued to increase. Laws against camping in vehicles and loitering are growing the fastest, but increases are significant across the board (with the exception of bans on camping in particular places, which have decreased as laws banning camping citywide have rapidly grown). See National Law Center on Homelessness and Poverty, *Housing Not Handcuffs*, 10; NLCHP, *No Safe Place*; Western Regional Advocacy Project, *National Civil Rights Outreach Fact Sheet*, April 5, 2013; Jouvenal, "Cities v. the Homeless," *Washington Post*, June 3, 2016, A01.

in 2013, some 14 percent of all arrests made in the city were of homeless people. As George Lipsitz summarizes,

> These policies of aggressive policing purport to protect poor people from crime, but in most cases, the only criminal charges that emerge are the ones that the officers bring against the residents they claim to be protecting. Aggressive policing subjects houseless people to unprovoked abuse and undeserved humiliation. A survey among residents of Skid Row in 2009 found that 89.3 percent reported being stopped and questioned by police officers, 82.8 percent reported they had been arrested. Respondents expressed more fear of harassment by the police than fear of criminal acts by other residents, a fear borne out by statistics that reveal a higher frequency of police harassment (37 percent) than assault (24 percent) or robbery (18 percent). A 2010 survey revealed that more than 50 percent of respondents reported being arrested in the previous year and losing housing, social services, or jobs as a result.

Of the hundred million dollars Los Angeles spent from its general fund on homelessness in 2014, eighty-seven million went to the police. Half of those surveyed in 2009 reported being physically or verbally abused by the police as they were being cited or arrested for jaywalking, sleeping on the sidewalk, or other minor offenses.[6]

All this money thrown at the police and there is little to show for it but shattered lives. Perhaps inevitably the Los Angeles Police Department's aggressive policing of "quality-of-life" laws on Skid Row has led not to "safer streets" but to death. Since 2006 a court order has restrained the LAPD from enforcing the city's anti-camping ordinance if not enough shelter beds are available—the judge's ruling essentially hews exactly to the Eighth Amendment theory the Department of Justice advanced nine years later in Boise—so police walk and cruise the streets before six o'clock each morning, ordering homeless people to get up, pack up their tents, cardboard shelters, and belongings, and get moving. Houseless residents are allowed to return after nine o'clock in the evening. The morning roustabout is a source of frequent annoyance and confrontation, and the symbolism couldn't be clearer as homeless peoples' places on the sidewalks are soon taken by store and restaurant employees with power hoses, cleansing the streets before the rapidly growing number of higher—usually upper—income residents descend from their lofts (the number of low-income housing units in Skid Row has halved since Bratton introduced the Safer Cities Initiative in 2006, even as the population of the district has grown).[7] Where they are to go is not entirely clear since the fifty-block Skid Row is, officially for the police, a "homeless containment zone."

Just after noon, on March 1, 2015, four police officers shot six bullets—two of them at point-blank range—into Charly Keunang, known on the street as "Africa." Mr. Keunang was unarmed. Video from surveillance cameras, police body cameras, and bystanders shows Mr. Keunang repeatedly pleading with two officers to just "let me express myself." One—Officer Francisco Martinez—responded by saying, "We're going to do things my way," and threatening, several times, to Taser him. Mr. Keunang then crawled back into his tent, a tent that should have been long since packed away, and this seems to have set the cops off. "The man got shot over a tent," said a witness.[8] And while this is certainly true, the facts of the matter are, inevitably, more complex (one of Mr. Keunang's comrades on the street had called the police after a dispute). After Mr. Keunang crawled back into the tent, the officers ordered him out. As he emerged, Martinez Tased him, twice. Mr. Keunang whirled and spun, likely reacting to the voltage coursing through his body. Another officer, Joshua Volosgis punched him "in the facial area," as Volosgis told police investigators, and the two fell, entangled, to the ground. Volosgis yelled that Mr. Keunang had grabbed his gun—he had not; the gun remained holstered throughout—and a third officer Tased Mr. Keunang all over again. Seconds later the cops opened fire. Mr. Charly Keunang, Africa, lay dead, and the police immediately got to work vilifying him (he's a convicted bank robber; he's in the United States illegally—all these are meant to justify his murder).[9]

"What did *this* man do to deserve to die?" He was black. He was poor. He was homeless. Like Eric Garner in New York the previous July, another victim of Bratton's quality-of-life, zero-tolerance policing, Mr. Keunang talked back—or, rather, tried to explain himself—when confronted with yet another instance of police intimidation.* (Officer Martinez, widely reputed on Skid Row to be a tough, sometimes violent cop, a "hard-ass bitch cop," a "Napoleon cop," according to locals, was known by name to Mr. Keunang.)[10] He lived on the streets where even a court order putatively protecting him from "cruel and unusual punishment" was not enough to keep him alive, to keep him from being killed by the very cops charged with protecting him. "To Protect and to Serve," the official motto of the department, it says on the side of all the LAPD cop cars. But, "Hell no, they're not protecting me," as one Skid Row resident told a reporter after Africa was killed (and before his real name, Charly Keunang, was widely known). "They should erase that off the side of the car."[11] Who—or what—then are the police protecting? With whom does the law align, such that someone like Mr. Keunang seemed to *deserve* to die?

A small part of the answer lies back in Boise. Less than two months after the Department of Justice filed its Statement of Interest asking the court to find the city's anti-camping law unconstitutionally cruel, the judge threw the case out. By September 2015 only two plaintiffs remained standing, and the judge declared

---

* Eric Garner was choked to death by New York City police as they attempted to arrest him for selling untaxed cigarettes, a quintessential "broken-windows" offense. Before being grabbed and choked, Mr. Garner was heard saying he was tired of the constant harassment he received at the hands of the police.

that, in fact, they had no standing.* On the "merits," he declared, they had no reason, or right—"no standing" as it's called—to bring a suit against the city. No decision thus had to be made as to whether the city's laws were cruel and unconstitutional. This decision was a long time coming. The suit had begun back in 2009 when eight Boise residents sued the city, its police department, and others after they had been arrested under a 2006 law banning camping. Over the ensuing six years, six of the plaintiffs dropped out of the suit; that is, they died, found housing, or moved away. For them the law was moot, so they no longer had standing. Of the two remaining, one, Robert Martin, had moved to another town but came to Boise regularly to visit his minor child. When he did he sometimes stayed with friends, at a Budget Inn (paid for by the pro bono attorneys in the lawsuit), or in one of Boise's emergency shelters, of which the Boise River of Life Rescue Mission is the largest. Those who want to stay at the Rescue Mission for more than one or two nights are required to attend chapel services and meet other religious requirements. But short-term "guests" are not. The judge found that though Mr. Martin objected to the religion requirement, that requirement was not enforced on him and so there was no reason he could not stay at the shelter. Since he could stay at the Mission, the anti-camping ordinance posed no potential of "harm" or "injury" to Mr. Martin and thus he had no standing to bring a constitutional challenge.[12]

The second plaintiff, Robert Anderson, was likewise found not to have standing because at the time of his most recent deposition (spring 2015) he was living with a girlfriend, not on the streets, and in the previous four years (back to 2011) he had not been warned by the police about any violation of the anti-camping ordinance. After the deposition was taken Mr. Anderson became homeless again and sought shelter at the River of Life Mission. Like Mr. Martin, Mr. Anderson objected to the religious instruction at the River of Life, but as with Mr. Martin, the judge found that Mr. Anderson did not *have to* attend chapel services or otherwise subject himself to proselytizers, just so long as he did not attempt to avail himself of any services other than the temporary, emergency services. Anderson thus also lacked standing: he could not prove actual harm or the imminent potential for harm.[13]

The judge went further. He noted that in 2014 the city of Boise changed its anti-camping ordinance to make it unenforceable if no shelter beds were available, making it accord not only with the injunction in Los Angeles and several other cities, but seemingly with an argument that the NLCHP and other advocates had long been making: that anti-sleeping and anti-camping ordinances were unconstitutional *when* there was no other shelter available within a ju-

*As will shortly be discussed, this decision was overturned by the Ninth Circuit Federal Appeals Court in September 2018. Yet it is nonetheless worth looking at its logic in some detail as it fairly succinctly lays out the contours of America's mean streets (and court rooms), a logic that, though contested, shows no signs of being entirely superseded.

risdiction.[14] Boise seemed to be meeting this requirement. The judge had little comment on the provision of the law that shelter space shall be considered available if homeless individuals are turned away "due to *voluntary* actions such as intoxication, drug use, unruly behavior, or violation of shelter rules" (presumably including those regarding religious instruction).* He noted only in passing that Boise shelters limit the number of nights each month a person can stay in emergency shelter, indicating that it is procedure (rather than law) that considers shelter to be unavailable to a person who has exceeded length of stay requirements, and so this provision too posed no unconstitutional threat.[15] Even if Mr. Martin or Mr. Anderson had standing, the judge concluded, the issue was moot because now Boise met objective standards of constitutionality. Though he did not say it, the city seemed to already meet the requirements pushed for by the Department of Justice in its Statement of Interest.

Left unaddressed was the whole question of past harm. The earlier citations and arrests of Mr. Martin, Mr. Anderson, and the six other plaintiffs in the original case now just did not count. Whatever harm may have occurred at the time—whatever violation of civil rights, whatever cruel practices—simply was no longer of any concern.

But it was of concern to the Ninth Circuit Court of Appeals meeting in Portland, as was the fact that Boise only *seemed* to be meeting the requirements the Department of Justice—and its own law—laid out to ensure any anti-camping ordinance would not be cruel.[16] The Court of Appeals disputed the Boise judge on almost every ground. In the first place, it found that Martin and Anderson indeed retained standing in the case since it was well within the realm of possibility that they could still be cited or arrested under the Boise statute. Whereas the city claimed that the three shelters in the city never reported being at or beyond capacity, the Appeals Court pointed out that, first, the only basis the city had for assessing these claims was the shelters' own reports, and there was good evidence in the record that such reports were, charitably, inaccurate. More importantly, the court noted that "whether or not the [Boise Rescue Mission] facilities are ever full or turn homeless individuals away *for lack of space*, they *do* refuse to shelter homeless people who exhaust the number of days allotted by the facilities." All three shelters in the city have stringent limits on the number of consecutive days one may stay and on the number of days in a month one may stay, and the two shelters operated by Boise Rescue Mission refuse to readmit men within a month if they leave the shelter *before* the seventeen consecutive days they are allotted.[17] Even discounting the religious requirements (which the Appeals Court also found burdensome), Martin and Anderson were found on appeal to have standing because they "demonstrated a genuine issue of mate-

* It has long been understood among medical practitioners and even in law that intoxication among the addicted and alcoholic is not, in any simple sense, voluntary (see *Robinson v. California*, 370 U.S. 660 [1962]).

rial fact regarding whether they face a credible risk of prosecution under the ordinances in the future on a night when they have been denied access to Boise's
homeless shelters."[18] Working its way through a torturous set of precedents, the
Appeals Court next held that Martin and Anderson not only had standing but
had legitimate reasons to seek both retrospective relief (relief for past harm) and
prospective relief (guarantees not to be harmed in the future) under the Eighth
Amendment's bar on cruel and unusual punishment and thus, most straight-
forwardly, asked (and answered): "Does the Cruel and Unusual Punishments
Clause of the Eighth Amendment preclude the enforcement of a statute prohibiting sleeping outside against homeless individuals with no access to alternative
shelter? We hold that it does," and it does particularly because the anti-camping
ordinance punishes a *status* (being homeless) if under the guise of punishing an
act (camping), and on largely spatial grounds: Martin and Anderson had potentially no *place* in which they could meet basic bodily necessities, like sleeping.*
The court explicitly noted that there was significant evidence in the record that
the camping ordinance was in fact strictly enforced, even after Boise amended
it to make it unenforceable if shelters were full and noted that it was frequently
used against people merely sleeping, maybe with a blanket, but with no other
"indicia of camping" as the ordinance calls such things as tents, cooking equipment, and so forth, which the ordinance itself says is *required* for an act of camping to take place. That is to say, in practice the city seemed to be citing and arresting people merely for sleeping.[19] The Appeals Court thus held the law to be
unconstitutional, while albeit (for various technical reasons) *not* reversing the
local court's denial of retrospective relief to Anderson and in part to Martin.†

  Yet at the same time the court stated plainly, "Our holding is a narrow one."
Quoting a case called *Jones* (which in fact was at the root of the injunction in Los
Angeles requiring the city to permit camping if no shelter space is available), the
court made clear that "we in no way dictate to the City that it must provide sufficient shelter for the homeless, or allow anyone who wishes to sit, lie, or sleep on
the streets . . . at any time and at any place," only that if people are turned away
from shelter, they cannot be arrested for sleeping anyway.[20]

  Under these narrow circumstances, one thing becomes abundantly clear:
while homeless people have a right not to die (at least in those states within the
Ninth Circuit's jurisdiction), they have a very limited right to *be* in the city (the
Appeals Court, as it narrowed its holding, certainly made that clear enough);
their presence is, at best, suffered. How much they suffer for the sufferance of
the rest of us is a question of just how elastic the law can made to be, not as it

---

*Besides Boise's anti-camping ordinance, its disorderly conduct ordinance barred "'occupying, lodging, or sleeping in *any* building, structure or place, whether public or private' without permission."

†One of the judges dissented in this part of the decision, arguing that if the law was unconstitutional past convictions deserved redress. Otherwise the appeals panel was unanimous.

serves and protects the homeless, but as it serves to deflect the threat the homeless seem to pose to the city, to "safer streets." For the district judge in Boise, the question was not how to push the law to protect those made vulnerable in our cities, but a smaller one. A meaner one. How can homeless people get only what they *deserve* and no more? The question for the Appeals Court, with its narrow holding, was actually not much different, as large and important as the basic declaration that punishing people for sleeping is indeed cruel certainly is.

And what do homeless people deserve? Apparently not much—not much more than, *at best*, not being arrested or even killed simply for sleeping. After all, they are "unproductive" citizens, filling up sidewalks, streets, shelters, and temporary or transitional housing.[21] They are, many of them, unemployed. Some are addicted to drugs or alcohol. Some are mentally ill. Some are all these things. They are disproportionately black and increasingly (in some parts of the country) Hispanic. A good number have physical disabilities. A lot are old. Or they are kids. They might be queer. They use up social services: shelter beds, social workers' time, hospital care, free meals, police patience and tolerance. When they are on the streets, hanging out, sleeping, begging, waiting for admission to a mission, or scavenging bottles and cans for deposits, they deter housed residents, incoming loft buyers, restaurant patrons, entrepreneurs looking to upgrade the neighborhood, and the creative types who make a city exciting—or so we are told.[22] Some, the "chronic" 10 percent, use up so many services—including emergency medical and police services—that it is a cheaper management strategy to just give them a damn apartment and be done with it.[23] The rationale for Housing First policies around the country are less rooted in a right to housing than they are in a cost-benefit analysis of how best to keep the homeless off the streets and out of visibility.[24]

The question of deservedness—the distinction between the deserving and undeserving—has long been central to how we understand the poor, of course. The earliest poor laws in Europe were based in this distinction. Between 1481 and 1530 the Council of Bern passed a series of edicts expelling "non-citizens": gypsies, wayfaring paupers, pilgrims, and French-speaking beggars. But the "wandering poor" continued to besiege the city and grew increasingly difficult to differentiate from Bern's homegrown poor. In 1527, therefore, the council required all local paupers—the deserving poor—to wear identifying badges, and the city kept a master list of badge holders in hopes of preventing fraud. Bern was not alone in such practices. Jurisdictions across Europe grappled with what to do with the poor and the seemingly rootless, the growing number of people who seemed out of place, not properly tied to the town or feudal land, and who were thus undeserving. By the 1530s, for example, beggars in England were required to carry tickets identifying them as legitimate paupers.[25] And by the dawn of the seventeenth century the English Parliament embarked on a project of codifying poor laws across England and Wales (the Elizabethan Poor Laws), developing a system of indoor relief (such as almshouses) and outdoor relief (the provision of food or clothing) for the "impotent poor" (those unable to work) and either confinement in houses of correction or forced labor for those who could work. Organized at the parish level, English poor law retained the distinction between the locally tied and thus more deserving poor and the wandering poor: the vagrants and vagabonds who were feared because they were out of place, because they could be a drain on public funds, stretching charity beyond its means, and, especially, because they were "masterless men" who seemed to have broken the old, hierarchical bonds tying a community together.[26]

Though poor relief and the "correction" of masterless men were organized at the parish level, the explosive growth of such men—*and women*—during the sixteenth and seventeenth centuries, which simultaneously signaled the waning of an older order, demanded national-scale action, and thus launched, in the words of Zygmunt Bauman, an era of "feverish legislative activity," in which "new legal notions were defined, new areas of legitimate state interests and responsibility charted, new punitive and corrective measures invented." For Bauman, the vagrant, the masterless man, the new, dangerous classes, were the central figures behind the rise of the modern, capitalist state.[27]

The distinctions between deserving and undeserving, neighbor and stranger, placed and placeless, mastered and masterless—and the laws and "punitive and corrective measures" that gave these distinctions force—were imported to the New World and became vital to the slavery-based racial regimes of the colonies that would become the United States, while extending well beyond the slave economy. Colonial poor laws called for "pillorying, branding, flogging or ear cropping . . . those migrants who could not give 'a good and satisfactory accounting of their wandering up and down.'" Those white paupers who could give a good accounting were sentenced to hard labor at the workhouse, on the rock pile, or in the harvest. Others, those for whom there was no local sympathy, those who were the truly undeserving, were simply "warned out"—forced back on the road—an expedient made possible, and plausible, by vast expanses of "wilderness" (the perhaps hostile indigenous territory that still marked the continent). If caught, Black men and women were, of course, returned to their masters or sold on.[28]

The Limits to Capital

The distinction between deserving and undeserving locates pauperism, beggary, and homelessness *within* the individual, as a characteristic of that individual, even as it admits through the back door that such a characteristic might have a broader social cause (men are "masterless"). Understanding homelessness primarily as a characteristic of individuals (their disorderliness, their addictions, their unproductiveness, their color, their age, their mental illnesses, their sim-

ple cussedness) and only secondarily as a condition of society, which is the pre-
dominant way of understanding homelessness in America today—what was it
about "Africa" that *he* deserved to die?—thus has a long, if ignoble, history.[29] It's
also wrong, as it will be one of the burdens of this book to show. To do so, in this
chapters and others, I instead make a strong argument for understanding homelessness primarily as a condition of society, one rooted not in homeless people
but in a set of political and economic structures and practices—logics of capital
and of capitalism—contradictory, complex, and fully mediated by all manner of
cross-cutting currents as these may be.[30]

Modern homelessness is often understood (at least by critics of the dominant mode of understanding homelessness as an attribute of individuals) to be
a function of housing, and it is. But it is not *primarily* a function of housing, as
the long concern with "masterless men" and "dangerous classes" hints: it is primarily a function of how the capitalist political economy operates, of the logic of
capital accumulation and perhaps especially capital circulation in the built environment. Homelessness, or something like it (since, as we will see, homelessness
shifts shape historically), is a *necessary* product of capitalism as it has evolved.
Historically, homelessness becomes a *crisis* at moments of vast, and rapid, political economic transformation. Consider those paupers (French-speaking or
not) and "masterless men" besieging Bern and the towns of England. Where had
they come from? Why were they on the road? The short answer (to what is actually a very long history) is that they were thrown onto the road, uprooted from
the land, by the breakdown of the old feudal order and its stuttering replacement
with a capitalist one. As the U.S. Supreme Court intoned in a landmark 1972 decision voiding vagrancy laws for being too vague, this "history is an oftentold
tale."[31]

One of those who told it with verve, and of course great political and theoretical purpose, was Karl Marx in his discussion of "the so-called primitive accumulation," a discussion that focused primarily on England. "The capitalist system," he argued, "pre-supposes the complete separation of the labourers from all
property in the means by which they can realize their labour," which primarily
was the land. Potential laborers in a capitalist system had to be detached from
the land as well as from bonds to feudal masters; in order to be freed up and
their labor power eventually to be made available *for sale*, they had to become
"masterless." As fast as this transformation was, it was also long and drawn out,
and it was geographically uneven. Expropriation happened in fits and starts—
it's still ongoing—though the latter part of the fifteenth century and the first
decades of the sixteenth were particularly momentous, as a war-drained, older
nobility could put up little resistance to usurpation by a newer noble order en-
riching itself by turning arable land into sheep pasture to feed rapidly growing
Flemish woolen mills. Peasants were thrown off the land, divorced from both
their smallholdings and the common grazing lands and woods. On the road they

went. They were homeless because they were placeless, severed from their old roots, alienated.[32] The transformation was, in social terms, revolutionary and "legislation was terrified at this revolution," as Marx put it. The sixteenth century was thus a century of radical legal experimentation: Bauman's "feverish legislative activity." Much of the legislation was geared toward tying peasants back into the land, limiting the size of sheep herds (so as to spread wealth), and ensuring peasant self-sufficiency by requiring that every house be surrounded by four acres of arable land.[33]

But forceful expropriation continued apace, given special impetus by the Reformation and the "consequent spoliation of the church property" (and thus the eviction of the church's tenants) and the emptying of the monasteries, which swelled the ranks of the new proletariat. The era was a time of social convulsion. Legally tying peasants to the land did not work, in the midst of the revolutionary transformation of markets sparked in part by the dawning age of exploration and colonization and its attendant mercantilism. New legislation—the Elizabethan Poor Laws—thus targeted the poor directly, seeking (at least to a degree) to reestablish the norms of an older, fading order. Yet the men and women thrown off the land and onto the road "could not . . . suddenly adapt themselves to the discipline of their new condition. They were turned *en masse* into beggars, robbers, vagabonds, partly from inclination, in most cases from stress of circumstances. Hence at the end of the 15th and during the whole of the 16th century throughout western Europe a bloody legislation against vagabondage." An evolving, new mode of accumulation produced a new homelessness. Vagabonds, vagrants, robbers, and the like were the *effect* as well as a *presupposition for* this new mode of accumulation. The homeless, some of whom would become the "fathers of the present working-class" (who could now use their wages to rent or purchase housing, however insecurely), others of whom would form the core of the reserve army of labor, were there, necessarily, at the dawn of capitalism. This was Marx's essential theoretical and political point, for which there is a logical corollary: as long as there will be capitalism, there will also be capitalist homelessness.[34] Not only that, but this class of people made homeless by the very workings of the capitalist system will continue to grow, as we shall see.

But it will also, as noted, change form, as the "tramp scares" of postbellum America made clear. The era between the Civil War and World War I was a time of massive economic restructuring in America, marked (over the long term) by the transformation of a largely agrarian economy into an industrial one, the concomitant "closing" of the frontier, and the more thorough knitting together of the continent by the railroads, and punctuated (over the short term) by economic panic after economic panic, recession after recession, depression after depression (the years 1865–1867, 1869–1870, 1873–1879, 1882–1885, 1890–1891, 1893, 1896, 1899–1900, 1902–1904, 1907, 1910–1911, 1913–1914 all saw economic panic and recession; the 1873 and 1893 panics launched full-scale depressions, unsurpassed in scope and severity until the 1930s). Each of these panics, recessions, and depressions threw people out of work, led to farm foreclosures, and sent thousands of men and women onto the road in search of employment, many illegally riding the newly built railroads or otherwise "tramping." Economic crises created armies of "tramps," and, as a seemingly new phenomenon, they deeply frightened the more respectable classes. In an argument that would find an echo a hundred and seven years later (when a Fort Lauderdale City Council member recommended sprinkling rat poison in all dumpsters in the city as a means of ridding the city of its homeless people), the *Chicago Tribune* suggested in July 1877 that the "simplest plan, probably, where one is not a member of the humane society, is to put a little . . . arsenic in the meat and other supplies furnished the tramp. This produces death within a comparatively short period of time, is warning to other tramps to keep out of the neighborhood, keeps the coroner in good humor, and saves one's chickens and other portable property from constant destruction."[35] Economic crisis produced dislocation; dislocation produced tramps, the robbers and vagabonds of their day, the superfluous, unneeded, and parasitic; and tramps scared America. Short of poisoning them, most jurisdictions instead revised and revamped their vagrancy laws in hopes of better controlling the wandering poor, as well as to better separate out the worthy from the unworthy (who were often labeled simply as "agitators").[36] As historian Todd DePastino put it, the tramp scares came to be understood as "struggles between the propertied and unpropertied over the use of public space, fears about the growth of a propertyless proletariat, and anxieties about the loss of traditional social controls in America."[37]

But that's only part of the story. The other part is that tramps and tramping were *needed* by the rapidly industrializing economy. They were not superfluous at all. As sons and daughters found there was no longer a place for them, no longer a chance of making a livelihood, on the family farm, they rushed to the mill towns, cities, and now massive, partially industrialized farms in search of work, joining hundreds of thousands and then millions of immigrants arriving from Europe also searching for work. And the industrial farms *were* massive. In California wheat farms and cattle operations regularly exceeded 100,000 acres; at its peak, the Miller & Lux cattle ranching company controlled 450,000 acres in the state. Wheat farms in the newly opened Dakotas and sugar beet farms across the Great Plains—funded by capital pouring in from Europe (especially Britain) and the East Coast—were not much smaller.[38] All needed massive amounts of labor but only in short, seasonal bursts. In the off season, very few workers were needed. Tramping workers were thus vital to America's growing agribusinesses, a pattern that held even as some of the massive wheat farms were broken up (especially in California) and replaced with smaller, more intense farms growing specialty fruits and vegetables.[39] Work in the timber industry, fisheries, canneries, and meatpacking plants, on the railroads, and even in the coal and ore mines of the West was likewise seasonal and episodic. The volatility of the economy, with boom soaring rapidly in the wake of panic and bust, meant that urban manufacturers also frequently relied on temporary and itinerant labor.[40] As historian Kenneth Kusmer concluded, "The increasing number of homeless men during the very period when the United States was emerging as an industrial nation was no coincidence. The new vagrancy was an indigenous aspect of a country in rapid transition from an agricultural and small-town society to one centered on great cities."[41]

Whole districts of towns and cities—Skid Rows—developed where temporary lodging could be found in boarding houses, flophouses, and single-room occupancy hotels, and where cheap restaurants, bars, pool halls, and brothels sprang up to serve workers between jobs (and increasingly as homes for those either beyond the age of work or disabled by it). Labor sharks (contractors who sent hobos and tramps off to day jobs or out into the country for work) also set up shop here.[42] Skid Rows evolved a whole *demi-monde* that, to more settled classes, made them impenetrable, unknowable (at least until the Chicago School sociologists like Nels Anderson and Alice Solenberger started peering into them), and more than a bit scary. Labor unrest and petty violence both seemed endemic.[43]

But Skid Rows were also sites of significant capital circulation. Capital circulated not only through Skid Rows' businesses—the flophouses, bars, and labor offices as entrepreneurs of various stripes saw plenty of opportunity to make money even off the small and intermittent wages of tramping workers—but through the built environment itself. Capital requires a landscape broadly suitable to its needs, both in terms of production of surplus value, the circulation of capital, and capital accumulation, and in terms of the reproduction of the working class (as David Harvey has driven home time and again). That landscape is itself produced as a commodity, or as Harvey put it in *The Limits to Capital*, as "a geographically ordered, complex, composite commodity" that "can be utilized for production, exchange and consumption." But the needs of capital and capitalist social formations continually shift (and in some instances arise out of, or must radically transform, environments created under noncapitalist conditions). Thus "at any one time the built environment"—roads, canals, and rail lines; factories, apartment buildings, and stores; parks, theaters, and schools—"appears as a palimpsest of landscapes fashioned according to the dictates of different modes of production at different stages of their historical development." Crucially, "under the social relations of capitalism, however, all elements assume a commodity form."[44]

Skid Rows in many cities (especially newer ones in the West) developed as speculative ventures, with developers, beginning in the 1870s, seeking to capitalize on the growth of a new, itinerant class of workers by building single room occupancy (SRO) hotels and flophouses, office buildings to house the labor sharks, unions, printers, bathhouse operators, and others who served this new class, and the restaurants, bars, poolrooms, and penny arcades where they spent their free time.* Even putatively non-profit-generating places—the police stations, missions, storefront churches, and charities—important for the regulating, disciplining, and perhaps the succor of this new class were also typically built by profit-making developers. Like any commodity, then, the built environment (Skid Row in this case) embodied value, both the existing value of materials and machinery transferred to the new commodity (the SRO, penny arcade, or union hall) and the new surplus value added by the carpenters, bricklayers, plumbers, and the rest. The difference between a commodity that is part of the built environment—a building, say—as compared to other commodities (a roll of newsprint or a roll of toilet paper) is that the building gives up its value (including its use value) relatively slowly. Capital is, comparatively, far more *fixed* in the built environment than it is in consumer commodities. Harvey, following Marx, thus also refers to the built environment as *fixed capital*, or more accurately, capital fixed in place.†

Such capital fixed in place holds its value and "releases" it only very slowly. This is both a problem and a solution for capitalism. It is a solution because a relatively permanent landscape is created that is *functional* for the circulation and accumulation of capital, in this case through the creation of a place that serves both the coordinating needs of capitalist employers (through the labor sharks) and the reproduction needs of the workers (through the SROs, missions, restaurants, and so forth). The Skid Row landscape developed as a place to *house* these highly mobile, and necessary, workers—a home for the "homeless." The workers, of course, were necessary in two ways: first necessary for their intermittent labor, as discussed, and second necessary to serve as a surplus, or reserve. In turn, such a reserve—the reserve army of labor, as Marx called it—performed two functions: to be available to be drafted into work as production

* In other cities, Skid Rows developed primarily in already-existing built environments, as, for example, fashionable classes and the businesses that served them moved to new districts, abandoning their mansions to be converted into rooming houses, their fancy clubs and hotels to be turned into pool halls and SROs, and their restaurants to become greasy spoons. Such processes, especially as they related to housing, were characterized by Chicago School sociologists and geographers as a sort of ecological successionism and by housing theorists as "filtering"—a central tenant behind the famous concentric zone model of the city—the very process reversed by gentrification. This sort of reuse of the built environment will be discussed more fully below. Of course—since the landscape is a palimpsest—plenty of cities' Skid Rows developed through a combination of speculative building and reuse.

† There are other kinds of fixed capital. Machinery, like a printing press, is fixed capital (even though a printing press can be moved from building to building or city to city), whereas a roll of newsprint is not, since it is consumed in its entirety in one go, as it were.

expanded and, by their very availability, to exert a downward pressure on wages (with a labor surplus it matters less if *this* particular worker returns to work tomorrow as long as *some* worker returns to work; workers become relatively interchangeable and end up competing with each other for jobs).*

There is actually a much more complex argument about the relationship between capital circulation, fixed capital formation, and the industrial reserve army worth developing (which will emerge over the course of the pages that follow), but for now the important point has been made: as American capitalism industrialized after the Civil War, a drifting working class (understood to be homeless tramps) was created that was necessary to this industrialization; in turn a place, Skid Row, developed to house this class, coordinate its movements (if only to a degree, as we are about to see), and ensure its reproduction. By both coordinating the movement of itinerant workers (who were both employed and unemployed) and providing an at least temporary home for them, Skid Row—and the kind of homelessness it made a place for, in the landscape and in the political economy—was a specific capitalist solution to a specific set of needs created by a specific evolution of capitalism. Skid Row, in other words, mediated a central contradiction within capitalism that was quite acute between the Civil War and World War I: on the one hand, capital needed (and still needs, if now in a different form) a highly *mobile* labor force, one that can follow the jobs or move to them; on the other hand, "the industrial reserve army can play its role in depressing wage rates only if it remains in place, as a permanent threat to those already employed" (see chapter 2). Indeed, "the reserve army of the unemployed . . . so unceremoniously 'freed' from its means of livelihood by technological change [among other means] can create conditions favourable to further accumulation only if it remains available to capital. This often means that it must stay in place. Escape routes must be blocked off by legal requirements or other social mechanisms." Crucially, "the industrial reserve army cannot be allowed to die off either, unless capital can absorb 'primitive and physically uncorrupted elements from the country' or mobilize the *latent* as opposed to the active reserve army," for example, women, the elderly, children, or others who, given the social circumstances, are not considered part of the regular labor force (like the large number of people of color who have simply been surplused and abandoned by capital and the state in recent decades). "Otherwise, capital must find ways to maintain a reserve army alive and in place by unemployment benefits, social security, welfare schemes and so on."[45] Before there were these bene-

---

*As Harvey argues (following insights from Marx's *Grundrisse*), a surplus population—a reserve army of labor—is a necessary condition for fixed capital formation, both machinery but especially built environments: "thus more to build railways, canals, aqueducts, telegraphs, etc., than to build the machinery," in Marx's words. While Skid Row is a home to the homeless, it is also in this sense a place they themselves built. Harvey, *Limits to Capital*, 217.

fits and schemes, however, there was Skid Row, and once such schemes were in place (the late 1930s), as we shall see, the function of Skid Row, and the nature of homelessness, changed drastically.

So Skid Row (as well as the itinerant workers who populated it) was a capitalist solution. Skid Row was also a capitalist problem. This is for a very simple reason. What capital wants and needs is labor power (the ability to do work). What it gets are people: the real, living, thinking human beings who embody that labor power. When it wears those people out—through age, or maiming during the industrial process, or whatever—the people persist, somehow. Skid Row became an important place for persistence. Short of letting them "die off," cities and states had to find some way to manage these persisting, now "useless" (to capital) denizens of Skid Row, a problem solved (if only ever partially) by charity, religious missions, and, significantly, the police.*[46]

People also scheme; they plot and they plan; they seek to take control of or shape their own lives; they learn to interpret their experiences and then to act. By concentrating itinerant workers and the reserve army, Skid Row became an important space for scheming, plotting, planning, experiencing, taking control, and acting, as did the labor camps set up by the railroads, mine companies, timber corporations, construction firms, and agribusiness that employed tramping workers, the rail cars in (or on) which they rode, and perhaps especially the hobo jungles (camping sites) where they often stayed when they did not have either the funds for a Skid Row flop or the desire to stay in one—or when, as was often the case, they preferred the comradery, sharing ethos, and freedom of the jungle to the often more constricted and surveilled spaces of the city proper. As will be detailed more fully in later chapters, jungles became significant sites for political organizing among migratory workers—the homeless—at the end of the nineteenth century and beginning of the twentieth as well as for experimenting in other ways to live besides merely succumbing to the "dull compulsion of economic necessity": they represented a *limit* to capital, to its ability to control entirely the lives of the people who embodied the labor power it so desperately requires. Tramps and hobos, migratory workers of all sorts, thus were as much a problem for capitalism as they were a solution, a problem always on the cusp of erupting into full-scale political revolt.[47]

Skid Row—the home of the tramping homeless—was, then, an essential node in the circulation of migratory workers, the general circulation of capital in the political economy, and the specific circulation of capital in and out of the buildings (the built environment) that composed it, as well as the tills of the businesses located in it. It was a space of rest and recreation, of social reproduc-

---

*Which is *not* to deny that sometimes capital, and the state, is actually perfectly content to let surplus populations "die off," just as long as sufficient active and latent reserves remain. See, e.g., Mitchell, "Work, Struggle, Death, and Geographies of Justice."

tion, of exploitation, of organizing and struggle. And in the years after World War I it changed drastically, as did the nature of homelessness. The war, coming hot on the heels of a deep, global recession in 1913–1914, sparked a significant restructuring of the American economy, in particular as the industrial system "matured," requiring less itinerant labor (e.g., for railroad construction and to a degree timbering), and concerted struggle among some workers (e.g., in long-shoring and shipping) led to an at least partial "decasualization" of work.

Structurally, and just as social scientists were beginning to discover and diag-nose the "casual laborer," the function of Skid Row began to shift. Skid Row had always been home to a significant "home guard"—workers and ex-workers who did not tramp for work—but as the need for tramping began to diminish this home guard increased in visibility. Skid Row seemed increasingly to be home to a permanent class of the unemployed and semiemployed, and its denizens were more and more characterized by social science as *disaffiliated*—that is, cut off from the ties and norms of settled bourgeois society. Homelessness was disaffil-iation. And it was understood to be largely a function of defects in the disaffil-iated individual (this argument was an extension and refinement of earlier ar-guments that held that the wanderlust of tramping workers was a function of character flaws that made them unwilling and unable to settle down like "nor-mal" people). Homelessness, as disaffiliation from family and bourgeois society more generally, was theorized by Chicago sociologists like Nels Anderson not so much as a question of housing or economic structure, but more as a chosen "way of life," and thus a (subculturally reinforced) expression of people's char-acters.[48] The effect was to classify homeless people as external to society, rather than produced by it and integral to its functioning. While it is certainly true that the proportion of Skid Row residents who occupied a place in the *permanent* re-serve army—who were seemingly unemployable because of age, disability, ill-ness, or lack of skills—grew in the 1920s, to understand this merely as a matter of disaffiliation rather than a shift in the nature of capitalist accumulation, was, at best, fallacious. Rather, Skid Row and the growing home guard expressed yet another limit to capital: a limit of capitalism, in its early twentieth-century lib-eral form, to provide for those spit out by its inevitable restructuring (or those who simply "aged out") and were thereby useless—or "redundant," to use a tell-ing term of art in industrial relations.

This limit became glaringly obvious when the 1929 stock market crash brought the 1920s liberal boom to a spectacular end. The eventual (Keynesian) means for overcoming the limit was exactly the "unemployment benefits, social security, welfare schemes and so on" that Harvey referred to above, even if his argument that "capital must find ways" to implement these is far too sanguine. Concerted class struggle mattered just as much to their creation and develop-ment, from the early massive marches of the unemployed (organized largely by communists), to the Bonus Marchers who descended on Washington, D.C., in

1932, to the strike after strike, sit-in after sit-in that finally won union recognition and contracts, to rent strikes in innumerable cities (also often organized largely by communists). As a result of such struggles, of capital's own need to resolve the deep contradictions that had brought the economy down, and of the state's dual efforts to jump-start capital accumulation and maintain its own legitimacy at a time of significant unrest, how labor markets operated was radically trans-formed (decasualization was promoted in many industries), unemployment in-surance and pension programs were developed, public housing (for working families, largely) was constructed, and make-work programs designed to sop up surplus labor (while creating important new infrastructures for both produc-tion and social reproduction) were developed. After first experiencing a mass influx of people—men, women, and children—impoverished and made home-less by the economic crisis, by the end of the 1930s (and especially with the con-siderable economic stimulus the growing war in Europe provided) Skid Row's raison d'être in the political economy, its function as a central node in the circu-lation of capital and workers, was considerably undermined. Of course Keynes-ian New Deal reforms in the United States were halting, incomplete (especially compared with post–World War II Europe), uneven, and deeply racist. Even so, as Todd DePastino concluded, "The Great Depression, which began by sending millions to the lodging houses, jungle camps, and public shelters ended by con-firming hobohemia's [Skid Row's] demise and recommitting the nation to the suburban domestic ideal."[49]

One way the reforms were racist was that, at the insistence of southern Dem-ocratic politicians seeking to protect the South's sharecropping economy that so benefited white landowners, New Deal employment reforms—the right to unionize, overtime guarantees, and the like—specifically excluded farmwork-ers.* An effect of this racist policy was to reinforce rather than ameliorate the episodic, casual, highly exploitative nature of farmwork, even as other indus-tries were decasualizing, and even though, to a degree, the federal government sought to ameliorate the horrid conditions of farmwork, especially for the mass of white "Okie" and "Arkie" workers tractored out of their homesteads and sent out on the road in search of work. As hundreds of thousands of Okies and Ar-kies alighted in California, first the state then the federal government intervened by constructing reasonably decent and somewhat self-governing labor camps to supplement if not replace growers' camps and the Hoovervilles (descendants of the jungles) that sprouted up on irrigation ditch banks and roadsides.[50] As some of these workers, in turn, were sucked into the rapidly expanding wartime in-

* It was racist in lots of other ways too, including in the administration of public housing, which was devolved to localities so that local "sensibilities" would preempt any sort of universal claim to a right to housing, in the directing of federally guaranteed construction loans and mortgages to racially ho-mogenous (and especially homogenously white) neighborhoods, in turning a blind eye toward newly legitimated unions' discriminatory practices, and in vigorously maintaining segregation in schools and make-work programs.

dustries of the West Coast, decasualization of the farming economy (and the re-form of the agribusiness landscape this would have required) was averted again by finding ways to guarantee, regularize, and manage in the farmers' interest the stream of migratory labor. In particular the bracero guest worker program (a "wartime emergency" program that lasted until 1964) assured growers ready access to large pools of highly controlled labor from Mexico that could be sent from crop to crop as needed. Such labor was still supplemented by workers sent out by labor contractors (in the case of California, such contractors were often state agencies) operating out of Skid Rows in cities big and small, but as the bracero program wore on, such "domestic" workers (white, black, Mexican American, Filipino) were increasingly sidelined—"dominated" to use the language of the law governing the program—by bracero labor. Skid Row's role as a functional space for the organizing of casual labor further declined.[51]

Those left behind on Skid Row in the postwar era were now understood in social science as the distilled and intensified epitome of disaffiliation. While women, children, and people of color never disappeared from the ranks of the unhoused, they were now simply not counted as part of the new postwar home-less. Those labeled "homeless" in the 1950s and 1960s were the residents of re-maining SROs, missions, and lodging houses on Skid Row, and they tended to be white, male, elderly, rarely transient, and unemployable. They were fre-quently alcoholic. They were modern society's outcasts, understood to be simply useless to the modern, productive economy.[52] By the early 1960s the men of Skid Row were joined by the first wave of the deinstitutionalized: the mentally and physically disabled freed from the total institutions of the asylum and state hos-pital, often for very good, humanitarian reasons. But since many receiving com-munities were unprepared to meet this new population (including especially Skid Rows where SROs, rooming houses, and the like provided cheap housing for newly deinstitutionalized people, who were typically poor), and since the money for community care that was supposed to accompany deinstitutional-ization rarely materialized, this new Skid Row population reinforced the sense that the "homeless" were "not like us."[53] Postwar urban sociologists "character-ized skid row as a world apart, an isolated enclave of damaged white men who had failed to take up their proper roles as family breadwinners," in DePastino's words.* They were the unworthy, the undeserving poor because they had failed to avail themselves of the benefits of the new postwar era.[54] In this way, de-spite the clearly incomplete, uneven, and contradictory nature of the New Deal reforms, the continued existence of homelessness could be made to fit a tra-

---

* Implicit in DePastino's conclusion is also the explicit re-sequestration of women in the home—their removal from the formal labor market—in the postwar era after expanding formal labor force participation during World War II. "Undamaged" white men could bring home a *family* wage, and their wives could devote themselves to the unremunerated work of social reproduction. Of course the "luxury" of a single household wage was finely parsed by dynamics of race and class; it was a "luxury" far less available to black women or white women in marginally employed households.

ditionally liberal ideology, in which opportunities for individual success were everywhere available (especially for white men), and thus lack of success was a function of either a character fault, a (bad) choice, or some combination of the two. But one salient fact remained the same: homeless people were people "whose presence represents unneeded labor," as urban anthropologist Kim Hopper put it, and as such, living right at the limit to capital, they remained "a drain on households [and] an affront to the peaceful enjoyment of civic space."[55]

Homelessness and Public Space

Police worked hard in the 1960s to contain the homeless to Skid Row or similar areas, adjusting policing by district: more stringent "move along" policing in the central business core and wealthier residential neighborhoods, which sought to ensure the more peaceful enjoyment of civic (or public) space for the bourgeoisie and housed working class, was coupled with a degree of tolerance for the street presence of homeless people in Skid Row (which is not to say policing was *not* sometimes brutal there). But two forces collided to radically transform the nature of homelessness and its geography. In turn so too did the nature of the city more generally shift, especially in the way capital circulated through it. These shifts were registered quite clearly in public space, which newly became a focus of social, legal, and policy concern as cities sought to promote not only "peaceful enjoyment," but especially inward investment.

The first shift was in law. Beginning in the late 1950s constitutional scholars questioned the legitimacy of targeting poor people, alcoholics, drug addicts, and others because of their "status" (as poor, alcoholic, or addicted) as opposed to targeting specific, sanctioned behaviors. The whole line of reasoning—the whole history—that penalized vagrants, "masterless men," since the time of the Council of Bern came under assault.[56] A concerted "constitutional revolution" (as conservative legal scholars like to call it) eventually led to the Supreme Court—invoking that "oftentold tale"—to invalidate vagrancy laws in 1972 because they were impermissibly broad and handed too much discretion to the cops.[57] It was now harder for the police to simply "move along" homeless people if they were found on the streets or in the squares and parks of districts outside Skid Row.

Simultaneously (this was the second shift) the deindustrialization of the American economy shifted into high gear. The massive restructuring that accompanied the deep, global economic crisis of the early 1970s threw millions out of work, many permanently.[58] The stable, lifelong (or nearly so) jobs, the family wage, the pegging of wages to productivity, state support for unionism, public housing, the welfare state—rudimentary and limited as all this was in the United States—all came under concerted attack in what David Harvey accurately describes as a thorough restoration of the capitalist class power that Keynesianism had weakened.[59] In an ugly irony, those least incorporated into the Keynesian

Grand Compromise between capital and labor that marked the postwar period—African Americans and other people of color—were, on the whole, most
strongly hit by this restructuring, losing toeholds up into not the middle class
but the relatively stable working class. Black men and women of all ages, a lot of
poor white women, a significant number of working-age white men joined the
old white men of Skid Row, the deinstitutionalized, and, indeed, growing numbers of Vietnam War veterans, on the streets and in other public spaces of the
city. Beginning in the late 1970s and accelerating in the early 1980s, homelessness
exploded. "So long as the appearance of unusual numbers of homeless men (in
addition to the accepted residuum of 'unemployables') can be framed as a temporary aberration," Kim Hopper wrote in the wake of this explosion, "the fiction
can be maintained that homelessness is nothing other than deranged mentali-
ties, bad habits, or faulty coping skills of those whom it effects."[60] By the early
1980s, the fiction could not hold. Homelessness looked like a crisis.

Yet as historian Thomas Sugrue has shown, the urban crisis (to which the
economic crisis and the homelessness crisis were inextricably bound) had in fact
begun long before the massive restructuring of the 1970s. As early as World War
II industrial capital began shifting out of the cities and into greenfield sites in
the suburbs, the Sun Belt, and, soon enough, overseas, often as a result of strong
governmental encouragement and explicit policy.[61] Besides capital's own interest in seeking out greenfield sites in low-tax, low-union, low-wage districts, federal policies subsidizing suburban housing development and the construction
of interstate highways, as well as the government's encouragement of the dispersal of industry for defense reasons (so major plants could less easily be targeted
by single nuclear blasts), led to an industrial and residential hallowing out of cities as early as the 1950s and rapidly accelerating in the wake of the urban unrest
of the 1960s. Downtowns were increasingly restructured to host the office work
that commanded, controlled, and managed the new economy. So-called bulldozer redevelopment played its part too as federal and state funds encouraged
the mass clearing of whole districts—slum clearance, as it was often called—and
their redevelopment as new skyscraper office districts, and sometimes as public
housing projects, convention centers, sports stadiums, inner-city expressways,
or just vast parking lots awaiting inward investment. This was, of course, a ter-
ribly uneven process that proceeded by fits and starts and was more "complete"
in some cities than others.

Often targeted was Skid Row, understood by now to be obsolete at best. But
the fiscal crises of the 1970s brought the era of bulldozer redevelopment to a
rapid, if not total, end. Some Skid Rows with their SRO hotels and cheap bars,
some working-class neighborhoods with their old housing stock and street corner bars and shops, and some old industrial districts with their complement of
warehouses and lofts were spared the wrecking ball, even as the outward expansion of the central business district ground to a halt. As elsewhere in the econ-

omy, capital circulation through the postwar urban environment—which included the capital necessary to knock down districts and their replacement with skyscrapers and stadiums—grew sclerotic.

By the time the arteries of capital circulation began to clear, patterns of investment in—and ideologies of—the built environment had shifted. Hardly expecting the return of industrial capital to inner cities and responding to a cultural shift in Americans' understanding of urban life, government at all levels increasingly encouraged the rehabilitation and reuse of urban landscapes, their remaking, their gentrification. Understood to be a "back to the city" movement of middle-class people, gentrification was in reality (as Neil Smith showed in his pioneering analyses) a back to the city movement by *capital* more so than people: not the industrial capital of yore, but now real estate capital, finance capital wrapped up in pensions and trusts, and, indeed, as is often the case during crises, productive capital retreating from the primary circuit of commodity production and seeking shelter in the secondary circuit of the built environment.[62] Gentrification was, and is, a *revalorization* process, whereby disinvested and devalued urban spaces—like Skid Row in the 1970s—are revalued, filling the "rent gap" between the land values that could be expected if urban spaces were put to something like their "highest and best use" and their current, disinvested values. Through gentrification (perhaps even more than other forms of redevelopment) the built environment *itself* became a primary space of accumulation (not just a space—"fixed capital"—that supported accumulation).[63]

SROs were converted into apartments and boutique hotels. Rooming houses were gutted and made into single- or double-family homes. Tonier restaurants moved in to replace the greasy spoons. Artists occupied lofts. The traditional denizens of working-class neighborhoods and Skid Rows were pushed out, economically as well as culturally. New government investment in nearby urban amenities (parks, improved streets and transportation options, historic features, museums or other cultural attractions meant to jump-start or solidify gentrification) were designed specifically to support the ongoing circulation and accumulation of capital *through* the built environment, while land more and primarily came to be "treated as a pure financial asset, a form of fictitious capital," rather than a *condition* for the creation of value or the harvesting of revenues.[64] Anything that threatened all this new investment, this new form of fictitious capital, locked up as it was for years and decades in the built environment, had to be eliminated, or at least managed.

Yet, radical economic restructuring and its attendant crises threw more and more people into homelessness; wave after wave of gentrification newly valorized the spaces where homelessness had once at least been partially tolerated, destroyed opportunities for cheap housing, and thus, perversely, made homelessness all the more visible in the public spaces of the city, even as these public spaces became all the more important for preserving and promoting urban land's function as a "pure financial asset." For all the talk of an urban renaissance in the 1980s, it was a renaissance built by squeezing significant numbers of people out onto the very streets and into the very parks that were meant to be evidence of this renaissance. The growing population of the homeless thus exposed the contradictions of the new modes of accumulation of the post-Keynesian city. Even more, it seemed to directly threaten that mode of accumulation itself.

Visible homelessness thus became a significant matter for urban management—and policing. On the management front, the first impulse was to create shelter. Pushed by advocates and activists and confronted with what looked like a humanitarian crisis at the beginning of the 1980s, cities quickly opened municipal shelters, supported religious groups that dedicated church basements and fellowship halls to beds for the homeless, and lobbied Congress, in an era of dawning austerity, to dedicate funds for homeless services. The latter efforts paid off in 1987 when Congress passed, and President Reagan very reluctantly signed, the Stewart B. McKinney Homeless Assistance Act, which provided some eight hundred million dollars in assistance to states and cities to establish emergency shelters or to support charities that ran them, to develop "continuum of care" transitional housing programs, and in some instances to preserve the stock of SROs.[65] The act also created the federal Interagency Council on Homelessness, charged with coordinating federal homelessness efforts. It did little to address the root causes of homelessness, however; nor, for various reasons, did it seem to make much of a dent in the visible presence of homeless people in American cities.[66]

Indeed, by the end of the 1980s a condition identified by pundits as "compassion fatigue" seemed to be settling in, as many city administrations, local property and business owners, gentrifying incomers, and suburban taxpayers worried that simply providing emergency housing did little to address the *personal* problems that they often saw as the root of an individual's homelessness and nothing at all to tackle a perceived growing disorder in city streets and other public spaces. For the former issue—housing—ever more elaborate transitional housing programs made the provision of supported group, and then more independent, housing dependent on successful participation in sobriety, job seeking, mental health, financial literacy, and other programs. Housing was not so much a right as a reward for becoming properly worthy, that is, for entering the ranks of the deserving poor.[67]

As for the latter matter—street disorder—now that blanket vagrancy laws seemed (at best) unenforceable, cities were forced to experiment. If homeless people could not be made to move along, then cities would make it difficult or impossible for them to stop. New curfews were implemented in parks; benches were subdivided with metal bars or otherwise shaped so that one could not lie on them, or they were made so uncomfortable no one would want to even sit on them (Mike Davis famously termed these "bum-proof" benches), or they were removed altogether; property owners were encouraged to festoon ledges with spikes, to overwater lawns or replace them with spiky plants, while cities did the same with their own properties; and business improvement district–paid "ambassadors" were coached on how to make homeless people, youth, and others keenly aware of how their presence was not wanted. Public space became exclusionary in new ways.[68]

Simultaneously, cities experimented with new legal regimes aimed at promoting "quality of life," itself now understood to be a primary and most valuable product of restructured cities and something constantly in danger of being ruined by those for whom the new city had no room. New laws sought to "protect" public space by targeting particular behaviors on the part of the homeless: sleeping in public; sitting or lying on sidewalks; begging near ATMs or businesses, during certain hours, or "aggressively"; offering to wash car windows or perform other trivial tasks for drivers; and so forth. Sometimes, as befits urban economies based in the circulation of capital, commodities, and people, such laws were justified on grounds of promoting traffic flow and pedestrian efficiency. As geographer Nicholas Blomley argues, city engineers often understand homeless people sitting on sidewalks, begging, jaywalking, or even sitting too long on benches as being little different from other traffic impediments like newsstands, café tables, merchants' sidewalk displays, advertising boards, street light poles, or bus shelters and thus deserving of the same level of regulatory oversight (café owners must secure permits and meet various requirements; city codes specify where newspaper boxes or pubs' chalkboards can and cannot be located; merchants' encroachments on sidewalks are heavily regulated; and so forth).[69]

But more often such laws seemed to arise out of something like an urban panic, especially since the "constitutional revolution" undermined cities' abilities to punish poor people simply for being poor. Listen again to former New York Mayor Giuliani: "You chase 'em, and you chase 'em, and you chase 'em." This is not a voice of rationality; it's a voice of abject hate, but also of fear, even paranoia. And it is not an uncommon voice. In this imagery the homeless are like dingoes stalking the perimeter of the village, ready to snatch babies; they are outside predators or invading parasites ready to destroy all that is good and healthy. The hard-boiled New York tabloid reporter Pete Hamill, for example, once urged that the homeless be rounded up and quarantined on mothballed military bases, a sentiment not infrequently echoed a generation later by members of San Francisco's tech worker elite—and in the comments section below just about any article in the press on homelessness.[70] In such a fevered atmosphere, proposals to ban sleeping in public or sitting on sidewalks or begging in the wrong manner all start to sound *reasonable*. So does stringent overpolicing of fairly innocuous behavior like jaywalking, littering, rummaging through trash cans in search of bottles, or selling loose cigarettes. "Quality of life" here can be read fairly literally as intervention into the (always public) behavior of the homeless (with homelessness understood as the etiology of an urban disease) so as to protect urban life itself.

At the same time, however (and as befitting a panic), "quality-of-life" laws and policing ought to be understood as desperate experiments in regulation—in "poverty management" as it is often called—not necessarily final solutions. We are once again in an era of feverish legislative activity, and just as before, quite often the regulatory experiments that result are a failure. Early anti-sleeping ordinances failed because people cannot be kept from sleeping and courts struck them down in part for that reason (but also because they were almost always selectively enforced). Early blanket prohibitions on begging fell afoul of First Amendment speech guarantees (and thus have since been refined to address the "time, place, and manner" of begging). Zero-tolerance policing in New York, Los Angeles, San Francisco, and innumerable other cities has shown, time and again, that it does nothing to address homeless*ness*, and so homeless people just do not go away (whatever the fantasies of mayors Giuliani and Lee). Nor, as the U.S. Department of Justice asserted, are camping bans—and the frequent sweeping up and destroying of homeless people's property that accompanies them—an effective tool for solving the problem of homelessness.[71] As a result some cities are now experimenting with either sanctioning homeless-governed encampments or creating government-run ones (often in far-afield places) in lieu of emergency shelters or permanent housing. The latter, as we shall see in chapter 3, seem to function quite like the quarantine Hamill hoped for, even as they provide for some level of stability in some homeless people's lives.

Other experiments in poverty management, especially the policy called Housing First, which reverses the continuum of care model that rewarded housing for becoming properly deserving, seeks perhaps more progressively to remove homeless people from public space. As against the continuum of care model, Housing First policies are based on the dual assumption that providing stable housing and *then* intervening in homeless people's lives will help them become deserving (and then maybe even self-sufficient) and that providing stable housing first is more cost-effective than the other way around. Despite its name, however, Housing First as it has evolved in both federal policy and local practice is less a housing program than a treatment program.[72] Housing First is aimed at the 10 to 20 percent of the homeless population who are considered "hard core": addicted or mentally ill people who "spend years cycling between streets, shelters, jail cells, and emergency rooms," and who, studies show, use a disproportionate amount of services, costing cities disproportionate amounts of money.[73] Promoted by both the Bush and Obama administrations as an important and cost-effective intervention into homelessness, Housing First has nonetheless been hampered by underfunding and by the fact that it tends to drain funds earmarked for the *other* 80 to 90 percent of the homeless.[74] While its pro-pagandists like to claim that homelessness *of this sort* is "not an inevitable price of capitalism," they have little to say about the homelessness of *the other sort*, the sort that affects 80 to 90 percent of the homeless population, which surely is.[75]

Housing policy since the crises of the 1970s has consisted of underfunding and eliminating public housing,* continuing to subsidize middle- and upper-class homeownership through tax policy, and (by the 2000s) encouraging stag-gering debt, both credit card and mortgage, for lower income families so that homeownership could "filter down" to them, as investors got rich, at least for a time, by investing in ever more complex and frequently fraudulent "securi-ties." We know how all that ended: changes in banking laws, coupled with slosh-ing surpluses of finance capital looking for investment opportunities in the built environment, led to a historic housing boom and an asset (and debt) bub-ble, which when it burst created a classic crisis of accumulation, marked by the rapid devaluation of capital that defined 2007–2008.[76] In the wake of the crisis homelessness has soared—New York now shelters more than sixty-five thou-sand homeless individuals a night, far more than it ever has before—even as some jurisdictions have had success in addressing it in limited circumstances (by, e.g., focusing energy and resources on homeless veterans who have often been pushed to the front of the Housing First queue, ahead even of the most "hardcore" homeless people).

Whatever the successes of experiments like Housing First and targeted inter-ventions toward certain groups of homeless people like veterans (and the suc-cesses are not insignificant, even as there remains room for critique), on the whole attempts to solve homelessness by focusing on individual characteristics (and characters) and to manage them by focusing on the behaviors they neces-sarily engage in while in public space have been a failure since they do not ad-dress the fact that homelessness is instead a condition of society, rooted in a set of political-economic realities (and their entwined ideologies of what makes a person deserving or undeserving, worthy or unworthy, or productive or unpro-ductive). The structures of capitalism *require* a large, growing, surplus popu-lation. The shift to an economy based in the development and redevelopment of the built environment—an economy based in the capitalist production of space—means we will inevitably be confronted by "the problem lying on our sidewalks," to appropriate the title of a law review article examining the limits to American's "compassion" for the homeless, and the increasingly mean-spirited laws that result.[77]

---

* Under the Clinton administration, the U.S. Department of Housing and Urban Development elim-inated a requirement that every unit of public housing destroyed had to be replaced. Local housing authorities and redevelopment agencies could now rip down public housing projects without worry-ing about building new ones. See Hackworth, *Neoliberal City*, 50.

Between Boise and "Africa"

The problem, of course, is that such experiments—such mean-spirited laws—which seek to regulate and manage the presence of homeless people in public space, simply do not work, as Obama's Department of Justice recognized. Bans on sleeping and now camping do not eliminate the need to sleep or do anything to address shortages of shelter that hit hard against significant numbers of the contemporary reserve army (for whom the chances of anything like even the itinerant labor of the early twentieth century are nonexistent).* Bans on sitting on sidewalks do nothing to slow the conversion of SROs and other cheap lodging into upscale boutique hotels or downtown apartments for the more wealthy or otherwise ameliorate displacements caused by gentrification. Aggressively citing poor people for jaywalking or peeing in public hardly compensates for the lack of public health care, decent pensions, affordable housing, or good and meaningful jobs. Demonizing people for being physically or mentally ill, for drinking or taking drugs, or for rummaging through garbage for salvageable items does nothing at all to create safe and welcoming spaces for the poor and outcast, while it does much to license, or at least excuse, remarkably violent policing against them, policing that sometimes leads to their death at the hands of the police as with Charly "Africa" Keunang and any number of others.

And it licenses the creation of what I have elsewhere called a "brutal public sphere," one that might most directly target the homeless, the unemployed, and the poor (and nonwhite) more generally—the undeserving who get what they are deserving—but ensnares all of us, as the chapters that make up part 2 make plain. Homeless people in urban space are a bellwether, an "indicator species," if such a dehumanizing appellation might be permitted, as to what's in store for all of us. We ignore them, and what we do to them, at our own peril. Yet, as the remaining chapters in part 1 show, the constant attempt to construct this brutal public sphere is just as constantly contested. Out of this contestation, intersecting as it does with the demands for capital circulation and accumulation in the urban landscape, the actually existing spaces of the city, the city's mean streets, come to be and new experiments in managing the poor, "deserving" or otherwise, arise.

---

*Some cities too have begun to recognize this and, as we will see in later chapters, have sought either to create official homeless camping areas or to sanction user-developed ones. Such attempts are long-standing, dating to the earliest days of the homelessness "crisis," but they do seem to have gained added impetus as some courts have turned a skeptical eye toward sleeping bans. It is important to note, however, that sanctioned homeless campgrounds are rarely established *instead* of aggressive anti-homeless policing in public space, but rather usually complement it.

CHAPTER 2

Footloose Rebels

> Those who command space can always control the politics of place even
> though, and this is a vital corollary, it takes control of some place in order
> to command space in the first instance. The relative powers of working-
> class movements and the bourgeoisie to command space [have] long
> been an important constituent in the power relations between them.
>
> —David Harvey, *The Condition of Postmodernity* (1989)

Homelessness is a condition of society, not a characteristic of individuals. Even so, those deemed by larger society to be homeless sometimes possess a radical potential to shape and reshape the political, economic, and social landscapes that define their lives. This was perhaps especially true in the years just before World War I when tramping workers and the Skid Row "home guard"—many of whom were linked to the radical Industrial Workers of the World (IWW or Wobblies)—made a bid for the political and social control of city streets of the American West and, thus, for significant control over the regional political economy. Understanding how and why they did so, as well as the opposition they met (from other workers as well as the bourgeoisie) is important for better understanding not just what homelessness means now, but also why battles for and over the mean streets of the city remain so fierce. It will also help us understand why urban politicians, policy makers, and many residents now so fear the subversive potential of tent cities (the modern-day hobo jungle), the topic of the next chapter.

The IWW had been founded in 1905 as a radical, syndicalist union determined to overthrow capitalism.[1] But it often had its best successes in bread-and-butter struggles for better wages, decent working conditions, and shorter hours in factories throughout the East, in lumber camps in the South, and on the docks of Philadelphia and other cities, especially among immigrant European (and to a lesser extent African American) workers, including women and girls. In the American and Canadian West, the IWW quickly became a strong presence not only among radical miners in the Rockies (whose unions had been central to its formation) but also among itinerant workers: the homeless who tramped between Skid Row, the burgeoning capitalist farms, the fisheries, and the lumber camps. In the West, Wobbly organizers "carried the local under their caps," as the saying went, authorized to enroll members and call strikes wherever they may have found themselves. This had the effect of turning their mobility subversive: because they were so often on the move and seemingly could turn up anywhere, Wobblies were often invisible to authorities.[2]

As vital as this subversive mobility was, Wobblies also had to stake a claim to city spaces if they were going to organize effectively. Skid Row was where the labor contractors were—labor sharks as the IWW called them—who served as subcontractors for agribusinesses, timber companies, railroads, and so forth. Highly exploitative, the labor sharks were frequent targets of Wobbly agitation. Likewise, Skid Row was where workers went when they were between jobs. Despite carrying the union under their caps and into the labor camps on farms or in the forests, Wobblies knew that city streets were the key to organizing, not just against this or that employer but as a class and across whole sectors. City officials, labor contractors, and employers knew this too, and so throughout the West (and occasionally in the East) cities passed street speaking bans, preventing IWW agitators from mounting the soapbox and extorting their "fellow workers and friends" to join the One Big Union—or to say anything else for that matter. In San Diego, Spokane, Fresno, New Castle, Pennsylvania, Centralia, Washington, and numerous other cities, Wobblies were hauled off their soapboxes and thrown into jail or run out of town. In response, "footloose rebels" would pour into the city to take their place. Jails quickly filled with raucous fellow workers—straining city budgets—even as city- and employer-organized vigilantes stepped up their violence against them, sometimes viciously attacking Wobblies and their allies (many liberals joined the struggle for free speech if not for One Big Union), forcing them to run the gantlet, tar-and-feathering them, or beating them senseless and then leaving them in the desert or mountains miles from town. These free speech fights, which lasted from 1908 until the eve of World War I, became causes célèbres on the left and frequently goaded city and state administrations (especially Progressive ones) into recognizing the IWW's right—and by extension the right of all—to street speaking. They are key moments in a long history of radical agitation—and bloody response—that has been vital to the struggle to achieve a promise enshrined in the Bill of Rights: the right to freedom of expression and assembly.[3]

The Denver Free Speech Fight

Yet Wobbly agitators usually had less abstract, more immediate goals in mind than securing Americans' right to free speech. They wanted control of the streets: they wanted to "control the politics of place" in order to "command space." This was especially true in the American West, as a closer examination of the Denver free speech fight in 1913 shows—assuming there ever was such a fight in Denver. According to George Creel, who had recently been appointed Denver's police chief, there wasn't.* Learning from the exceedingly violent 1912 San Diego free speech fight and others, Creel later claimed that he had instituted a policy of toleration in regard to street speaking, realizing that by doing so the IWW would lose one of its key foci for agitation: the bullying tactics of the police and employers. "These 'wobblies' with their American version of Europe's communism," Creel wrote in his memoirs,

> had been turning other cities into bedlams by street meetings that invited arrest. Jail was exactly what they wanted, for it gave them an opportunity to raise a cry against "America's Cossaks" and attack the whole democratic process. Knowing this, and happening to believe in free speech, I gave the wobblies the right to talk their heads off. . . . As I expected, nobody listened to [IWW president] Big Bill [Haywood's] orators after the first day, and he actually came to see me, begging for a "crack down." When I refused, the hulking agitator and his followers left town.[4]

Early historians of the IWW and a study of mainstream newspapers seem to support Creel's account. Paul Brissenden, the author of the first scholarly history of the IWW, for example, reported that given Creel's permissiveness, in Denver "there was free speech but no fight."[5] To a limited extent this is true (the bulk of the fight occurred after Creel was fired by Denver's mayor in March 1913).†

But the fuller truth is otherwise: the 1913 Denver struggle had its origins under Creel's watch, and IWW speakers were, in fact, arrested on several occasions while Creel was police chief.[6] On December 26, 1912, Frank, Jacob, and Arthur Rice were arrested as they addressed a crowd of casual laborers near Larimer and Seventeenth streets.[7] According to one of the IWW's papers, the *Industrial Worker*, Arthur Rice was arrested for "taking as his subject the brutalities of the police in Little Falls, N.Y.," sardonically suggesting that the Denver police "were so conscious stricken by their own brutalities in the past that they thought the speaker was referring to them."[8] Whatever the validity of this claim, the Rices' arrests set off a low-grade struggle for the control of the streets, with IWW speakers sporadically being arrested throughout the early months of the winter.[9] The city's main papers—the *Denver Post* and the *Rocky Mountain News*—evinced no interest in the battle. Beyond the report of the Rices' original arrests, and until the battle really heated up in April, the two papers, along with their politically

* Creel later became famous as America's chief propagandist during World War I.

† According to the IWW press, Creel, "who believes in free speech as long as no acts of violence were advocated," was "discharged" from his duties by Mayor Henry Arnold so that the IWW could be silenced. "With Creel discharged, the battle began, and the employment sharks and recruiting officers both are backing the attempt to throttle the I.W.W." "Marching on Denver to Fight for Free Speech," *Industrial Worker*, March 27, 1913.

oriented counterparts, the *Democrat* and the *Republican*, paid no attention to these ongoing arrests.[10]

Such silence in the "capitalist press" (as the IWW invariably called it) about IWW actions was not unusual and was one reason Wobblies put so much emphasis on holding street meetings. As the labor historian Philip Foner noted, "It was essential that the right to speak on the streets be protected, because this was the method the Wobblies relied on to gather new recruits among the itinerant workers who poured into the cities of the West every winter."[11] Control of the streets was key to organizing, and in Denver, according to some of those involved, the employment agencies, constructions firms, and others that relied on "casual" labor understood this well. "A contractor by the name of Dooley, representing some of the construction firms of Denver, and some Employment Offices appeared before the Fire and Police Board and demanded the IWW be stopped from speaking on the streets just before the first arrest was made."[12]

The means by which the Denver police sought to limit the Wobblies' use of the streets, and hence to undermine their ability to organize, are telling. According to Wobblies Dave Ingler and Joe Perry, on February 2, 1913, the IWW "called a meeting to order on the corner of 17th and Market Streets . . . about 12 o'clock noon. . . . [A] uniformed police officer appeared and asked the speaker if he had a permit [from] the 'Fire and Police' Board. The answer was 'yes.'" Nonetheless the officer ordered the meeting disbanded and the speakers to appear before the board, which "informed them that the permits of the IWW had been revoked." Since permits for other street speakers (like the Salvation Army) were still valid, the IWW decided to defy the ban. The following day the police arrested eight IWW speakers and—tellingly—charged them not with speaking without a permit but with "vagrancy."[13] This is why it is telling: vagrancy law in Denver simply, and tautologically, made it "unlawful for any person to have the status or condition of or to be a vagrant," that is, to be without a permanent home or to be a beggar.[14] Vagrancy punished Wobblies for a "condition" induced by precisely those economic and political circumstances they sought to transform through their organizing of casual laborers on the streets. Yet their very condition—their homelessness—made it illegal for them to even be on the streets.

This was hardly an unusual circumstance. As detailed in chapter 1, wave after wave of industrial restructuring—from the end of the Civil War forward—had created a massive reserve army of migratory labor.* Indeed, 1913 and 1914 were particularly bad years for unskilled workers, and as unemployment skyrocketed, more and more people were forced onto the road, forced to become, in the eyes of the law, vagrants. Joyce Kornblugh's succinct description of the mi-

---

*Eric Monkkonen correctly reminds us that the "reserve" army in the United States was never fully coterminous with the army of "industrial tramps." Like now, it was composed also of a large proportion of men and women, both unemployed and marginally employed, who never took to the roads or rails—who never became "homeless." Monkkonen, "Introduction."

gratory life at this time gives a clear sense of what it was like for many men (and some women) on the road:

> Moving across the country, the itinerant workers harvested crops, sawed trees, cut ice, built roads, laid ties. In the Midwest, they followed ripening crops from Kansas to the Dakotas. On the West Coast, they gathered the fruit, hops, and grain, canned the fruit and vegetables of California, Washington, and Oregon, and found whatever out of season employment possible. Most of them "beat their way" by freight car from one place to another, and railroad companies estimated there were half a million hoboes riding the rails, walking the tracks, or waiting at railroad junctions to catch trains at any one time. Carleton Parker noted, "This group might be a fraction of the migratory millions actually in transit."[15]

The sheer distances traveled by migratory workers searching for jobs could be staggering. Over the course of a few years, for example, a worker might travel a circuit from the fields of California through the woods of the Northwest, on to the wheat fields of North Dakota, the packing plants and ammunition factories of Iowa, and the mines of Colorado before returning to California.[16]

The very mobility required of them defined migratory workers as criminals: they were vagrants. And selective arrests for vagrancy was one of the key tools in employers' and police departments' attempts to undermine migrant organization and to enforce social control and order—attempts that were often quite successful. Indeed, Wobbly Charles Ashleigh wrote about "the unceasing, gnawing fear of arrest for vagrancy or of a beating up by the railroad police in the yards of the town of destination."[17] And once a hobo made it from the rail yards to the city streets, things were scarcely better. While "transient men found on the main stem [of any city] all the places they needed," they also found their control over the spaces of even Skid Row highly circumscribed. In the first place, "the line between the main stem and the rest of the city was clear—spatially and socially."[18] And it was well policed, with beat policemen given a great deal of discretion in ensuring that tramps and hobos—the homeless of their day—remained confined to certain parts of the city.[19] Second, as with contemporary homeless shelters, lodging on Skid Row (in flophouses, police stations, municipal lodging houses, SROs, and so forth) was usually temporary, and quite frequently residents were not allowed to remain in the lodging during the day.[20]

In Denver, the Larimer Street Skid Row between Sixteenth and Twenty-Second streets served as the center of migrant labor. Here one found a number of employment bureaus, outdoor employment markets (the "slave market" in the corner of Nineteenth and Larimer lasted until the urban renewal of the 1950s), flophouses, missions, and dozens of saloons.[21] Encompassing Market and Lawrence streets to either side of Larimer, the Denver Skid Row area was key to the IWW's organizing plans. Indeed, in the midst of the free speech battle, the IWW relocated its headquarters from Eighteenth and Arapahoe to the more central Seventeenth and Lawrence. As elsewhere in the West, the IWW head-quarters served as a clearinghouse, a meeting place, a library, a canteen, and more. Wobbly stalwarts met their comrades there; new recruits found not only a hive of union activity but a place of real comradery that complemented what could be a rather fractious comradery of the streets.

Back out on those streets, while authorities sought to criminalize it, Wobblies sought to turn vagrancy—homelessness, footlooseness—in their favor and make it a central weapon in the class war. On the one hand (as already briefly noted), the peripatetic nature of migrant work meant that casual, migratory workers were relatively invisible to authorities who rarely knew where those "migratory millions" might turn up next. With no fixed address, they could not be pinned down. Migratory workers maintained a degree of power just by dint of their ability to slip away, to move on, to hide. On the other hand, high rates of mobility allowed radicalized workers to act quickly, moving from scene of confrontation to scene of confrontation with relative rapidity—a point that is key to the whole story of the Denver free speech fight. When the first February arrests were made in Denver, for example, IWW Local 26 quickly sent "out a call for men to help them win the fight."[22] And by February 20 the *Industrial Worker* was exhorting, "On to Denver You Rebels" at the top of its front page, and it followed two weeks later with "Recruits Needed for Denver Fight."[23] "Come on to Denver, fellow slaves," the IWW urged, arguing that with "the help of a few footloose rebels from each of the live locals" in the West, the Denver local "can win the fight."[24] And on to Denver they came.

As early as mid-March "numerous fellow workers" from two locals in California's Central Valley, led by Frank Little (a veteran of the bloody Fresno free speech fight and soon to be martyr in Butte, Montana),* left for Denver, plotting a route through California, Nevada, Utah, and Colorado towns, in hopes of "gaining recruits as they go." Each town at which the "army" stopped was to become "a center of agitation while the band is mustering additional strength."[25] By April 7 an advance guard of the army of free speech fighters had reached Grand Junction, where, the *Rocky Mountain News* reported, they demanded to be fed before moving on to Denver.[26] On April 11, a large vigilante mob—the *News* reported it was three thousand strong—forced some one hundred Wobblies out of Grand Junction and began a recall of the mayor, who, many felt, had treated the IWWs too kindly.[27] When a contingent of sixty-six Wobblies approached Denver on April 14, they were met on the outskirts of Englewood (well beyond Denver's city limits) by sixty Denver police officers, the chief of police, and two of his top aides. For those Wobblies who eluded capture in Englewood and made it to Denver, "as fast as they are found the chief has given orders to throw them in jail."[28] The arrested Wobblies were fined from $60 to $120 each (an astronom-

---

*As a result of his effectiveness as a union organizer, Frank Little was hung from a railroad trestle by company-hired vigilantes in Butte in 1917.

ical sum), and unable or refusing to pay, seventy-one were thrown in a single cell designed for twenty-four.[29] One apprehended Wobbly predicted that their fate would be determined in the "time honored Colorado way—deportation," but that deportation "will have no terrors for the California fighters. They have braved the desert and snow-capped mountains, day and night, and will do it again."[30]

Such threats, coupled with the fact that more "footloose rebels" were on the way, as well as the bad publicity the overcrowded jails were garnering Denver (sixty IWWs had begun a hunger strike in the city jail), seemed to work.[31] On May 1, 1913, the city of Denver capitulated to the IWW's demands and granted the Wobblies the right to speak on the streets. "The city authorities will grant the I.W.W. permits to speak on the streets of Denver," the agreement between a committee of Wobblies and the police read, "at four designated points from the hours of 12 noon to 11 p.m., provided all men who took part in the free speech fight will leave town if unable to get work." The *Industrial Worker* reported that the terms of the permits were more favorable than the originals, and that as a result of the struggle "several of the most active workers have remained in Denver to help build up the local. . . . A new headquarters has been secured at 1909 Lawrence street. Street meetings are being held every night and the crowds are greater than ever."[32] Controlling the streets of cities like Denver, then, was essential to the Wobblies' desire to make mobility fully subversive. And conversely, the Wobblies cemented their power in a fixed local space—Denver's Skid Row—only by *mobilizing* their power elsewhere.

In short—and in the short run—the Wobblies won. By harnessing the power of their subversive mobility, the IWW—organized workers who were also the footloose, homeless outcasts of the era—had secured for itself a "space *for* representation," a space that allowed them to gain some control over the social forces that shaped their lives and determined who they were, how they worked, and what they did.[33] In turn, gaining some control over the space of the street allowed the Wobblies some semblance of control over the conditions of their mobility. More than a month after the end of the fight, the *Industrial Worker* reported that "Pat Noonan is the principal speaker on the streets and he is getting a fine result. The way the slaves are discussing the I.W.W. makes it look as though Denver is surely being put on the map."[34] It was being put on the map, it should be clear, by two intersection processes. First, there was the seemingly local battle to control the streets and make them available for agitation. Second, there was the organization of mobility at quite large scales—a mobility, and indeed (as we shall see) a use of geographic scale itself, that implied no little increase in *power* at the local level.

But the IWW's victory was hardly complete. For even as the IWW was seeking to consolidate its newfound power to use the streets of Denver for political mobilization and labor organizing, so too were the political and economic powers of Denver mobilizing resources of their own—capital, police power, and people—at multiple geographical scales to reinforce *their* ability to control place and command space. And when we turn to that history, the rather heroic picture of the Wobblies' fight for control of the streets I have painted so far gets considerably more complicated (with important implications for both the evolution of homelessness and the nature of labor organizing). Before turning to those complications, however, it is worth pausing a moment to assess the political and geographical importance of the story just told, a process that will also entail examining the specific political economy of the American West as its industrialization was completed around the turn of the twentieth century. For whenever the structure and struggles of the homeless and the reserve army of labor are at stake, so are the patterns and logics of circulating capital.

Producing Space and Scale in the American West

Physical space—from the specific landscapes of Skid Row to the more or less coherent regions that make up the American West—is socially produced. Showing how and why this is the case (theorizing precisely *how* space is produced) has been, perhaps, the signal contribution of the field of human geography over the past generation. David Harvey long ago laid out the general proposition: "Capitalist society must of necessity create a physical landscape—a mass of humanly constructed physical resources—in its own image, broadly appropriate to the purposes of production and reproduction." And, moreover, the specific "relation between labor and the built environment can be understood only in terms" of the "domination of capital over labor" in any particular setting.[35] The "domination of capital over labor," however, is neither simple nor guaranteed; it is, rather, a point of constant struggle—over what Marx called the "historical and moral element" that is so crucial to determining the rates and forms of the exploitation of labor power.[36]

The built environment—the produced space of city and countryside—is thus at least partly the result of the intersection of capital circulation (and capitalist domination) and struggle against that circulation (and domination) by social groups that must live in that built environment.[37] Yet if capital is able to circulate only by ensuring at least some capital is fixed in place, then this contradiction necessarily engenders struggles "over the definition and meaning of use values; the standard of living labor; the quality of life; consciousness; and even human nature itself."[38] These struggles are at least in large part struggles over the landscape: over who controls it, who may use and live in it, how they may live, and the degree to which the landscape will be more or less integrated into the production of surplus value. Here we can begin to understand Henri Lefebvre's polemical insistence that it is class struggle "alone which prevents abstract space [the commensurable space of capitalist accumulation] from taking over the whole planet and papering over all differences which are not intrinsic to economic growth *qua* strategy, 'logic,' or 'system'—that is to say, differences which are neither induced by nor acceptable to that growth."[39]

Yet Lefebvre's formulation remains too abstract,[40] too removed from the particular historical and geographical processes at work in particular places and at particular times—which is not to say that historical materialist accounts of the production of space should devolve into pure particularity, into an argument that there is nothing *but* the particular historical and geographical processes and that generalization is impossible. The missing link between philosophically abstract discussions of the production of space and more empirical and closely wrought studies of particular spaces is the middle ground not only between abstraction and specificity, but also between local and larger geographical scales. This is an especially important issue in the historiography of the capitalist transformation of the American West—and hence for understanding the nature and importance of the Denver free speech fight (and thus for how homelessness fits into class struggles). If the historiography of the American West has long been presided over by the ghost of Frederick Jackson Turner, despite efforts in the 1980s and 1990s by so-called New Western Historians to dislodge it, then it is because the major question he raised, namely how to account for the development of the West as a region and a landscape within the larger history of American expansionism, remains pertinent.[41]

But many of those who take this question as their guide, according to Brian Page, tend to work themselves into theoretical and methodological corners by misspecifying the *scale* at which linkages are made between and among places, and between places and the workings of capital in general. Critiquing key works in New Western History, Page finds that much scholarship on the American West (including its cities) theorizes economic development as the product of a "giant, vague and homogenous industrialism that envelops the west" and as the product of a "hyper-structuralist" world system that allows little room for agency within nation-states and regions. Either that or it relies on a model of generalized capital circulation that is not attentive enough to the specific and "distinctive process[es] of regional industrialization" that are situated within a complex hierarchy of geographical scales. Page argues that the study of the capitalist transformation of the American West ought to become more sensitive to the different scales at which "social life and individual experience [and] broader economic and political forces" are linked together.[42]

In other words, "geographical scale" is a crucial theoretical concept and methodological tool for understanding struggle and the production of space—the space of Denver's Skid Row, for example—both in particular localities and in terms of broad processes. As geographers have long shown, however, it is easy to take scale for granted: there are the local, the regional, the national, and the global, each obvious and clear. This is misleading. While it is the case that interesting questions about the production of space—and about struggles over the control of space—arise out of the study of how different scales act recursively on each other (how, for example, the local is imbricated in the global), even more interesting questions about the production and control of the landscape arise when we understand geographical scale, like space, to be actively and socially *produced*.[43]

To the degree that a critical theory of scale penetrated the broader reaches of cultural theory (if not necessarily western historical scholarship), it was in some ways due to Neil Smith's evocative arguments about how social movements were sometimes able to "jump scale"—how they were able to transform their actions from ones that impinged on processes at one scale to ones that were effective at other scales. Indeed, Smith argued (in specific reference to homeless people's political struggles), the ability to jump scale is essential to the success of any social movement. Yet much of the work that has built on Smith's notion has tended to reify scale as if it is simply obvious that an urban street corner (for instance) is "more local" than the whole of the city, or the space of the region. It has seemed to take for granted that the regional or national was simply *there*, waiting to be jumped into, both feet first, and hence repeated exactly the error of misspecification that Page identified in New Western History scholarship. But Smith's point was exactly that scale is and must be produced and reproduced: any reification of scale (and scale is continually being reified) is a social achievement always in the making. As Smith wrote, "The point [for analysts and activists] is not to 'freeze' a set of scales as building blocks of a spatialized politics, but to understand the social means and political purposes through and for which such freezing is accomplished—albeit fleetingly." The production of scale, therefore, had to be understood as just as necessary for the reproduction of capital (for the patterns through and by which capital circulates) as it was for the success of social or class struggle.[44] Geographical scale, as Andrew Herod notes, is a "*contested social construction*," in which all manner of social struggles "modify the law of value in different geographical locations."[45]

In one sense then, geographical scale—when reified, that is, produced—can be thought of as a container. "In a literal as much as a metaphorical way, scale both *contains* social activity and at the same time provides an already partitioned geography in which activity *takes place*," Smith argued. "Scale," he continued, "demarcates the sites of social contest, the object as well as the resolution of contest."[46] So while scale sets the boundaries within which competition and cooperation, struggle and acquiescence, are determined, so too do those processes of competition, cooperation, struggle, and acquiescence in turn determine the boundaries of scale. This leads to an obvious question: what is it—what processes, what sort of activities—that not only produces and demarcates relatively stable scales, but binds them together in some sort of a "nested hierarchy"?[47]

One answer to that question that is particularly germane to the case at hand might be developed by focusing on processes of circulation—the circulation of capital, of people, of images and ideas. Indeed, in his important *Nature's Metropolis*, founding New Western Historian William Cronon went a long way toward showing how the "Great West" (a designation that describes a particular regional scale) was produced through the circulation of commodities and capital. Cronon argued that to understand the making of the Great West, one must first look east: "Repeatedly in the nineteenth century," Cronon wrote, "western cities came into being when eastern capital created remote colonies in landscapes that as yet contained relatively few people." As capital moved west, it necessarily put people in motion, both Native Americans and others it dispossessed and workers from beyond the region (and often beyond North America) to provide labor when and where it was needed. Yet as Cronon showed in a part of *Nature's Metropolis* nicely titled "The Geography of Capital," once implanted in the West, the circulation of capital created (and was created by) processes of *regional* circulation—through credit flows and banking linkages, warehousing, and the retailing of finished commodities sold through catalogues. Crucially, as Cronon rightly concluded, such a "geography of capital expressed itself not just in . . . physical structures"—the production of space—"but as the ways people lived, worked and traded within them." Such a relationship between the circulation of capital, the determination of lived social relations, and the production of space was often quite mystified, even as it was being constructed. "The paradox of nineteenth-century Chicago," and by extension other places in the American West, was that "the same market that brought city and country ever closer together . . . also concealed the very linkages that were making it. The geography of capital produced a landscape of obscured connections."[48]

Yet that "landscape of obscured connections" was not quite so simply the production of "capital." It was even more directly the product of labor, and thus of laborers. If capital must create the conditions necessary for its own circulation, then it cannot do so on its own. Capital can conjure nothing into being without the work of live people. To the degree that capital can circulate among multifarious circuits, some small and some quite large, to the degree that it can circulate through the land, machinery, people, and commodities of a single enterprise as well as across vast spatial reaches, it can do so only because the arteries of circulation have been built, been labored over. The various circuits of capital are constructed, not simply given.[49] The regional scale (or any other scale), when defined through the circulation of capital, is an achievement—but it is an achievement built on a contradiction. For, as previewed in chapter 1, without a certain fixity of some capital (in laborers' bodies as well as in the ossified labor that is worked land, machines, buildings, or other elements of "fixed capital") other factions of capital are in no sense able to circulate "freely."[50] Whatever the eventual (and always ongoing) resolution of this contradiction between circulation and fixity, the important point is that "channels" are opened at particular scales that allow capital to circulate *within* that scale. And the continual drive to-ward the expansion of capital, linked as it is to the imperative force of competi-tion among individual capitals, implies that one means of gaining competitive advantage is to remake, transcend, or transform the ossified scales created by earlier rounds of capital circulation, earlier rounds of capitalist production.

Just as the circulation of capital is a necessary precondition for the produc-tion of value, so too is the circulation of labor, or more accurately labor power. Like the circulation of capital, the circulation of labor power—and especially the workers who embody that labor power—defines a number of scales, from intra-firm movement to global labor migrations. And also like capital, the move-ment of some laborers demands the fixity in place of other workers. The differ-ence between capital and labor, of course, is that people are not machines or dol-lar bills: they feel the contradictions of competition between mobility and fixity most keenly, and hence the internecine *politics* of labor (and labor mobility) can be quite fierce (as we shall see in a moment when we return to Denver). This in-ternecine politics, too, is crucial to the politics and production of scale and to the productive circulation of capital.

How best, then, to understand the relationship between capital circulation, labor circulation, and the production of scale? To take just the case closest to hand—the migratory, casual, and often surplus homeless workers of the Ameri-can West before World War I—the importance of the circulation of labor power to the expansion of capital is obvious. As Eric Monkkonen neatly summarizes, "The story of the tramp is the story of mass population movement caused by the industrial transformation of the urban United States."[51] The migrant laborer was essential to the eventual development of a "mature" industrial system both in the West and nationally. It was the sweat and blood of "footloose," often immigrant workers that welded the region and nation together. They built the networks of railroads, telegraphs, and power—the very infrastructure that made possible the efficient geographical circulation of capital (as money and commodities). They mined the ores and harvested (and still harvest) the fruits and vegetables that fueled the expanding economic system. And they did all this under often appall-ing conditions. Quite literally, mobile workers *made* the city, region, and global economic system. But so too did processes of capital circulation make *them*. "As employment declined or shifted location, young men took to the road, walking or riding the rails where possible, seeking not their fortunes, but simply jobs."[52]

Such mobility clearly has its costs, and it was precisely the conditions of this mobility against which the Wobblies in the West frequently organized, seek-ing to turn footloose workers into footloose rebels. Yet these costs were borne by capital too. I have already indicated the loss of surveillance and control im-plied by mobility turned subversive. But there were other concerns too. For ex-ample, it is something of a truism that the circulation of capital must always be *faster* than the circulation of labor. Fixing labor in place is often part of the arsenal of capital. In the words of geographer Jamie Peck, "Strategies of *local-ization* (in industrial relations norms and conventions, in welfare entitlements and programs) play an active role in the subordination of labor. Just as the rela-tive immobility of labor vis-à-vis capital—its rootedness in place—is the source of asymmetrical power between labor and capital, so strategies of localization are . . . used to extend managerial domination and state discipline."[53] The pro-cesses of localization—an important production of scale—can be quite com-plex, both materially and ideologically. In the case of migrant labor in Califor-nia during the Depression, for example, the construction and policing of the "legitimately local"—the deserving poor and deserving workers—was a key tool for delegitimizing the claims to power of migrant workers. By declaring radical migratory workers (the political descendants of the Wobblies) to be "outsiders" and hence not legitimately members of the "community," agribusiness interests (which, of course, depended on their right to move extra-locally for their very survival as capitalist firms) and their allies in the state could better control *some* places so as to better maintain control over processes of circulation (of capital, people, ideologies, and so forth) across vast spaces of the economy. Hence the multiple scales of economic activity—for capital and for labor—are produced through ongoing struggles over precisely how and where each should circulate, as the Denver press's talk of "invading armies" of IWWs made plain: folks with claims understood to be locally legitimate will not be seen as invaders.[54]

In other words, just these struggles—between the fixity and mobility of cap-ital, between the mobility and fixity of labor, between the scales of legitimacy and identity—were at issue in the Denver free speech fight (and others like it in the American West), even as all these struggles seemed to dissolve into a rather more simple struggle over the control of the streets. With that in mind, it is time to return to the streets of Denver, but now seeing them as part of a larger skein of interrelationships that bound Denver to the larger region, nation, and world, even as these interrelationships produced these scales in the first place.

Controlling the Streets

What, then, were the processes and systems of circulation that constructed the regions of which Denver was a part? How was geographical scale produced in the American West? What was the role of the production of space in Denver in these productions of scale? And what does all this mean for the footloose work-ers and rebels, the unemployed home guard of Denver's Skid Row and others who were part of the homeless class?

Like many western cities, Denver developed in the first place around trans-portation. Besides the small deposits of gold that brought prospectors and ad-venturers to the site of Denver in the first place, its founders were most enthusi-astic about Denver's location as a crossroads. "Denver is situated at the mouth of

Cherry Creek, where it forms its confluence with the South Platte," William Larimer wrote to his wife. "This is the point also where the Santa Fe and New Mexico road crosses to Fort Laramie and Fort Bridger, also the great road leading from the Missouri River: in short, it is the center of all great leading thoroughfares and is bound to be a great place."[55] Indeed, Denver's prosperity was predicated on the mobility of capital. One the one hand, "Denver was an ideal supply center and break-in-bulk point for goods from the east." On the other hand, the "rapid emergence of banking was one of the most impressive features of Denver's early development, helping to achieve the 'initial advantage' that urban geographers regard as crucial to a city's long-term growth."[56] Like Chicago, Denver served as an entrepôt for both goods and capital, with its growth closely linked to the expansion of railroads in the last two decades of the nineteenth century. Denver gathered to itself economic control that reached at least to central Utah and covered much of Wyoming, northern New Mexico, and western Kansas.[57] As the journalist William Allen White put it in 1902, Denver was "the clearing house for everything West of the plains. Money, Indian blankets, scenery, mining stocks, statesmen and news from the desert and mountains, from the coast and from the cow country in the southwest are dumped in the hopper in Denver. Whatever the Powers there find fit to go east goes; other things are lost."[58] Coupled with a vibrant industrial sector (especially smelting), the growing transportation, banking, and warehousing sectors of the entrepôt city led to a population of more than 140,000 by 1900. But also coupled with this growth was the increasing prominence of outside capital from the east and from Europe.[59] Denver thus existed as a node in a network of capital and commodity flows that extended across the globe, but which was particularly thick in its own backyard.*

As a point of capital control, and as a stopping point for capital in its ceaseless wandering from place to place,[60] Denver also served as a point of control for the movement of labor. Denver served as a "turnstile town" for many workers in the late nineteenth and early twentieth centuries.[61] In the early 1880s, "perhaps 1000 workers per month passed through the city, bound for grading camps on the Denver and Rio Grande railroad alone." While demand for railroad construction crews had surely declined by the turn of the century, Denver was still a resting—and a living—point in the midst of seasonal and permanent migrations for countless workers.[62] Even so, as a center of industry, warehousing, and other localized economic activities, Denver was also home to a more settled and at times quite powerful, working class. And it was not infrequent that the needs and desires of these different factions of the working class—the fully mobile tramps,

---

*Obviously, "capital and commodity flows" is only a shorthand for the fact that produced *things*—like ore—moved in and out of Denver. Denver's regional prominence owed much to Denver-based capitalists' ability to organize and control production—specifically ranching and mining—elsewhere in the area. Denver's wealth was a function of economic production across the region; it was not just a function of "circulation." See Wyckoff, *Creating Colorado*, 54.

the semimobile workers who shifted between work in the smelters and seasonal work in the beet refineries, the relative "labor aristocracy" of permanent railroad employees and clerks in the banks, department stores, and hotels—clashed with each other as the regional circuits of capital mobility solidified, and especially as the importance to western capital of tramping workers declined in the twentieth century.

The free speech fights of the IWW must be understood within this context. The IWW's use of "direct action," connected as it was to the condition of mobility, to the ways in which class struggle produced spaces, and to the tug of war over creating the scales that "contain social activity" (including the productive circulation of capital and labor), was about a lot more than "free speech." Yet ideologies of free speech *were* vital to the IWW's evolving strategies of labor militancy in the West. They connected the IWW to long-standing (if contentious) American traditions of radical republicanism. By the 1870s many radical labor unionists merged a critique of industrialism with a version of American republicanism to call for an end to "wage slavery," and the achievement—at least—of an independent citizenry of associated producers. The end of wage slavery would inevitably lead to the end of capitalism and the creation of "a republicanization of labor, as well as a republicanization of government" as one advocate for the eight-hour day put it after the Civil War.[63] Such republican ideals rested on related ideals about the use of public space by radical workers to advance their cause. In public space workers could *become* associated and use the control of space to mount attacks on an established order that worked diligently to separate citizens and workers one from another (a theme returned to in chapter 5). Freedom of speech and freedom of assembly were necessary planks in the republican platform.

But that republicanism was built on a certain form of localism that asserted that the legitimate community was the local community. And by the turn of the century, "few realistically believed any longer in the nineteenth-century republican ideal of a nation of equal citizens made up of small independent producers. Even the most ardent critics of industrial capitalism now recognized that the large-scale production and distribution of goods had rendered obsolete these older social ideals."[64] The IWW, therefore, explicitly sought to build on the language of republicanism while expanding the scale of organizing and protest to become coterminous with the scale of the lives they actually lived—and with the scale of capitalism itself.

"Call a mass meeting of all men who are out of work," the national-circulation *Industrial Worker* beseeched its readers, "and ask them to come to Denver, on the cushions if they can, on the rods if they must. But come!"[65] One of the Wobblies who rode the rails to Denver put the point quite clearly: "This is a critical time to have advocates of One Big Union in Denver, as the entire state is strike-ridden. . . . Scatter out, live ones of the Coast! Get posted yourself, then come to the middle west and post others. The field is broad and fertile. Happiness must replace misery; the right to earn plenty must replace want and suffering."[66] The desire for One Big Union, the ultimate goal of the IWW, neatly summarized the degree to which the IWW understood the necessity of extending the scale of labor organizing, both vertically through all sectors of the economy, and horizontally across ever-greater reaches of geographical space.

But in Denver this task was not to be so easy. In the midst of the free speech fight the *Rocky Mountain News* announced at the top of its April 4, 1913, issue, "Heads of Unions Here to Prevent War on D. & R. G." According to the article, "One of the fiercest struggles in the history of organized labor is on between the American Federation of Labor and the Industrial Workers of the World." At issue was a presumed plot by Wobblies to foment a strike on the Denver and Rio Grande Railroad. Five presidents and vice presidents of AFL craft unions and a number of "lesser lights in the labor world" "rushed to Denver to take up the cudgel against the I.W.W." The labor leaders came from as far away as San Francisco, Chicago, and Kansas City in hopes of convincing local workers that, in the words of one official, the "Denver and Rio Grande is the fairest road to its shop employes [sic] of any road upon which union men are employed." Speakers at a series of meetings urged workers to "let the leaders settle our difficulty," making it clear that the IWW's vision of radical, democratic, syndicalist control over work—the modern form of earlier republicanism—no longer had a place in the "respectable" labor movement.[67]

Interestingly, in reporting on the labor leaders "rush to Denver," the *News* made one of its few references to the ongoing free-speech fight in Denver, making clear one of the reasons local officials and business interests (and now some leaders of the AFL) were keen on eliminating the IWW's public agitation. "The Industrial Workers of the World have been gathering in Denver for months," the paper reported.

> Driven from San Diego and other California towns, they came eastward and gathered in Denver. Members of the organization declare they can gain more recruits by being "persecuted" than by speechmaking, and for that reason in every city they make inflammatory speeches on the streets, and if sent to jail, are happy. Last week a telegram was received declaring that if their members were jailed in Denver 1500 other members from other cities and towns were prepared to march on this city. There are several hundred members here now, and they are scattered in cities and towns along the Denver and Rio Grande as far as Salt Lake.

The threat to the interests of capital and the "conservative faction" of labor was palpable. The very mobility of radical workers threatened established labor and capital the length of the railroad. Even though the IWW would seemingly rather be "persecuted" than organize, they still seemed to be a real threat to the AFL, which "stands for the interests of working men, and which is fair in its consideration of capital," as one of the AFL leaders put it. The AFL, he declared, "only wants a square deal for those who work and is willing to give a square deal in return."[68]

The irony, of course, was that to protect the *local* interests of Denver workers against a threat posed by mobile workers (and the unemployed) rushing in from afar, the AFL itself had to mobilize its leaders around the country and rush *them* to Denver. "Strike talk . . . has been mostly among men who have no families to support," one "grand officer" of the AFL argued. He asserted that those with roots and families, the legitimate workers on the railroad, would only be harmed if they failed to "leave grievances to their grand officers for settlement."[69] These same grand officers, however, promised they would "ask nothing hard" of the D&RG, because it was "an easy road to deal with."[70] The question at hand in Denver, then, was clearly one of the conditions under which the construction and maintenance of the *means* of circulation was to be accomplished. Not only was the control of these conditions vital to capital, it was vital to the respectable labor movement as it sought to ensure a square deal as much for capital as for labor.

Only in this context can a curious article that appeared on the first page of the April 19, 1913, Denver *Democrat* be understood:

> The International Harvester company has its biggest twine plant in Auburn, Cayuga County, N.Y. For this factory most of the raw material comes from the Philippines, and the finished product is sent to every country in the world where agriculture is conducted on a large scale. In a city of 30,000 the so-called Harvester trust has been the largest employer of labor. A strike, still going on, has paralyzed its work, and about $1000 a day has been lost to the workers. Now, the concern announces that it will dismantle its plant and move all its machinery to Germany. The dismantling has begun and the City of Auburn is much agitated.
>
> The Tariff change impending does not materially affect the Harvester company. It gets its raw material free of duty now. It would have the same advantages under the proposed law. In Germany, it would have to pay a slight duty on hemp. But settled labor conditions are more vital than anything else to such an interest.
>
> Labor agitators are very valorous in killing the goose that lays the golden egg. They are not to be scared by the vanishing payroll. They refuse to think before they order strikes. The penalty has to be borne by the wives and children of those who accept their leadership.*

This commentary had first appeared as a front-page editorial in the *Brooklyn Eagle*, but why was it published at this moment in Denver? The *Democrat* sought to make it crystal clear, it seems, that labor agitation, in this case including agitation by "rebels" nearly as "footloose" as capital itself, threatened not just the

---

*Those who think of capital flight—or the threat of it—as a fairly recent phenomenon would do well to notice this editorial. Obviously capital has long understood the disciplining power of its own mobility.

continued accumulation of capital, but places themselves. To the degree capital could simply move away itself, workers' movements had to be regularized and controlled—left to responsible leaders, not "labor agitators."[71]

The role of migratory workers in places like Denver had to be redefined, but this could be done only by establishing "respectable" rather than subversive labor, a process in which the AFL's labor leaders were fully complicit. In the midst of the Denver battle, for example, the *Rocky Mountain News* opined that the "mill weavers of Paterson seem to have regained a measure of their equilibrium when they ask[ed] the American Federation of Labor to take the place of the I.W.W. The saboteurs and 'direct action' leaders of the I.W.W. made a sorry mess of the strike.... [The AFL] will rescue the cause of labor from the clutches of its worst enemy, the apostles of the un-American policy of sabotage, which brazenly invokes criminal violence in the adjustment of labor disputes."* Two days later the *News* ran a full-page editorial on the evils of "syndicalism and sabotage"— words "you won't find ... in any English dictionary."[72]

The *News*, however, was not entirely unsympathetic to those attracted to the radicalism of the IWW. "For whether you like Syndicalism or Sabotage or not there must be a cause for their birth. The atrocities and indifferences of the trust system in this country have been the chief provocation." Even so, any resort to sabotage or syndicalism (the two are fully conflated in the *News*'s account) had no place in America. Even more, despite a "crassly foolish trust system [that] refuses to listen to the teachings of reason," the attempt "to stop or reduce production is a relic of an old appeal to ignorance and stunted reason." The proper course, according to the *News*, was to follow the AFL in its belief in "the sacredness of the contract."[73]

In this quite fascinating editorial are still further hints as to what was taking place on the streets of Denver that winter and spring, even if the city's streets were never mentioned. The prime example of the "old appeal to ignorance and stunted reason" given by the *News* was the Luddite and other crusades of industrializing England. Workers there were not protesting the loss of control over their working conditions or simply the loss of jobs; and they were not seeking through their protests to determine the conditions under which they lived and labored. Instead, in the *News*'s rendering, they were engaging in futile riots against inevitable progress.[74] The destruction of a "way of life" seemed to mean far less to the *News* than the destruction of a weaving machine in England—or in Paterson, New Jersey.

*The Paterson strike was a protracted silk workers strike in New Jersey led by the IWW. The union and the strikers were ultimately defeated, but not before they were arrested for reading the free speech clause of the New Jersey state constitution and a spectacular fund-raising pageant was held at New York City's Madison Square Garden that attracted the interest of the press around the world. As with the railroad in Denver, Paterson silk mill owners secured the assistance of craft union leaders in breaking the strike.

Importantly, then, the circulation of images—by Wobblies on the streets speaking about outrages in Little Falls or Paterson and about conditions in the nearby railroad camps and mining towns, and by print media reminding readers of the proper place of labor (that it should be conservative and cooperative, not agitational)—complemented and contested the circulation of capital and labor so as to define "the ways people lived, worked, and traded" (as Cronon put it). Struggle for the control of public space was central in this process of cementing patterns of circulation to patterns of production—or disrupting them—whether we define "public space" metaphorically as the sphere of communication within which dominant and contestatory ideas circulate or as the material spaces of the city.[75] The streets of Skid Rows in cities like Denver sat at the intersection of these patterns of circulation and production, as necessary to capital as they were to labor. For as the IWW Charles Ashleigh wrote, in such districts

> as you walk down the street you notice that the loungers are all "stiffs." Sun-tanned, brawny men, most of them in early manhood or in the prime of life, dressed in blue overalls or khaki pants and blue cotton shirts . . . are standing in knots around the doors of the employment sharks, watching requirements chalked up on the blackboards displayed outside. . . . Numbers of disconsolate ones may also be observed who have not the price of a job and who are waiting in hope of that much-desired thing—a free shipment. There may be a dozen [employment] offices in a town of three blocks.

Along with the employment offices and dozens of bars, lodging houses "crawling with vermin," and cheap cafés, Ashleigh continued, the military had its recruiting offices on Skid Row "offering a desperate refuge for the jobless, homeless, starving worker; vultures hovering over the swamp of poverty, ready to sweep down on some despairing victim, probably some lad lured to this country by booster-fed visions of the 'Golden West.'"[76]

The moral is simple. Controlling the streets of Denver was necessary to gaining some control over life within the region as a whole. And this simple fact was as well understood by the radical, footloose workers of the IWW as it was by the agents of capital and the state. In turn, control over the streets of Denver was possible only through liberating or controlling the subversive mobility of workers throughout the West. Yet given that, it is perhaps surprising that I could find no surviving records of the direct outcome of the AFL leaders' attempt to undermine the IWW organizing on the Denver and Rio Grande. One of the "fiercest struggles in the history of organized labor" seems to have left no traces in either the establishment or the radical press. Once the IWW won the right to speak on the streets, the *Rocky Mountain News* stopped covering its agitational activities and the *Industrial Worker* turned its attention to the need to organize the upcoming wheat harvest in eastern Colorado and western Kansas.

While it is impossible to know the reason for this silence—or more importantly the outcome of the labor leaders' work to still the agitation along the railroad—perhaps it is possible to conclude from the silence that the struggle had little to do with work conditions along the D&RG and more to do with who spoke for which workers. It may be that the IWW's agreement with the city that control over the streets would be bought at the price of ensuring that Wobblies without employment would leave the city undermined its ability to organize railroad workers.

Whatever the validity of that speculation, the IWW did not hesitate to claim an important victory on the streets of Denver: "Things are beginning to move in this dead burg of Denver—the best lighted cemetery in the world," Denver's Local 26 reported in June 1913. "Since the settlement of the free speech fight, extensive agitation has been carried on with splendid results." Even so, "there is room for good street speakers here and job agitators are needed badly. All agitators will be accorded a hearty reception. All rebels who intend to go into the Kansas harvest should be sure to communicate with local 26."[77]

If, as William Cronon argues, the key to understanding regional development in the West is to keep our "compass sights on the paths into and out of town," then surely the paths worth tracing include those of migratory workers as they meander through hobo jungle and skid row, work camp and factory.[78] For those of us interested in the intersection of labor relations, capital accumulation and circulation, the sort of marginality that gets named "homelessness" in different eras, and the making of geographies, this ought to be as worthy a project now as it was then for those who sought to unleash or contain the radical potential of persistent mobility. For it is these movements and the work of laborers that bind together the geographical scales that structure our lives (whether we are comfortably housed or, like so many, living in the tent encampments, shelters, or always-threatened SROs of contemporary Skid Row). And it is these movements too that continually transform those scales, reframing and reconstituting the world in which we live.

In the end the movements of migratory laborers who beat their way to Denver for the right to speak and assemble on the streets are not very strange at all, especially to those of us raised on the traditional images of the American West. Listen to Wobbly Richard Brazier as he recalls his days shifting between jobs in the developing West:

> The West was a wide open country, the open spaces really existed. There was plenty of room to move around in, and there were scenes of great grandeur and beauty, and there were journeys to be made that took you to all kinds of interesting sections in the country. That's the feeling we all had. I think that's one of the reasons we kept on moving as much as we did. In addition to searching for the job, we were also searching for something to satisfy our emotional desire for grandeur and

beauty. After all, we have a concept of beauty too, although we were only migratory workers.[79]

The irony of this recollection becomes clear the moment we recall the struggles for the streets of Denver and other actions like it. To experience that beauty, many workers had to pay with police beatings, jail time for vagrancy, and frequent resort to the lousy flophouses of the "dead burgs" of the region.

Between Denver and Auburn

Class struggle, Lefebvre said, is all there is that prevents the world from being "papered over" by the abstract space of capital, that prevents the total capitalist control of the spaces of grandeur and beauty Brazier was seeking, as well as the contentious streets of the city the Wobblies sought to organize. Such struggle is, as we have seen, organized spatially, in and across scales. Crucially, it is organized around differential mobilities of different factions of capital and labor (including the reserve army): the AFL's leaders summoned by telegraph rather than weekly newspapers did not have to steal rides on freight trains or march across mountains and desert to get to Denver as did Wobblies. And it is organized by seeking ways to control and discipline those differential mobilities in favor of one party or another. When the Denver *Democrat* wrote about how "settled labor conditions are more important than anything," and when it gave such prominent play to the ability of capital to "flee," as soon as labor gets militant, it was frankly recognizing the precarious position of any city or town under the logic of expansionary, mobile capitalism. For although Denver was built by the labor of countless workers, both migratory and relatively settled, it was also constructed by the ability of capital to flow: by the movement of English capital into the manufacturing concerns of the city and the stockyards of the surrounding countryside, of Chicago and New York capital into the warehouses and railroads, and of financial capital from all over the world into the banks along Seventeenth Street.[80] But as some of this capital became fixed in place, it became vulnerable to the movements of other capital—which threatened not only the owners of locally fixed capital, but locally based workers too.

The protection of locally fixed capital—property—the experience of Auburn, New York, seemed to suggest, rested precisely on the ability to control labor, including controlling the size, nature, and movements of the reserve army as well as ensuring the stability and proper conservativism of the settled working class. Yet, and this is crucial, stability might not preclude the mobility of labor; indeed, it might demand it. Thus, it demands the construction of particular geographical scales of activity: scales of social and economic control. But when that mobility turns subversive, when those scales of control become unbound and thrown into question, first by organizing on the streets, and then by organizing across the region to protect that right to organize on the streets, then measures must be taken to ensure a return to more settled labor conditions, a return to a more systematic and orderly production of scale. These measures include, of course, working to regain control over public space. The struggle for the production and control of public space is intimately tied to the struggle for the production and control of scale. Each is defined and made possible by the other.

In 1913 in Denver, the struggle for the control of space and scale entailed revoking the right of Wobblies to speak in public, the "rushing in" of conservative labor leaders to help quell an incipient revolt on the railroads, and a strong ideological, and at least nationally organized, offensive in the papers to remind workers (and other citizens) of the proper ways labor is supposed to behave. That offensive implied continual reference to struggle in other places (Auburn and Paterson, but also Akron and innumerable other industrial towns). And such an offensive was also clearly limited: within a year the coal fields of southern Colorado would erupt into a violent strike culminating in the Ludlow Massacre, proof positive that capital realized that mere persuasion often had to be replaced by actual physical violence in the effort to control the space and scales of production and circulation.[81]

If capital could call on the experience of distant places to support its ideology of compliant labor, radicalized workers—especially the footloose rebels of the IWW—could call on a fund of other places (in the case of free speech, places like Fresno, San Diego, Kansas City, and Spokane) not just in ideological terms, but also in terms of material connection. They could productively and subversively use the "paths into and out of town" that they produced through their labor and reproduced through their very mobility as migratory, "casual," homeless laborers. *These* paths were every bit as vital in connecting up the West, in allowing for its development at the scale of the region, as were the paths of capital. And the two working together both shaped and were shaped by the struggles on the streets of Denver (and numerous other places). "Marching on Denver to Fight for Free Speech," the *Industrial Worker* labeled the 1913 action. But, as the analysis in this chapter has shown, as important as free speech was, this march, this subversive mobilization, was about a great deal more than that. All the *other* things it was about connect it to a long history, and a present reality, of ongoing mobilizations and struggles by the poorly housed and the seemingly footloose, as we are about to see.

CHAPTER 3

Power Abhors a Tent

> Tent City is less a single location than a nomadic but constant phenomenon,
> a shifting blue-tarped shadow to the glass and steel American metropolis.
>
> **—Ben Ehrenreich, "Tales of Tent City" (2009)**

The existential threat International Harvester posed to Auburn, New York, in 1913 has, of course, long since come to pass. Twine is no longer made in that small Upstate town; the silk mills long ago departed Paterson. There is no smelting in Denver. The "Great U-turn" of American manufacturing that marked the 1970s and 1980s (see chapter 1) was in reality merely a quickening and generalization of what was always potentially there in the logic of capital: *its* inherent (if nonetheless contradictory) footlooseness; *its* inherent vagrancy that actually and with little compunction *does* destroy whole cities and regions.[1] During the ascendency of President Donald Trump in 2016, the exemplary case was the Carrier Corporation's plans to abandon production of air conditioning and heating units in Indianapolis, Indiana, in favor of cheaper labor in Monterrey, Mexico. Those of us watching events from Syracuse, New York (where I lived at the time), could not help but note the irony. Syracuse had lured Carrier away from its New Jersey base in the 1930s, only to see its Central New York production closed down and jobs shipped to other states (including Indiana) and overseas after it was purchased by United Technologies, based in Hartford, Connecticut, in the 1980s. While a few engineering jobs remain in Syracuse, Carrier's once-sprawling campus is now little more than a wind-blown plain with a few old husks of manufacturing buildings, part of the desolate landscape of deindustrialization that defines much of the region. As Carrier, along with General Electric, Allied Chemicals (Honeywell), New Process Gear, and so many others were shutting down shop in this part of the world—often complaining about high labor costs and recalcitrant unions—few brand-name politicians shed many tears, crocodile or otherwise. Such restructuring—"disruption" as we've now been taught to admiringly call it—is simply the way of the world.

Even in cities where workers and their allies made valiant efforts to keep their jobs as the asset strippers and hedge-fund managers came calling (like Youngstown, Ohio, or Pittsburg, California), sometimes sparking campaigns to buy out the vultures and turn factories into cooperatives, the eventual result was, typically, abandonment. Along with abandonment of factories came dilapidation and abandonment of homes, evictions and foreclosures, and growing numbers of homeless people. Even as some cities, like San Francisco, Brooklyn, Boston, and indeed Denver, boomed in the post-deindustrialization era, others—especially small manufacturing cities—descended into what looked like terminal decline, a decline only hastened by the economic catastrophe of 2007–2008.*

Camden, New Jersey, is paradigmatic. In the words of an exposé in the *Nation* in 2010, "Camden, New Jersey stands as a warning of what huge pockets of American could turn into." Stealing some of Detroit's thunder, perhaps, editors at the *Nation* called Camden the "City of Ruins." Besides Detroit (or Syracuse), they could have been talking about Cleveland, Gary (Indiana), not a little bit of Los Angeles, or, until very recently, much of Oakland. They could have been talking (perhaps a bit more surprisingly) about large pockets of Seattle, San Diego, Atlanta, or, again, Denver. As told by former war correspondent Chris Hedges (and illustrated with penetrating comics by Joe Sacco), the *Nation*'s story of Camden's destruction by the forces of capital makes for sobering reading. Two years after the economic meltdown, Camden's real unemployment rate likely stood between 30 and 40 percent, median household income was $24,600 (a little more than half that of the United States as a whole), the high school dropout rate was 70 percent, and city services were being radically slashed: the police force in a city routinely described as America's most violent was soon cut in half,† library budgets were cut by two-thirds, and all departments were slashed by at least 25 percent. Matters have hardly improved in the years since.[2]

If all that were not enough, the political establishment was deeply corrupt (the political boss ran the place from a suburb, not even bothering to live in the city he dominated). Though Campbell's Soup has retained its headquarters in the city, there is virtually no manufacturing in what had once been "an industrial giant." Shipbuilding, electronics, food manufacturing, and more have all fled for greener pastures and distant shores. As Hedges puts it, "Camden is the poster child of postindustrial decay. It stands as a warning of what huge pockets of the United

---

*For a while it looked like cities such as Syracuse might have avoided the worst of the effects of the Great Recession: after all, they seemingly could not go any lower. But as the crisis has roiled on, its effects have become obvious, with the governments of both the city of Syracuse and its surrounding county of Onondaga effectively bankrupt, housing abandonment continuing apace, jobs continuing to dry up, and (apart from a small "revitalized" downtown and a booming bubble of student housing near the university) storefronts, restaurants, and office parks standing empty.

†A week after Camden slashed its police and other budgets in 2010, President Obama reached a "compromise" with Republicans in Congress extending a tax cut to the most wealthy Americans.

States could turn into as we cement into place a permanent underclass of the un-employed, slash state and federal services in a desperate bid to cut massive deficits, watch cities and states go bankrupt and struggle to adjust to a stark neofeudalism in which the working and middle classes are decimated."[3] Donald Trump's startling victory in the Republican primaries and then his Electoral College win in the general election can be attributed, at least in some part, to a revolt against exactly these sorts of conditions as many of the alienated and disaffected turned to him in the absence of any sort of creditable political alternative to the world footloose capital had made (or just abstained from voting at all).*

Beyond turning to a certain kind of populism, the ways people find to cope with the ugly world footloose capital has made can be glimpsed in many places, from the food pantries and soup kitchens churches have set up to the gardens growing on abandoned lots, the dollar stores that move into run-down strip malls, the illicit markets in drugs, sex, counterfeit brand-name clothes, and basic consumer goods that thrive in many city neighborhoods—and perhaps especially in the overfull homeless shelters, the innumerable people bedding down in doorways of closed shops, and the homeless encampments that are springing up in every city.

Camden is no exception. In the wake of the economic crisis dozens of home-less people, perhaps sixty of them, set up a camp of tents and tarpaulin shelters under an interstate highway on-ramp. They called their encampment Transitional Park. This was just one redoubt of the city's homeless; there had to be others. Camden City Council counted 775 people as officially homeless, but there were only 220 shelter beds in the whole of the county. According to Hedges, the "mayor" of Transitional Park "ran the tent city . . . like a military encampment." The mayor had an assistant, whom he called his CEO, and together they conducted inspections every weekend, held a camp meeting every week and posted rules banning drugs, fighting, selling food stamps, and prostitutes bringing their tricks into the camp, as well as requiring trash to be picked up. Repeat violators were expelled from the camp. A guard detail was established to keep residents safe at night.[4] Amid the ruins, this was survival. This was self-organization, if perhaps not as immediately political in orientation as the self-organization of the Wobblies a century earlier. Though an alternative to the abject, isolated, disorganized life of the street, it was not really an alternative to the world that capital and its flight likes to make, but it was something.

And it was something the city tolerated through the winter of 2010, perhaps because it seemed to have no other option.[5] But the visibility of that something,

---

* Trump's voters were destined, of course, to be disappointed. His first budget promised even more massive cuts in the taxes of the wealthy and in social services for the rest. Nor, beyond occasionally publicly shaming companies contemplating moving jobs overseas, has the Trump administration contemplated any sort of comprehensive industrial policy (though he has engaged in a sort of ad hoc and incoherent, if ever-expanding trade war); indeed, Trump's government is most noteworthy for being stocked by a large number of corporate raiders sourced from Wall Street.

perhaps the potential of the occupation of what might be called interstitial spaces of the capitalist city, and organizing in it to erupt into something more powerful (as had often happened in the past), eventually became too much. With spring's arrival, therefore, also came the wrecking crews. "Those tossed out scattered, and about a half-dozen migrated to the squalor under the concrete ramps of Route 676, where it runs across the river into Philadelphia."[6] The alternative that was no alternative was now no more—destroyed for no good reason except the city leaders thought it was a blight on their already thoroughly blighted landscape. This is often the fate of tent cities, not only in Camden but also in Fresno or Phoenix, Sacramento, or St. Petersburg (Florida). As soon as tent cities spring up, as soon as they get organized well enough to provide a bit of security—at least in most cities—they're destroyed.*

Why?

Tent City—A Historical Geography

Every time we get leadership, they get a bus ticket out of town.

   —Tent city resident Brad Bradford (2006)

In a lengthy but still highly partial (and deeply problematic) account, prominent law scholar Robert Ellickson asserted that in the Skid Row of the 1960s police had homeless men—bums as he called them—right where they wanted them.[7] As long as homeless people stuck to their district, the city provided a space for them. Aspects of this argument can also be found in Jim Duncan's still insightful analysis of tramps' classification and use of space. But Duncan goes a step further, showing how it was precisely the marginal, or interstitial, spaces of the city that made it possible for homeless men to survive.[8] In this struggle for survival, visibility mattered. To the degree homeless men were confined to Skid Row, then they could be kept out of sight—or perhaps transformed into merely a picaresque, colorful remnant of a bygone era. To the degree their numbers were not huge and they remained in their single room occupancy hotels (or otherwise their encampments were hidden away under bridges, in back alleys, or behind abandoned buildings) they were tolerated.[9] Episodic visibility—to panhandle or cadge cigarettes, to visit soup kitchens or take an occasional day job—was at least partially tolerated in non–Skid Row locales. But it was primarily the interstices of Skid Row that were, in Jeremy Waldron's terms, the spaces where homeless people could *be*.[10] Even more than the public property

* Some West Coast cities, notably Portland and Seattle, have begun to understand encampments as a form of "transitional" housing and have begun to make it legally possible for them to exist as such. Other cities, notably Los Angeles, have been restrained by the courts from totally destroying tent encampments and allow individuals to set up overnight on Skid Row sidewalks under very stringent conditions (as noted in chapter 1).

that Waldron felt kept homeless people from the annihilation that would face them if we truly lived in a "libertarian paradise" of only private property, the abandoned, in-between, unsurveilled spaces of the city—whether publicly or privately owned—together with the relatively benign policing of Skid Row provided the very conditions of possibility for being "men without property," to use Duncan's term. Or so the argument went.

Ellickson's and Duncan's accounts of Skid Row are partial because Skid Row was not really an abandoned space: as we have already seen it played a vital economic function in industrial-era America, and continued to do so, if in much reduced capacity, into the 1960s (though temporarily diminished in economic importance, day labor markets and labor contracting of casual labor continued, and Skid Row remained a center for such functions). And neither was Skid Row such a benign place: the police could be impressively violent in their control of tramping workers, homeless men, and alcoholics on the street, and the private violence of jackrollers and muggers took its steady toll. And now, of course, in city after city (if not Camden, which, in the shadow of Philadelphia, never really had a well-developed Skid Row), Skid Row has been thoroughly gentrified, brought in from the margins, from the interstices, and placed right at the center of the new city.*

Nonetheless interstices in cities remain—under bridges, in abandoned lots still awaiting redevelopment, on the grounds of old factories, in the scrub and silt of the riverbeds that run through town—and they remain vital for homeless people and their pursuit of life (see chapter 4). Sometimes these interstitial spaces become, for homeless people, absolutely central. They become tent cities: relatively stable encampments of the desperately poor.

Poor people's encampments have a long and important history in the United States. During America's post–Civil War industrialization, tramps "slept just about anywhere they could," as Tim Cresswell has put it.[11] Municipal lodging houses, jailhouse floors, rescue missions, SROs, and "cage" hotels on Skid Row; bunkhouses provided by employers; and sometimes park benches or storefront doorways all formed part of the tramps' archipelago of housing.[12] But of particular significance was "the jungle"—or hobo encampment. Usually tramps' jungles developed in wastelands near the railroad. "Hobo sociologist" Nels Anderson described the conditions that made for a good jungle: "It should be located in a dry and shady place that permits sleeping on the ground. There should be plenty of water for cooking and bathing and wood enough to keep the pot boiling. If there is a general store near by where bread, meat, and vegetables may be had, so much the better. For those who have no money but enough cour-

---

*Meanwhile, reinvigorated day labor markets (catering largely to immigrant casual laborers) and day labor agencies like Manpower, Inc. (the new labor sharks for the very poor and catering largely to people of color), following the economy, have shifted location to suburban parking lots and poor African American neighborhoods, respectively.

age to 'bum lumps,' it is well that the jungles be not too far from town, though far enough to escape the attention of natives and officials."[13] Jungles might have been permanent or temporary, but they existed by a strict code of mutuality, even if this mutuality was also organized around a hierarchy (especially in sexual relations): sharing was sine qua non. If someone had a decent "stake," he was expected to look out for his brothers who did not, in the knowledge that the tables would soon be turned. According to Anderson, the jungles were frequently multiracial.[14]

Importantly, the jungle was a political place (especially after the founding of the Industrial Workers of the World in 1905) on par with the Skid Row street corner, or union hall.* No doubt tramping casual workers who lived off and on in the jungles were a despised class, condemned as mental inferiors, lousy workers, habitual drunks, beggars, and other no-goods—a kind of condemnation that has lived down through the years and more or less continues to define many popular perceptions of homeless people (especially men).[15] Against such characterizations, however, tramping workers created their own political culture, within which the jungle was central. Seeking to both capitalize on and revolutionize this culture, IWW organizers—carrying the union under their hat—sought to turn migratory and homeless workers into a revolutionary class, or if not entirely that, then at least a radical one ready to fight for its rights as workers and as outcasts. In so doing the IWW developed a particular renown among migratory workers. Indeed, as one undercover agent in California wrote of the IWW, "The extent and activity of this organization's workings are almost beyond belief. One sees notices everywhere. You hear 'Wobblies' spoken of favorably in 'jungle' conversations. There is widespread knowledge of and interest in any consideration of the problems concerned with this organization."[16] The jungle was a space of organizing for the IWW; it was a space of worry and danger for the bourgeoisie. Its hiddenness together with the seeming impenetrability of its mores—its very status as an interstices in the capitalist political economy and culture—together with the obvious fact that it was a space of radical organizing added to its threatening power. To eliminate this power, the federal government,

---

* By all accounts, before the IWW was suppressed by the federal government in 1917, their union halls were remarkable places, for the group was an intellectual as well as a political and labor organization. According to Philip Foner, "The typical hall, especially in the West usually contained dog-eared copies of Marx, Darwin, Spenser, Voltaire, Tom Paine, Jack London and a variety of government documents." Progressive reformer Carleton Parker wrote of the IWW, "Presumably they were better acquainted with American social statistics than the academic class." And another historian (quoted by Foner) wrote of Wobblies, "Entering a hall in the evening one might see several shabbily dressed young men reading from books taken from shelves of the library in the room. Others crouched over a makeshift stove brewing a mulligan stew, its ambitious odor permeating the hall. While they tended supper, they argued some point in economics or religion." A similar culture permeated the jungles, even if the books may have been fewer, being typically replaced by a range of newspapers carried in by workers and hobos come to bed down for the night. Foner, *Industrial Workers of the World*, 151; Parker, "I.W.W."

drawing on undercover work by agents of the California Commission of Immigration and Housing and the theories of its executive director Carleton Parker, sought—during World War I—to eliminate not only the IWW but also the jungle, to bring tramping workers into visibility, as it were, and to thereby weaken their subversive potential.[17]

Jungles were only one form of political encampment for tramping workers, hobos, and homeless people. In the midst of economic depressions various "armies" formed to march on state capitals and Washington, D.C., where they often camped at length, making demands on the state. Coxey's and Kelly's armies of the 1893 depression provided the precedent, but a further Kelly's Army in California in 1914 and the Bonus Marchers of the Great Depression (cleared out of their encampment by the U.S. Army) showed the threatening power that organized, destitute workers and homeless people could sometimes possess, especially if they were successful in controlling both the spaces and places of their radicalism.[18] Coxey's and Kelly's armies commandeered trains; they camped en masse in empty lots, city streets, and farmers' fields; they marched.

It is not surprising, then, that the 1914 Kelly's Army met such fierce resistance when it camped in Sacramento. The 1914 army had begun in San Francisco, but was soon violently expelled, as it also quickly was in Oakland. But as it marched into Sacramento it was at first met with a fair degree of sympathy and tolerance. Indeed, its large encampment near the capitol building became something of an attraction with tourists and radicals alike descending on it. But as the marchers became more militant, the sheriff deputized hundreds of "upstanding citizens" who formed the core of a counter-army that eventually grew to eight hundred members, including several fire crews. The firefighters took the lead when city leaders determined to roust Kelly's Army, swooping into the camp, spraying their powerful hoses, arresting identifiable leaders, and "routing" the marchers. Kelly's Army's occupation of prime space in California's capital—which had been attracting a good degree of public sympathy in the midst of a deep economic crisis—had become intolerable. The Progressive administration of Governor Hiram Johnson, which only two years before had actually showed some restraint and a good deal of political savvy in brokering an end to the IWW's bloodiest free speech fight (in San Diego), now cheered on the routing of Kelly's Army from behind the scenes, as did much of what the IWW called the "kept press": the reports in the *New York Times* on the violent routing of the army in Sacramento were practically gleeful.[19]

Yet in this instance it was not only the interstices that mattered to poor people's ability to be, but also the way that organized poor and homeless people managed to transform a center into the interstices: into a tent city at the heart of the city that had real political effectivity (as witnessed in the ferociousness of the assault when it came), and was thus a real threat to bourgeois business as usual. With its rout, Kelly's Army dissipated, but the political and economic currents it symbolized continued to roil. In rural California (as elsewhere) en-campments of dissatisfied or striking workers were a regular part of the land-scape throughout the latter part of the 1920s, especially as ethnically Mexican agricultural workers grew militant in the last two years of the decade. Often forced into strikers' camps as they were shut out of company housing in the la-bor camps, militant workers found that taking and occupying space was vital to organizing resistance against and within the very spaces of injustice that defined their lives. They were met, up and down the state, with impressive violence, vio-lence designed not only to break up their power but also and especially to reas-sert control over the spaces that made their power possible—power that by the mid-1930s seemed to portend a radical change to the long-standing structure of injustice and deep exploitation that marked the California valleys.[20]

As with the IWW a generation earlier, the demands of such strikers were of-ten deceptively simple—a small raise in wages, a demand that the government disarm the farmers—but they implicated a whole spatial system of production (and reproduction), and as such could not be tolerated either by organized agri-business, or the larger state apparatus. Thus, for everything else they were, the Farm Security Administration labor camps in the late 1930s (made famous in John Steinbeck's *The Grapes of Wrath*) were as much a means to quell dissent to business as usual as they were a means to protect the rights of itinerant, destitute, homeless farmworkers.

On the national front, the well-known Bonus March of 1932 also made clear the limits of tolerance for poor and working people's movements. When Pres-ident Herbert Hoover grew tired of the fifteen to twenty thousand veterans and their families who set up a protest camp in Washington (some after a long cross-country trek) to demand that a payment promised for 1945 be moved for-ward to meet immediate needs, he sent in General Douglas MacArthur and the U.S. Army—not used against the American people since the Battle of Blair Mountain in 1921—to clear out occupied buildings along Pennsylvania Ave-nue. Riding the tanks, directing soldiers armed with live ammunition, and di-recting volley after volley of teargas, MacArthur ordered troops into Anacos-tia where the Bonus Marchers had established their racially integrated, orderly, carefully organized camp (a camp that authorities nonetheless claimed endan-gered health and safety) and set it on fire.* By the time MacArthur's scorched-earth policy had run its course, two veterans and two babies were dead, the Bo-nus Expeditionary Force (as the Bonus Marchers called themselves) had been routed, and its leaders had been either bought off or sent into hiding. Once

---

*As I wrote these words, the state and federal governments were preparing to attack the Standing Rock protest encampment established to deter the completion of an oil pipeline across the Missouri River. The script prepared for this presumed rout could have been written in 1932, or 1914, or, as we will see, all through the 1990s and 2000s when homeless people created camps and politicized them, or 2011–2012 with the global assault on Occupy encampments. Power truly abhors a tent.

again, as with the IWW, the Bonus Marcher's demands were quite simple, but they implicated a deep structure of inequality—an ubiquitous geography of injustice that extended well beyond these immediate demands, as was made plain in the very racial integration of the Bonus encampment in the midst of hyper-segregated Washington.[21]

Of equal importance to the Bonus Marchers as the Great Depression deepened were the innumerable "Hoovervilles" that sprang up in cities and countryside alike. Squatters built shacks in New York's Central Park, and other Hoovervilles climbed up the banks of the Harlem River (to which they would return in the 1980s). In California shack towns filled empty lots in all the major cities; encampments of tents, wooden or cardboard boxes, and brush filled the river bottoms and irrigation ditch banks in the agricultural countryside. These margins too possessed the potential to unleash a new and scary politics, as Steinbeck's Tom Joad—perhaps America's most famous Hooverville denizen—made clear in his ringing soliloquy near the end of *The Grapes of Wrath*: "I'll be ever'where—wherever you look. Wherever they's a fight so hungry people can eat. I'll be there. Wherever they's a cop beatin' up a guy. I'll be there. . . . An' when our folks eat the stuff they raise an' live in the houses they build—why, I'll be there."*

After World War II, however, such mass interstitial living began to evaporate. In some instances (rural California, for instance) tent and shack cities in unincorporated areas were gradually transformed into more settled, more permanent districts, more or less on the model of informal settlements the world over.[22] Labor markets were altered, as much labor was decasualized, and that which was not, such as agricultural work in California, was handed over to Mexican "guest workers," in a federally sponsored plan to drive "domestic" (that is, citizen and long-term resident) workers out of the fields and replace them with what was essentially an indentured labor force; agribusinesses also assiduously recruited armies of undocumented workers (as the immigration authorities mostly looked the other way), many of them living in brush encampments in the desert and ravines, or squatting in (or under) abandoned farmhouses.[23] As chapter 1 indicated, the face of homelessness in the cities changed. Skid Row became largely the haunt of elderly, not infrequently alcoholic men, soon joined by very poor residents recently released from mental institutions in the first bout of deinstitutionalization. The one-two punch of urban renewal and gentrification further marginalized Skid Row and its residents. With the exception of rural en-

---

*No doubt some of those in California's Hoovervilles had earlier been driven out of the large—several thousand residents—tent city in the River Bottom section of Oklahoma City. In 1931, in the wake of a rare order from the governor demanding the Oklahoma City mayor and police stop arresting unemployed people on charges of vagrancy and sentencing them to either finding a (nonexistent) job or leaving the jurisdiction, Oklahoma City police resorted to the much more direct expedient of shutting down the tent city on the grounds of "unsanitary living conditions." After the sweep, a large number of unemployed families were reportedly "leaving the city" and heading west. See Presthold, "How We Solved It at Oklahoma City"; Steinbeck, *Grapes of Wrath*.

campments of undocumented workers, tent-city-like encampments—and jungles—seemed to fade from the scene in the postwar but pre-neoliberal era.*

With the Reagan Revolution, tent cities returned. Already declining during the Carter administration, the public housing budget was cut in half in the first Reagan budget, and slashed and slashed again in the years that followed.† Disability and mental health support budgets were likewise slashed, and the inevitable effects of unsupported deinstitutionalization quickly made themselves felt in city after city (the 1980s marked a new, intensified wave of the deinstitutionalization that had begun in the 1950s).[24] Deindustrialization played its role, eliminating jobs and livelihoods, leading to foreclosures, and sending thousands of workers and their families out on the road looking for better opportunities.[25] All these processes hit people of color the hardest, and the next new face of homelessness was increasingly dark and increasingly female. The old fact of homelessness expressed itself in the old form: shantytowns and tent cities.

One of the most famous of the 1980s tent cities was in Los Angeles's Skid Row. Called Justiceville, originally located on a sidewalk and led by the charismatic Ted Hayes, it in some ways reflected the cult of personality that developed around him.‡ This cult had important effects, bringing significant attention to the plight of homeless people in Skid Row and the city's ongoing attempts to uproot their encampments, memorialized in a documentary film and Motown song. For some, the cult of personality—and indeed the rather dictatorial manner in which Justiceville was run—encouraged defection even before the LA city government moved to close the tent city down. Not far away, therefore, Love Camp, another encampment of homeless people, developed (with at least some support from nearby businesses). Love Camp was more cooperatively organized than Justiceville, and for some homeless people, according to geographers Stacey Rowe and Jennifer Wolch, "the camp became so supportive the residents attempted to remain on the sidewalk and build quasi-permanent structures (plywood homes) as a personal long-term 'solution' to more transient homeless existence. The intent was not to rejoin mainstream society, but instead to remain as a member of a homeless street community." Such a move to stability and autonomy, however, is something most cities cannot countenance. As with Camden's Transitional Park a generation later, Love Camp was swept away,

* By the 1970s hobo jungles had been rendered so rare and impotent as to become quaint, nostalgically reconstructed in an annual Hobo Convention in Britt, Iowa.

† Since 1996 there has been absolutely no money budgeted for new public housing, though Section 8 housing vouchers still exist, with waiting lists of tens of thousands; and cities now mandate that some number of units be set aside as "affordable housing" in new developments.

‡ Hayes is a controversial figure. A strong supporter of President George W. Bush in the early 2000s, he stood for Congress as a Republican against long-serving Los Angeles progressive Democrat Maxine Waters; later he formed the Crispus Attucks Brigade, an African American organization that agitated against "illegal" immigrants and sought to disrupt the immigrant rights rallies in Los Angeles during the immigrants' uprising of 2006.

its residents dispersed. "It took so long for us to build that up," one resident told Rowe and Wolch, "and it took five minutes to tear it down."[26]

Innumerable similar Justicevilles, Love Camps, Dignity Villages, Reagan-villes, and more developed across the country, pushed and shoved around the wastelands of the city, as city officials at times tolerated their presence as the least bad option, and at other times sought to shut them down. They were supplemented by thousands of less organized, though sometimes quite large, encampments in riverbeds, under on-ramps, and on disused rail lines. And they grew in number, size, and precariousness as the Reagan-Bush era gave way to the Clinton era. Such spaces moved around, but they never disappeared, even when the economy picked up in the wake of the economic crises and recessions of the 1980s. "In good times and bad, Tent City comes and goes," as investigative reporter Ben Ehrenreich has written; "it forms and scatters and takes shape again."[27] Sometimes tent city takes official shape, with architects' help. After Justiceville was chased around Skid Row a few times, for example, Ted Hayes managed to secure a fenced site and a quarter-million-dollar grant from the oil company ARCO to erect twenty geodesic domes for homeless people, designed by an acolyte of Buckminster Fuller. Dome Village lasted until 2006, when the owner of the land it was on reclaimed it—part of an anti-Republican campaign, according to Hayes.[28] Dignity Village in Portland, Oregon, now more than twenty-five years old, calls itself a "campground for the homeless" and boasts a flashy website, a board of directors, and a Facebook presence. Like Dome Village, it is an official nonprofit organization and has garnered a great deal of popular and critical attention.[29] These are (or were), no doubt, vital spaces—important attempts to secure a space for homeless people's survival.

But they are, often, also fenced and carefully policed spaces. And the historical geography of tent city is replete with attempts to corral and contain the homeless. As street homelessness continued to grow in Los Angeles in the 1990s, the city made plans to develop a "drop-in center" funded in part by a large grant from HUD. A city official described the drop-in center as a "fenced-in urban campground where up to 800 people could take a shower and sleep on a lawn."[30] The city planned to purchase a hidden-away vacant lot in Skid Row, put a fence around a large lawn on the site, and build a fifty-bed shelter that would also house some social services. Homeless people would be bussed to the site from various places around the city and locked up for the night. Homeless advocate and UCLA law professor Gary Blasi called the plan "a first step on a slippery slope to concentration camps in rural areas for homeless people."[31] Eventually the plan for the overnight camping lawn was dropped (though more due to merchant than homeless advocate opposition) and the drop-in center itself was long stalled.[32]

Plans for such fenced encampments are not rare, and they continue to this day. In the wake of the 2008 economic crisis, Ontario, California, built one. Its

Temporary Homeless Services Area (THSA) began as a fenced-off camping area that police directed homeless people to (perhaps "pushed" is a better term). Yet

> in March [2008], after herding the local homeless population to Tent City, police and code enforcement officers descended on the encampment and required its inhabitants to prove they were residents of Ontario. Those who could not—all but 127—were evicted. The city bulldozed and graded the field, erected orderly rows of matching green tents, issued ID cards to those who remained, fenced the encampment and posted a list of rules: no re-entry after 10 pm, no alcohol, no pets, no minors, no visitors. Now private security guards patrol the THSA's perimeters, ejecting anyone who doesn't have permission to be there, including reporters.[33]

As Ben Ehrenreich detailed,

> None of the Tent City residents I interviewed from just outside the fence complained much. They were fed three meals a day and were otherwise left alone. The rules were infantilizing, but the people largely shrugged them off. Still, more than a third of those permitted to stay in the THSA have left for good. No new arrivals have been admitted. Isaac Jackson, coordinator of the county's Office of Homeless Services, credited Ontario with doing a "great job" of reducing Tent City's population. Neither city nor county officials, though, knew if any of those who have left the Tent City have found a better source of shelter than a tent. It seems unlikely.*

Ehrenreich's in-depth account of struggles over tent cities in contemporary California came in the wake of massive publicity surrounding Sacramento's bulging tent city on the banks of the American River in early 2009. The media turned its glare to Sacramento's tent city after daytime TV guru Oprah Winfrey suggested it was paradigmatic of a new, growing poverty made visible by the burst financial and housing bubbles.[34]

But as Ehrenreich makes so clear, the residents of Sacramento's tent city were largely *not* the newly evicted but people who had long since been evicted from the mainstream economy and from standard housing. Tent city, he writes, "tells the grueling backstory of the current recession—nearly thirty years of cuts in social services to the poor and mentally ill, the decimation of the industrial economy and the cruel underside of the housing boom."[35] Contemporary tent cities, then, are evidence not of capitalism in crisis but of capitalism in full flower.[36] They are what they have always been: deeply troubling interstitial spaces only by dint of which capitalism's reserve army can survive, whether that survival has

---

*In another official tack, city officials in San Diego, under a court order to provide winter shelter for homeless people, spent the 1990s scrambling each year to locate a disused warehouse or office building in that rapidly redeveloping and gentrifying city; by the dawn of the new century they had thrown in the towel and taken to erecting large "sprung shelters"—giant tents—on the only space they could find: a couple of dead-end streets near where the new baseball stadium was being constructed. After the stadium was finished, the homeless were chased from there too. See Staeheli and Mitchell, *People's Property?*, chap. 3.

radical or revolutionary potential, is merely infantilizing, or, now with a space to *be*, just *is*.

Tent City—A Space of Survival

Survival is the biggest time-filler here. Tents must be shored up against the wind and rain. The schedule for meals, clothing giveaways and shower times at local agencies must be strictly followed.

—Maria La Ganga, "In Sacramento's Tent City" (2009)

Tent city is not the crisis. It's the conditions that caused tent city that's the crisis.

—Homeless advocate Eric Rubin (2007)

Ben Ehrenreich was correct, of course, when he argued that Sacramento's tent city was not *only* a symbol of the economic crisis, but part of the "back story" of that crisis, the result of a long history of disinvestment, upward wealth redistribution, the attack on the state, and the veneration of markets. It was proof positive of the very nature of the good life neoliberalism had made. It was also proof positive that the bourgeoisie *still* had no more of a solution to the housing problem than it did in Engel's day.[37]

Sacramento's tent city merely made the case. Transient encampments of greater or lesser extent had long existed on the wasteland by the American River that Oprah Winfrey brought to the world's attention in early 2009. The iteration she found had grown to some two to three hundred residents over the past year (out of more than twelve hundred homeless people in shelters or sleeping rough in Sacramento). Some residents had long been homeless in the city; others became homeless or moved to the city more recently. Tent city residents had self-sorted themselves into "neighborhoods" based on interests, affinity, tolerance for drugs or alcohol, and the like. Joan Burke, who worked at the nearby Loaves and Fishes homeless services agency, told a reporter, "There is a sort of very pure democracy and self-governance at play. People are just making up the rules of their clusters of tents, deciding what's permitted, just as in any sort of community. . . . You don't want to romanticize this—it isn't camping—but there is a community and a sense of helping others. We've had a series of storms here recently, and if there's somebody new who doesn't have a tent, people will take them in. It's that understanding that, you know, there's somebody worse off than I am."[38] In other words, something like the ethos of the old hobo jungle was being re-created.

The global attention Sacramento's tent city garnered made it intolerable to city authorities. New (neo)liberal mayor Kevin Johnson soon announced plans to clear it out. While admitting that the city had to show some compassion toward the homeless, Mayor Johnson declared that Sacramento needed to begin exercising "tough love" (classic urban-right code for stripping homeless people of their humanity while simultaneously reducing homelessness to a character flaw, here adopted by a putatively liberal mayor) as well as adopt a "zero-tolerance" policy toward homeless encampments.[39] He therefore announced a plan (in late March) to open a wintertime emergency shelter on the grounds of the California State Fair—a shelter that would be highly regulated, fenced, and locked up at night, but within which residents would not be separated from their partners and pets, and where there would be at least some provision for the safe storage of belongings. Many of those in the tent city resisted the plan. "People out here are not going to go anywhere where they are going to lock you in," as one put it. "Would you go anywhere where they are going to turn the key and lock you in for the night? No." And as another said, "I'm not sure what's going to happen. . . . I'd just like to be left alone myself. I like it right here where I am at. So I don't know what's going to go on. . . . But I am not really very happy about it." Yet as Richard Gonzalez, the National Public Radio reporter covering the issue, closed one of his stories, "being left alone isn't in the cards,"* given Mayor Johnson's talk of tough love and zero tolerance.[40]

Sacramento's tent city was duly closed at the end of March 2009 and some two hundred homeless people—not all of them tent city residents—moved to the winter shelter at the fairgrounds. On July 1 the winter shelter was closed, and the residents found themselves back on the streets. In the wake of the closure homeless people (including many who had never moved to the fairgrounds, but instead retreated more deeply into the brush) marched through Sacramento and demanded a right to camp. Setting up a symbolic tent in an empty lot next to a police station, they demanded "a civil liberty that ought to already exist, which is [that] people have a right to be, to live without the constant threat of being incarcerated in their own country," as one marcher put it.[41] Another marcher described his life since the American River tent city was cleared out at the end of March: "When we moved out we moved over to a private area two fields over. They wanted us off of there too. Just like shuttling cattle, that's all it is. . . . We're supposed to be the eyesore, but actually we're citizens and we're human beings. We're supposed to have rights like everybody else; it doesn't matter what we have in our pockets."[42] He had spent his time one step ahead of the police, seeking out any sort of shelter.

He likely lived, off and on, in one or another of the dozen or so small tent encampments that "continue[d] to pop up and just as quickly" were shut down by

---

*The U.S. Supreme Court has more than once declared the "right to be left alone" to be one of the "most comprehensive of rights and the right most valued by civilized men." There is much to question in this formulation (and some of its political implications are troubling, as we will see in chapters 5 and 6), but it does point to an autonomy in social life that citizens of the country seem to have by right—unless they are homeless.

the police. Advocates for the homeless thus stepped up agitation for what they called "safe ground, a legal campground, so they're not hounded from place to place. And they're not subject to citations and arrests."* Mayor Johnson said he was open to the idea, but also that "I do not believe that people should be allowed to camp, you know, illegally, anywhere in the city at this particular time."[43]

The creation of such "safe ground" is not a novel idea. More than twenty-five years ago the city of Miami was required by court order to create a safe haven for homeless people and eventually set aside an area under a highway overpass where homeless people could be free from arbitrary sweeps, the confiscation of their belongings, arrest for loitering or sleeping in public, and—as in the event that led to the lawsuit from which the court order resulted—being roused from their sleep in a park and handcuffed while their belongings were thrown in a pile and lit on fire.[44] They have, however, sparked new interest, as the question of the very survival of homeless people continues to force itself into the consciousness of city managers and the public alike.[45] By the time Oprah turned the world's attention to Sacramento, for example, homeless people in Nashville had been living in encampments under an interstate overpass near the Cumberland River for perhaps two decades. According to a Nashville City Council member, the camp was "pretty extensive," with some shelters possessing roofs and stoves, and pirated electricity occasionally available. "Over the years," he said, "we've found that it is a lot of individuals who are trying to find some sort of refuge from the mean streets from the violence and disorder they see in other parts of the city as they're homeless." The out-of-the-way space of the encampment served as a safe haven for the city's homeless population as it grew during the economic crisis. When the growing population of the encampment and the new national attention Oprah brought to such places meant greater local scrutiny, the city decided not to raze it, but to "monitor it" and to "put case management services around these people" to help move them out of homelessness.[46]

The problem of safe havens is a difficult one. On the one hand, the creation of safe havens is both a frank admission that Engels was right (in homelessness, capitalism runs right up against one of its limits: a limit to providing even the basic necessities of life for significant numbers of people) and an evolution in poverty *management*. By containing homeless people in a defined area and "put[ting] case management services around these people" cities are seeking to "neutralize homelessness," a primary aim of poverty management, as Peter Marcuse long ago noted and as the city of Ontario's actions made clear.[47] Against such neutralization and containment, homeless people want two things: infra-

*In the end, no safe space was created, though homeless people did band together to gain access to portable toilets at one of the American River encampments, which the city eventually removed because neighbors complained of a growing "homeless infrastructure"; see Speer, " Right to Infrastructure," 10.

structure and control over their own lives, neither of which, geographer Jessie Speer makes clear, is independent of the other.[48] Speer's analysis of homeless people's struggle for clean, serviced, reasonably autonomous tent cities in Fresno (California) is worth paying attention to.

By fighting for infrastructure (garbage cans or dumpsters, portable toilets, maybe water), Speer argues, homeless Fresno residents were implicitly and sometimes explicitly questioning the individualizing logic of the provision of housing alone. While neither Speer nor the homeless residents she talked with dismissed the importance of efforts to provide some of the homeless population with their own apartments (through Housing First–type programs), they disputed "the provision of housing for the homeless . . . [as an] extreme manifestation of 'turf' politics in which individuals are assisted in securing their own domestic spaces while the larger problem of capitalist housing remains unchallenged" as well as the growing circumstances in American cities where "sanitation provision was only available in exchange for money." The struggle for infrastructure was thus a struggle for a different form of life and by (at least temporarily) "building alternative infrastructures in the encampments, homeless Fresnans and activists collectively created the encampment as an oeuvre that reflected their own interests and demands." Speer concludes, "In this sense, an effort that appears unambitious in the moment—the provision of sanitation to homeless encampments—can be seen from a broader temporal lens as the beginning of a move towards untying the bonds between private property and domestic life."[49]

It can also be seen as threatening—to property and the values it represents, to bourgeois sensibilities, and to city administrations' abilities to control and regulate space within their jurisdictions—which is why in Fresno as elsewhere (or in fact even more intensely than elsewhere), the city had engaged in a never-ending bulldozer and dump truck assault on homeless people's encampments, unable intellectually, emotionally, and ideologically to differentiate homeless people and their encampments from the very trash homeless people would like to have had collected.[50] And it is why cities have fought vigorously against court-mandated "safe havens," or sought to take total control of them, as in Ontario.

The dynamics at work could perhaps best be seen in St. Petersburg, Florida, when the homeless population burgeoned as the housing bubble began to burst in 2006. In December of that year church groups distributed tents to some thirty homeless people living under Interstate 375.[51] At the New Year, the tent city—now called "Coming Up"—moved across the street to a vacant lot owned by the St. Vincent de Paul Society, where it grew to about 140 residents.[52] Residents (the majority of whom worked full-time) signed a contract with each other pledging four hours of community work a week to keep the grounds clean, clean the portable toilets, cut hair, mediate disputes, and so forth. Such self-organization quickly prompted city officials (over the objections of some council members) to declare a "crisis"* and order St. Vincent de Paul to evict the residents under an old law prohibiting people from living in tents anywhere in the city, even on private property. The city pledged to find a vacant building to use as a winter shelter but had no intention of delaying the eviction until it did, a position that led to strenuous protests by local homeless people and their advocates, including a large protest at the mayor's church. Threatened with daily fines of $250 for code violations, St. Vincent de Paul complied with city orders to shut down the camp. Some residents moved back to one of two camps under the interstate; others accepted one-time rent vouchers of $550, which would allow them to stay in a motel for two weeks or more. Others merely disappeared.

Soon after the St. Vincent de Paul site was closed down, two homeless men were murdered in a single night. An extraordinary city council meeting followed, shedding further light on the dangers faced by homeless people living on the streets. Even so, a week after the murders, with no suspects yet apprehended,† city police entered the two small tent cities that had sprung up in the wake of St. Vincent closing, slashing the tents from their bases and moorings with knives, box cutters, and scissors, and confiscating them. They claimed fire code violations (though precisely which ones and whether they actually applied or not remained unclear in official explanations). The police claimed they cut up the tents to avoid "physical altercations" with homeless people, who might have refused to let them confiscate them if they asked.‡ The move was ineffective; homeless advocates secured new tents within eight hours and the camps were quickly reestablished.

Moreover, videos of the raid were quickly posted on YouTube, attracting significant national attention and encouraging furious backtracking by the mayor and other city officials.§ In turn, nearby businesses and residents organized to ensure the permanent elimination of the tent cities, holding rallies and protests nearby, at which they claimed the tent cities encouraged crime, threatened property values, and undermined business. As a result, the city held a "homeless summit," an effect of which was a change in city codes—outlawing tents on public rights of way, but allowing them under certain conditions on private prop-

---

*To which residents responded, "We are not a crisis. We are a success and a solution! . . . For many of us the tent city provides not only protection, but also a nurturing community." Quoted in Sabastian Grimmage and seventy-two others, "Tent City Residents Are Part of the Community," *St. Petersburg Times*, January 20, 2007, 2.

† Two arrests were eventually made a month after the murders; robbery may have been the motive.

‡ Apparently it did not occur to city, fire, and police officials that the operation entailed seizing and destroying private property, a significant constitutional violation. "In hindsight we didn't discuss the actual property issue," according to Police Chief Chuck Harmon (whose job it is to uphold the law), "and we probably should have taken that into consideration." Quoted in Abhi Raghunathan, "Mayor; Tent Raid Was Not My Plan," *St. Petersburg Times*, January 23, 2007, 1A.

§ Eventually, the police major who came up with the idea of the raid was commissioned to investigate it and write a report. In the report she exonerated herself and declared the slashing of tents and destruction of property to be legal.

erty—and the opening of negotiations with St. Vincent de Paul to have it once again host a tent city on the site the city had forced to be closed only a few weeks before, this time as a collaborative effort among the city government, homeless advocates, and the St. Vincent de Paul Society.

In the meantime the city and various charities worked to move those living in the tent cities into other housing (and in some instances to provide jobs). By late February more than a hundred tent city residents and other homeless people had been moved to apartments and treatment centers (with the aid of a half-million-dollar grant from the Catholic Diocese). But as each homeless person or couple was found a new place to live, another arrived—from somewhere—to take their place in a tent, doing nothing to dampen the growing backlash. The city worked on tightening laws against camping and sleeping in public spaces and announced plans for a "temporary use permit" for the St. Vincent site, which would allow seventy-five tents for no more than ninety days.* Tent city residents and their advocates demanded, however, that the St. Vincent tent city be allowed to remain open indefinitely—for as long as there was need. They also demanded an equal voice for homeless people in running the camp, the entrance of new residents as old ones departed, that the city abandon plans to require all residents to wear identifying armbands, and that none be placed in a new shelter being built, which they felt would be unsafe and represent a great loss of autonomy. The city refused all demands and threatened to arrest those who refused to move from the underpass under the city's conditions. Nonetheless, when the new laws were passed and the St. Vincent tent city opened in mid-March, "the two-satellite tent cities appeared abandoned," and the new site quickly filled.[53] Other homeless people moved to a new tent city on church property in another district that parishioners created despite objections from neighbors.

The new St. Vincent site—called New Hope City—ran by strict rules. The lot was fenced. Residents had to wear identifying wristbands at all times. Alcohol was forbidden. There was a midnight curfew (when the gates were locked). When residents moved out, new ones could not take their place. Together, these rules posed a problem. Twenty-seven residents were evicted for drinking or violating the curfew (which is to say, it was not just that they could not enter or leave the grounds after midnight, it was that they could not be *out* after midnight). Seventy-two residents received housing vouchers for one month. As these ran out (or as other vouchers given at previous tent cities ran out), former residents could not return; many ended up once again living furtively on the streets. By early May New Hope City was empty, though the homeless pop-

---

*The proposed law in St. Petersburg was an early adopter of language making it enforceable only in the event that sufficient shelter beds were available—anticipating the position the Department of Justice adopted in 2015 and that Boise, Idaho, had moved toward a few years earlier. See chapter 1.

ulation of the city had not shrunk at all. City council thus turned its attention to passing a new anti-panhandling law to police those still living on the streets. Homeless people and an advocate responded by setting up a protest encampment on the site of one of the satellite tent cities, leading to three arrests. Simultaneously, homeless residents who had had their tents slashed in the original tent city sued the city for damages, which the city sought to settle with a payment of two hundred fifty dollars. Over the summer, with no other place to go, dozens of homeless people took to sleeping on the sidewalk in front of city hall, which the city was unable to do anything about because its anti-camping ordinance could be enforced only if there were shelter beds available. There were not, not even in a tent city.

Determined to learn from this experience, the city of St. Petersburg and surrounding Pinellas County began planning early for the following winter's homeless "crisis." They planned to "encourage[e] the homeless to live in" a controlled encampment built "so far out of the way you will never see it unless you search for it" (while continuing to make no progress whatsoever on a promised indoor shelter). A central plank in the county's federally mandated "Ten Year Plan to End Homelessness," the Pinellas Hope tent city was to be built on ten acres of litter-strewn scrub owned by the Catholic diocese in an industrially zoned area more than ten miles from the city center. It would consist of 125 tents (housing 225 people), three excess modular buildings donated by the school district for laundry facilities, a kitchen, and administrative offices, and two large communal dining tents. It would be fenced and security guards would be hired to patrol the perimeter and to check those coming in and out. Background checks would be performed on all potential residents. Neighbors—a scrap yard, construction companies, trucking companies, and the like—nonetheless raised concerns about theft and safety.

Despite worries that homeless people would not accept the distant Pinellas Hope, with its strict rules, fences, and security guards, the tent city quickly filled to near capacity when it opened the following winter (even as a fairly large encampment remained in front of city hall occupied by those protesting city and county policies and who refused to go to the distant camp). Catholic Charities, which managed Pinellas Hope, nonetheless stuck to its promise to close it on April 30, 2008, the winter homelessness crisis by then presumably over. Or, rather, "One of the things we want to do is have the people in Pinellas Hope think, 'What's my next step.' We are not trying to create a tent city that people can live in permanently," in the words of the Catholic Charities president.[54] By the time its scheduled closing rolled around, Pinellas Hope had housed 490 people, of whom 148 found other housing, 122 found jobs, and more than 200 simply went missing—probably returning to the streets. Because need remained, Catholic Charities relented and used recently raised donations to keep a scaled-down version of the camp (housing fifty to seventy-five) open through September. The reduction in population was to be achieved by evicting homeless residents who "show[ed] no signs of progress"—though in what was not specified.[55]

Meanwhile, St. Petersburg not only expanded its anti-panhandling law but also passed an ordinance giving the police the right to confiscate homeless people's property without a warrant "as sympathy for homeless people wane[d]" in the words of one reporter. According to a city council member, "People are simply tired of these antics"—of homeless people establishing their own tent cities and finding other ways to survive in an increasingly hostile city.[56] Perhaps it is for this reason—to protect the sensibilities of the housed in St. Petersburg—that the city and county eventually decided to make Pinellas Hope permanent. By the end of the decade it had an annual budget of a quarter million dollars and was a large—and growing—stand-alone program of Catholic Charities that continued to run the tent city for two hundred fifty residents, and increasingly involved itself in building supportive housing. At the camp itself tents were first replaced by garden sheds and now by "repurposed" metal shipping containers—"an exciting new temporary housing concept," in the boastful words of the Pinellas Hope website.[57]

Indeed, despite initial concerns, officials came to consider distant Pinellas Hope such a success that cities in the county collectively donated a million dollars to it (or about $12 per tent city resident per day, as compared to jail costs—for, say, someone arrested because of outstanding warrants for public urination or trespassing—of $126 per day). The county also changed its zoning laws to allow for the creation of more permanent campgrounds like Pinellas Hope. And adjacent Hillsborough County, home to Tampa, which hosts the largest homeless population in the state, sought to build something similar, though it was quickly met by a firestorm of protest. In other words, with the support of some local officials, Catholic Charities has sought to create a network of authoritarian camps in out-of-sight and out-of-the-way places to warehouse homeless people—though it has primarily succeeded only in consolidating facilities at the Pinellas Hope site. Gary Blasio's worry in 1980s LA—that soon there would be rural concentration camps for homeless people—seemed close to coming true in 2010s Florida.

Between Camden and St. Petersburg

From Camden to St. Petersburg: these mark out the ends of two trajectories of tent cities in the contemporary United States, and they represent two different outcomes in the ongoing "war of position" that is the permanent condition of homelessness in capitalism's heartland. As homeless people have been chased from doorstep to public park, and from public park to abandoned lot or interstate overpass, as shelters—and even sometimes semipermanent tent cities—for the homeless and hungry are now more or less tolerated by city elites, housed residents, and businesses (at least in some cities like Portland and Seattle), and as homeless people themselves have been variously positioned as either deserving of aid (as in the wake of the destruction of St. Petersburg's first tent city) or not (as was the case a year later, and remains the case in cities like Fresno), tent cities, shantytowns, and new "jungles" have remained a constant. Indeed, as California's record drought came to an end in the winter of 2016–2017 with equally record rain and snowfall, the hidden encampments along Sacramento's American River once again made headlines when floodwaters ripped away the shielding scrub and exposed the city's large population of homeless people sleeping rough to view: "All of a sudden they are visible to the rest of us," as Joan Burke of Loaves and Fishes remarked. While Sacramento's current mayor speaks a more progressive game (especially in the wake of the death of two homeless men outside City Hall in a week during that winter) than did Kevin Johnson back when Oprah came to town, there are plenty of politicians in the city who would rather just see homeless people disappear.[58]

Many on the political and academic left want just the opposite, seeing such encampments as important not only for survival, but for autonomy and organizing (as I myself argued earlier in this chapter).[59] The space of the tent city must, for that reason, be preserved. There is, obviously, much to commend this argument. The history of homelessness in the United States shows that jungles and camps have indeed been vital to poor people's (sometimes radical) organizing—and to their dignity. Indicatively, in St. Petersburg Pinellas Hope was promoted by some of its advocates precisely as a means of quelling more radical demands by homeless people and their advocates, and it persists, with its guards, fences, curfews, rules on sobriety, and charity-led governance as a means (among many others, of course) of ensuring the social control of homeless people. Pinellas Hope has created a more orderly, more controlled, and less political space of homelessness, and its directors are in fact quite clear that this is one of its primary advantages.[60] So too was Sacramento's emergency shelter at the State Fairgrounds: it was (in part) a breaking apart of both a social and a political community that had formed along the banks of the American River—and so too, of course, was the dispersal of Camden's Transitional Park. These moves against the encampments of homeless people suggest indeed that such spaces need to be fought for and defended.

And yet, it must be remembered, as one St. Petersburg tent city activist put it, "Tent city is not the crisis. It's the conditions that cause the tent city that's the crisis." At the same time, as the rights of homeless people to occupy and mobilize in the interstices are struggled for, we must recognize tent cities for what they are: evidence of the utter failure of the capitalist city to provide for its residents. Existing at the limits of capital, they, and the people who live in them, show the limits *to* capital, and are eloquent testimony that something must be done. What must be done—what must be fought for—is not (only) the protection of tent cities, but (especially) the destruction of a system that has made them an *inevitable* part of the urban landscape. We need to start to find ways to eliminate tent cities from the urban landscape—not to clear them out as the neoliberal urban right would have us do, and not to replace them with fenced-off campsites hidden away in the scrub and run by charities, but rather to make them superfluous rather than necessary. If the bourgeoisie *still* has no answer to the housing question, then we need to find *non*bourgeois answers. And here, ironically, tent cities, though they must be eliminated if a just city is to arise, provide a model: as a taking of land, as a noncommodified and cooperative form of property and social relations, as (potentially) an organizational space, tent cities and their progenitors like the hobo jungle have much to teach us about what it will take to create a city that does not express the limits of capital but overcomes them.

CHAPTER 4

The Criminalization of Survival

We're going to help those who can't help themselves and run those
who are able-bodied and sound of mind out of our community. I
want potential violators to know, the mayor means business.

—Las Vegas mayor Oscar Goodman (2006)

The fear that homeless people, together with allies, might somehow both expose and overcome the limits of capital to make a just city is perhaps nowhere better expressed than in the constant attempts by American urban authorities to criminalize survival itself. These efforts have continued to expand as we saw in chapter 1, even though the absolute number of officially homeless people in the United States as a whole seemed to decline during the Obama years (a fact that masks just how uneven this process is).[1] During the Obama years there was federal recognition of the futility of anti-homeless laws, as the Department of Justice's intervention into the Boise case (chapter 1) made clear, and after he retired, Obama's first attorney general, Eric Holder, could be quite blunt: "The criminalization of homelessness must end. It is costly, unjust, and clearly not a solution to homelessness." It is "not worthy of our great nation. It is unconstitutional and, moreover, it is bad public policy."[2] And yet the use and spread of these laws continue, slowed not at all by such arguments and interventions.

At the same time, it is abundantly clear that the landscapes of care—shelters, food pantries, drop in centers, even whole homeless services campuses like San Diego's St. Vincent de Paul Village—remain inadequate to the task. The nightly "bed shortage" in emergency shelters across the country extends into the tens of thousands—while nightly shelter-bed "vacancy" hovers around 1 percent. In some cities like Los Angeles, unmet shelter-bed need reaches nearly 80 percent. Rents across the United States have risen at an annual rate of 3.5 percent over the past decade (well in excess of inflation), and of course much faster in hot markets like San Francisco, New York, and Portland, Oregon, and it is now the case that "there is no single state, or even county, in the nation where a worker earning the federal minimum wage of $7.25 an hour can afford a modest two-bedroom apartment at market rent." There is a nationwide affordable housing shortage of at least 7.2 million units. Just as the shortage of shelter beds stretches into the tens of thousands, so too do the public housing waiting lists in major cities, like Miami-Dade, where more than twenty-eight thousand people wait their turn for a unit.[3]

A similar story can be told about hunger. Though, for example, the percentage of U.S. households that were "food insecure," a frequent corollary of housing insecurity, declined in 2015 to 12.7 percent (that is, 15.8 *million* households) from its 2011 peak of 14.9 percent as the economy finally began to recover after the 2008 crisis, the rate is still above the pre–Great Recession level of 11.1 percent in 2007.[4] Those celebrating this decline might forget that already in that pre-recession year, anti-hunger activists were raising the alarm about rapidly growing food insecurity. Indeed, the U.S. Department of Agriculture's own statistics indicated that between 1999 and 2004 (roughly George W. Bush's first term), hunger in the United States increased by 43 percent.[5] During 2007, as the economic crisis was just beginning to bite, food insecurity increased in New York City by 20 percent over the previous year, with some 1.3 million New Yorkers—one in six—unable to afford food at some point in the year. The USDA estimated that 10 percent—that is, 29.8 *million* people—went hungry at some point in 2006.[6] Christmastime news reports in 2007 detailed the increasing inability of North America's volunteer food security system—the regional food banks and networks of pantries—to cope with rapidly growing demand. In New York's borough of Queens, 76 percent of food pantries and hot-food sites reported that they had to turn people away during 2007.[7] Then the crisis hit.

Taken together, the continuing fact of massive homelessness and housing insecurity along with massive hunger and food insecurity means that for significant numbers of people, working *within* the normal relations of capitalism leaves them in a position of being unable to fulfill their social reproduction needs, while those at first makeshift but now permanent interventions that have arisen to offer a safety net—city-run and volunteer shelters, food banks, food pantries, and hot-food sites—are simply inadequate in relation to demand, even as they remain an important means of alleviation for hungry and homeless individuals and families.[8] Limited as they may be, they are a central part of what could be called a "geography of survival" in American cities. In a political economy that demands ever-increasing inequalities of wealth, where welfare functions of the state continue to be "rolled back" (even if this rollback was slowed a bit during the Obama years) and new modes of discipline—so-called poverty management strategies—continue to be "rolled out," and where neither nutrition nor shelter are considered human rights, all manner of ad hoc arrangements have emerged to address the most basic needs of the homeless, hungry, and poor.[9] But this geography itself remains highly precarious, under threat from NIMBY movements seeking to move services (and poor people) out of their neighborhoods, the relentless march of gentrification and increasing rents, decreased funding, and aging volunteer staffs who are physically incapable of keeping pantries and shelters open as much as they should be.[10] Increasingly, stringent rules governing funding have the effect of turning social service agencies into outlaws if they continue to serve the people who may need their services the most.* Clearly, the ad hoc geography of survival is at risk in American cities, and long has been.

And yet, of course (and as we have abundantly seen already), the homeless and hungry do continue to survive, somehow, at least as a whole, as a class. But many individuals do not. Those who do survive do so both because of the ad hoc institutional geography that has arisen since the current homelessness "crisis" erupted in the late 1970s, and despite it. In other words, people in poverty continue to activate their own geographies of survival, to construct pathways of survival through the urban landscape that link together places to sleep or rest, locations to eat a meal or forage food, hidden corners of safety and security, and, of course, sometimes such relatively permanent fixtures as homeless encampments or shantytowns.[11] These geographies of survival are structured not only by the changing institutional landscape, but also by the altered legal landscape of anti-homeless laws. Laws and increased policing that make sleeping more difficult and dangerous, panhandling riskier, and tending to bodily needs all but impossible push the homeless as well as the housed poor more deeply into the urban shadows, the hidden abodes of poverty that continue to mark every North American city no matter how shiny its gentrified appearance.

The saga of survival in American cities is not, however, simply a one-way story of oppression, restriction, and decline, though this side of the story remains deeply important. It is also, as with the development of tent cities, a story of coping in the shadowed interstices of the city and fighting back. As pressures have mounted on food pantries and traditional shelters, numerous activist groups have arisen to address changing needs. For example, Food Not Bombs has long distributed free meals in public spaces in countless cities, dedicating itself not only to providing meals for the hungry (any hungry person, with no questions of eligibility or requirements that certain rules be followed), but also to a radical critique of the American food system in particular and the

---

*Anti-drug and anti-alcohol policies, often enforced by funding agencies in response to donor demands, are the most obvious example; but there are others. In Columbus, Ohio, at the end of the 1990s, for example, the Open Shelter was forced underground—and eventually out—when it maintained its open policy of admitting anyone who needed a bed. The consortium of agencies that funded and coordinated homeless programs in Columbus, responding to pressure from politicians, withdrew funding from the Open Shelter when it refused to follow a mandate not to serve "sex offenders." Open Shelter advocates argued that it was better to have "sex offenders" housed in a relatively stable environment than completely shunned—made completely outcast—but to no avail.

unjust political economy in general. Similarly, housing-based "right to the city" movements have arisen to advocate for radically transformed housing policy that starts from what seems to be a quite radical foundation: that *all* people have a right to be in and part of the city, with none priced out.[12] And of course poor people—housed and unhoused—find whatever means they must, legal or illegal, temporary or relatively permanent, to pay their bills, rest their heads, and meet their basic needs. *Because* they cannot survive through the normal modes of making a living in capitalism and the landscape of care is inadequate, homeless and hungry people resort to other strategies: rummaging in dumpsters for edible food, recyclable materials, and clothing; sleeping rough in hidden corners of parks or in unlocked basements; taking care of bodily needs in back alleys and overgrown lots; or just hanging out in places where they are otherwise free from the constant surveillance of the police and other authorities.

The geography of survival for poor people—living right at the limits of capital—is thus a dialectic. As new legal restrictions arise, as new techniques of poverty management are devised, as new challenges present themselves in the urban landscape, people in need as well as activists and service providers invent new strategies for coping—strategies that sometimes directly confront the relations of power that structure everyday life, and at other times seek only to make life tolerable within them. It is worth examining, then, convolutions in this dialectic, and to provide some speculations about what they might mean for the geography of survival.

Three Transformations in the Geography of Survival

The dialectic of survival—and thus the nature of contemporary class struggle as it relates to homelessness—is increasingly shaped by three interrelated processes: the increasing saturation of urban space by surveillance, legal innovations related to trespass, and the criminalization of *intervention* (as opposed to the criminalization of homelessness itself). The first two often, but not always, target the more hidden or furtive spaces of survival; the third targets those who would intervene *in public* rather than in the more hidden, more private, and thus less politically and economically charged spaces of the mission, shelter, or food pantry.

The interstices of urban space are important not only for hosting tent cities and other informal settlements. As noted in the last chapter, homeless men have historically used in-between more or less public spaces of the city like alleys, some sidewalks, hidden corners of parks, covered doorways, and abandoned lots for their own survival.[13] But so also are certain kinds of private spaces vitally important in this regard, like fenced-off dumpsters or remote, fenced-in parking lots. These sorts of spaces, together with shelters, friends' rooms or apartments, drop-in centers, dive bars, and the like, compose homeless people's urban habitat, their geography of survival. But these spaces (even including a relative's couch if it is in a public housing unit or otherwise governed by a restrictive lease) are the ones that broader capitalist society, and perhaps even the lion's share of urban residents, are most nervous about.

During the summer of 2006, for example, the City Council in Minneapolis seriously considered passing a law that would have outlawed "strangers" from setting foot in any of the 450 miles of alleys in the city (see chapter 7 for more details). According to the Minneapolis-based urban planner Ann Forsythe, such a proposal made sense because "an alley tends to be blocked off from view. . . . There's often not a real reason for people to be walking out there except to do antisocial things."[14] These antisocial things include youth hanging out, homeless people urinating or sifting through trash and recycling bins, and, of course, petty thieves trying out car door handles to see if one has been left unlocked. But the real issue, as Forsythe suggests, is one of visibility and control. Alleys "tend to be blocked from view" and thereby are not legible to authority. As spaces out of control, they are necessarily "antisocial." Or, to put that another way, the reason that alleys are valuable to homeless people (and others) is precisely because they are blocked off from view, illegible to authority. Although they may be part of the urban habitat necessary to the survival of homeless people, they are also perceived to be dangerous places. The question for authority, then, is how to make alleyways (or any other space important for homeless people's survival) visible and bring them under control. There are at least three possible ways to achieve this: by subjecting alleys to surveillance, by regulating who can be in them (the proposed Minneapolis solution), and by regulating what can be done in them.* Let's look at each in turn.

SURVEILLANCE

Urban foraging is a critical survival strategy for homeless and other poor people in North American cities. "Dumpster diving"—searching through garbage dumpsters for reusable goods or relatively unspoiled food—is not only an end-of-term ritual in college towns across the United States (as relatively well-off students dispose of everything from TVs to clothes to furniture as they move out of their dormitory rooms and apartments). It is also a mode of survival.[15] Dumpsters are resource collectors. As such they are also contested sites.

It is not uncommon in American cities, therefore, to see dumpsters "protected" not only by razor wire but also by CCTV cameras. These cameras have many purposes: to deter industrial sabotage and identity theft, to catch restaurant employees who use dumpsters to stash goods stolen from the kitchen, to discourage others from dumping their trash in your dumpster (and thus increasing your costs), to discourage both "freegans" and homeless people from

---

* In the end, despite a great deal of popular support for it, Minneapolis ended up not passing its alley law. See chapter 7.

scavenging,[16] and, sadly, to prevent homeless people from using dumpsters as beds, where they all too frequently meet their deaths.* Such cameras have variable effects. Although promoters often talk of them in a Foucauldian language of behavior modification—video surveillance will encourage employees to self-govern their behavior—they also have the effect of bringing interstitial spaces of the city into the spotlight, bringing hidden spaces of survival into visibility. Through such surveillance, the geography of survival in the capitalist city is altered, and the ability of homeless people to inhabit the city is transformed.

The same is true for the more general use of CCTV in the city. The reasons for its use are many (discouraging crime through self-regulation and thus encouraging a certain sense of safety and security among many users of urban space, allowing for greater policing of protest, even promoting the city as spectacle), but its effects are differentiated.[17] For the housed, exposure to the unblinking (if not always all-seeing) eye of the of the surveillance camera may provide either a sense of security or a sense that certain civil liberties, especially those tied to the ability to remain anonymous in public or to engage in activities not directly regulated or approved a priori by the state, are being undermined. Both are important effects of surveillance. But for the homeless CCTV has the additional potential to close off the use of previously available spaces (hidden spaces used for sleeping or bodily functions), to alter the deployment of private and public police forces as they seek to enforce anti-homeless laws, or to eliminate the diurnal differentiation of the urban landscape (with nighttime spaces now as visible as they were during the day).

The fencing and CCTV surveillance of dumpsters is particularly instructive here. In debates that erupt from time to time in city councils over whether to require businesses to fence and/or surveil their dumpsters—such as a proposed 2007 law in Vancouver, British Columbia, that would require all the dumpsters in the city to be locked—it is clear that two main concerns preoccupy lawmakers. First, lawmakers worry that accessible, unobserved dumpsters *enable* homeless people to live outside the gaze and perhaps even control of settled society (in a way that a shelter, with its rules of behavior and need to please funders and the state, does not). Second, they intuit that the commodity world that defines capitalist life is, in fact, quite insecure and continually threatened by people seeking to live off the wastes of that very world—by people finding ways to live a decommodified life in a hypercommodified world.[18]

We typically do not think of surveillance cameras (or fencing) in these terms, largely because they are now fixtures of the urban landscape that many of us have come to expect and even desire.[19] CCTV cameras have proven their worth.

*Across the country, homeless people are not infrequently injured, and occasionally killed, while sleeping in dumpsters. Compared to other city spaces, dumpsters are relatively dry, warm, and, indeed, clean. For a recent report and discussion, see Alastair Gee, "Death in an Amazon Dumpster," *Guardian*, December 28, 2017.

Along with cell phone videos by bystanders (and victims), they have been essential, if not always reliable, in exposing would-be and successful terrorists, police brutality, and everyday crime. CCTV is in fact a huge and popular business. In the first half dozen years after the September 11, 2001, terrorist attacks, the federal Department of Homeland Security distributed "tens and probably hundreds of millions of dollars" to cities to install CCTV networks. At the time the *Boston Globe* reported a poll that found that 71 percent of the nation's population approved of the use of security cameras in public spaces "as a means of fighting terrorism and other crime."[20] And case law in the United States is making it increasingly clear that in publicly accessible spaces people have no right to privacy: we have no right to absent ourselves from surveillance, except to avoid spaces monitored by cameras, which is, of course, a practical impossibility.[21]

If it is a practical impossibility for the housed to avoid the gaze of CCTV, it is a daily reality for homeless people that more and more of their movements as well as their life moments are under surveillance (shelters are increasingly installing CCTV as a way of monitoring communal—and even private—sleeping areas). In a world where there are simply not enough beds for homeless people in shelters, apartments are unaffordable, hotels and other sites off the streets can only intermittently be accessed, where fresh rather than discarded food is out of the reach of many, the expectation of many of us housed is that there will be greater *urban* security through surveillance. But this might just further undermine some other people's *human* security—their very ability to survive in the contemporary city. The urban habitat these other people—the homeless—now must inhabit is one of total exposure.

TRESPASS

Surveillance of urban spaces is propelled by many forces, and these have multiple social and political effects. But on its own, surveillance of urban space is rarely a sufficient mode of regulation. As the proponents of the Minneapolis alley law recognized, many spaces remained too easily beyond the gaze of the state and sedentary society. The goals of the Minneapolis law, therefore, were to regulate who could be in such spaces and to empower the police to arrest all those who seemed not to belong. Had the law passed, any "stranger" in a back alley of a city could have been arrested for trespassing, even though alleys remained, putatively, publicly accessible property.

To "trespass," of course, is to "disobey, violate (a law, etc.)," and to "wrongfully enter on a person's land or property." Figuratively, to trespass is to "make an unwarranted claim, intrude, encroach (on or upon a person's time, attention, patience, domain, etc.)." This sense of making an unwarranted claim (to which we will return in later chapters) is important because "warranted" means "permitted by law or authority, authorized, justified, sanctioned."[22] The Minneapolis law sought to ensure only those who were authorized, who were permitted by law, would set foot in back alleys. This reverses a normal assumption about public space: that people have an a priori right to be in it and that exclusions must be justified.

The Minneapolis law may not have passed, but the reversal of assumptions about public space it encapsulated seems only to be gaining force. In 2004 Hawai'i passed Act 50, a law that empowered police and other "authorized individual[s]" to ban persons from public property for up to a year by issuing a (verbal) "warning statement advising the person that the person's presence is no longer desired on the premises." According to the *Honolulu Advertiser*, "The state law does not define what conduct would justify a year-long ban or place any limits on which public property, and there are no court hearings or other judicial reviews."[23] Persons who return to property they were banned from would be subject for arrest for trespass. Quite obviously, they are not authorized or permitted by law to be in spaces from which they have been banned. The impetus for the law was the desire to remove homeless people camping in Mokule'ia Beach Park. But it was also used to ban a man from the Honolulu Public Library because he accessed a gay chat room from one of its computers. The Hawai'i attorney general defended the law by stating, "The state has a right to protect its interests. The state can't bar somebody because they are exercising their First Amendment rights, but that does not mean a trespass statute which allows the state to bar someone for perfectly legitimate reasons, is unconstitutional." The attorney general went on to say that the law was in line with other trespass policies around the United States.[24] Though he did not say so explicitly, it is likely that the attorney general—and the state legislature that passed the law—was mindful of the 2003 U.S. Supreme Court ruling concerning similar banishment policies in Richmond, Virginia, in which the court unanimously upheld the right of even semipublic authorities to ban people *for life* from particular (often vast) public spaces if they did not have a "legitimate social or business purpose" and had been orally warned before (this case is analyzed in detail in chapter 6).

Other jurisdictions have eagerly followed suit. In March 2006, for example, San Francisco announced new plans to patrol city public housing projects to arrest and issue banishment notices to "non-residents hanging out on the streets, people outside 'playing dice,' and those with criminal records."[25] Seattle has long been issuing banishments to homeless people in city parks, but police have been known to complain that they do not have enough resources to rigorously enforce them.[26] Nevertheless, according to a legislative analysis prepared for the San Francisco Board of Supervisors in 2002, San Francisco looked enviously toward Seattle. In the latter city, police were empowered to arrest for trespassing people who remained on private property (e.g., doors, stoops or porches, hallways), whether or not a complaint from the property owner could be obtained. In other words, arrest could be immediate. San Francisco law, by contrast, required both a complaint from the property owner and a written or oral notice to be served to the trespasser that "s/he is requested to leave, and further, that such notice must describe the specific area and hours to keep off or away."[27]

The problem with trespass-banishment notices in general and San Francisco–style trespass laws in particular, at least from the point of view of those who seek to more fully regulate who can be where on city streets and publicly accessible property, is that they are targeted. Trespass and banishment notices must be served to and enforced against specified individuals. They require what might be thought of as a much more personal and bodily (i.e., in Foucauldian terms, an almost premodern) form of enforcement.* They rely on neither the self-governing nor the kind of generalized policing that mark modern discipline. Tailored to specific individuals and spaces, they require police and other enforcement agencies to possess an enormous amount of individualized information—knowledge that this specific person cannot be in that specific space or area.† Attractive though they may be to many jurisdictions (in part because they authorize a wide range of agents, such as a library guard in the Honolulu case and housing authority workers and city police in the Richmond case, to make a first banishment and/or arrest), they are also in some respects inefficient— hence the San Francisco Police Department's complaint that they have for too long had inadequate resources to properly enforce trespassing laws as part of their overall "quality-of-life" policing.

Partially as a means of addressing such inefficiencies, cities in North America are seeking ways to streamline and rationalize trespass enforcement. In San Francisco, the North of Market/Tenderloin Community Benefit District began encouraging property owners to acquire a "No Trespassing" sign from the Tenderloin Police Station. These "signs"—actually photocopied pages on which the property's address and a date could be entered—conform to Municipal Code Section 25, which allows a general written notice to stand in lieu of individualized notification of trespassing violations. Posting these signs allows police to take action even in the absence of a direct complaint by the property owner.[28] Such practices became common in the first decade of the twenty-first century, and they remain a key tool in many cities' toolboxes.[29] In British Columbia, such notices are increasingly popular in both Vancouver and Victoria. As the Homeless Nation advocacy group in that province as well as the National Law Center on Homelessness and Poverty in the United States have both noted, however,

---

*Indeed, Katherine Beckett and Steve Herbert make the fully plausible argument that American cities are seeing a *reemergence* of banishment (of which trespass-barment is a species). Though they do not trace the history back this far, banishment was a primary mode of policing unwanted people from the Edicts of Bern, through the colonial era (when "warning out" was a key way of dealing with the wandering poor), until the dawn of industrialization, as we saw in chapter 1. Beckett and Herbert, *Banished.*

†Police have, of course, become highly interested in developing means—from computerized crime mapping to facial recognition technology—to do this more efficiently, but it is still far from a perfected system of control. See, e.g., Lippert and Walby, *Policing Cities.*

these are blunt tools. Just as a homeless person sitting or sleeping in a doorway is trespassing, so is any shopper who enters through the doorway to the store beyond.[30] But it is to their advantage rather than disadvantage that they are so blunt because discretion for enforcement is passed on to the police (or other semiofficial and private authorities).[31] Needing neither a formal complaint nor knowledge of a specific banishment, such notices on city buildings allow for a generalized—and thus self-governing—enforcement, as well as greater efficiency in policing.

In reality, what matters is the combination of these two trends in governing publicly accessible (and often publicly owned) space. Enforcement can be either tailored or generalized as circumstances require, and what is "warranted" in public space can thus be more thoroughly structured. Many claims on property, attention, time, and so forth are, it seems, potentially unwarrantable and therefore unauthorized. As with CCTV surveillance, for many of us—the comfortably housed—such encroachments on our a priori right to the city might seem minimal (though part 2 of this book will in fact argue otherwise). For those who live their lives in public, however, those whose very survival is a function of moving between, but also staying on, spaces most of us only have to pass by, such developments represent a further transformation and constriction of the interstitial spaces that constitute their geography of survival.*

In another example, the ongoing battle between homeless people seeking to survive and city officials in Fresno seeking to spruce up their city for economic development (which Jessie Speer has done so much to explicate—see chapter 3) has long been defined by the issue of trespass. When the city was enjoined in 2006 from directly destroying homeless people's personal property, and because of that it found it could not (at least for a time) use its traditional method of moving homeless people along (confiscating and destroying their belongings), it instead resorted to trespass law. After California Highway Patrol officers (some with their guns unholstered) evicted about twenty-five people from a strip of land owned by the California Department of Transportation, the evictees moved to an empty city-owned lot near a park. In response, the city posted a "Notice of Trespass and Clean-Up" announcing the city would conduct a sweep on April 5, 2007, that would entail the "removal of all individuals, personal property, junk and/or garbage." The notice seemed to threaten any individuals remaining at the site on that day with arrest for criminal trespass. As a contributor to the "Indybay" website wrote, "The ordering of homeless people off one prop-

---

*As insightful as they are, thus, Nicholas Blomley's recent arguments that we need to stop seeing the city as do legal scholars or geographers and pay much more attention to it as do engineers—who tend to see beggars and homeless people as obstructions to flow on par with bus stops, kiosks, and café seating—come up short in this regard, for a kiosk and a café table are decidedly *not* people who need not just a place to be (in Jeremy Waldron's famous formulation) but a place to *live*. Blomley, *Rights of Passage*; Waldron, "Homelessness and the Issue of Freedom."

erty ends up with them going someplace else. All property is owned by some-one—it might be public land [or] owned by an individual or a business. There is no place in Fresno where homeless people can go and be left alone."[32] That, of course, is exactly the point; trespass laws and enforcement are becoming a primary means to sort as well as authorize who can be in what space in the contemporary city—and to "warn out" those who are simply undeserving.

INTERVENTION

In July 2006—once again *before* the economic crisis hit—the Las Vegas City Council unanimously passed a law that made it illegal to provide food in public parks to "indigent" people "for free or at a nominal fee." It remained legal to serve food cheaply or gratis to well-off—or even merely comfortable—people. Asked how the police would tell the difference between indigent and non-indigent people, Las Vegas mayor Oscar Goodman replied, "Certain truths are self-evident. You know who's homeless." A councilmember made it clear that the law was targeted not at well-meaning citizens but instead at activists who, he thought, tended to enable homelessness: "'The marshals will get special training on enforcement,' [councilmember Steve] Wolfson said. 'If you brought a couple of burgers and wanted to give them out, you would technically be in violation, but you would not be cited.'"[33]

The impetus for the law had been the arrest, a few months earlier, of two women, Gail Sacco and Lyla Bartholomae, for providing a meal to homeless people in the city's Huntridge Circle Park. Since there was no ordinance against such activities, the women were cited for holding a gathering of more than twenty-five people without a permit.* They were also banned from entering the park for six months and warned that if they did they would be arrested for trespassing.[34] Their banishment was eventually rescinded in response to public pressure and a lawsuit filed by the American Civil Liberties Union. But at the same time the city stepped up enforcement of city park closing hours, seeking to keep homeless people from sleeping in them (in Las Vegas there were then between ten and twelve thousand homeless people and only about seven hundred shelter beds).

And it developed the new law to prohibit giving away food to homeless people. The mayor hired special consultants to train police in detaining homeless people under provisions of Nevada state law and delivering them to a private mental health care facility. Of the facility, he said, "If they do not want to treat [the homeless], I want to know why because we give them a lot of funding." That the facility was already filled to capacity did not seem to concern the mayor, who was more intent on joining police at Huntridge Circle Park before six o'clock in

*As it turned out, the city did not issue permits for Huntridge Circle Park; the two women were charged for not doing something that it was impossible to do.

the morning to arrest for trespass homeless people who were sleeping rough. At the time of the arrests, he said, "We are going to help those who can't help themselves and run those [homeless people] who are able-bodied and sound of mind out of our community. I want potential violators to know, the mayor means business."[35]

Whatever business the mayor promised, it seemed not to have too great an effect throughout the spring and summer of 2006. Even after the law was passed, activists—as well as just ordinary concerned people—continued to provide food to the indigent. Strategies of resistance varied. Bartholomae and Sacco continued to provide food to poor people (just not in the park). One longtime activist adopted a strategy of collecting several homeless people in her car, taking them to the supermarket, letting them select their food, paying for it herself, and then returning them to the park so they could have a picnic. The idea was not only to provide needed food but to visibly assert the right of homeless people to survive in a troubled city.[36] (Even before the economic crisis became apparent in the rest of the country, Las Vegas was already experiencing a growing tide of foreclosures.) The local chapter of Food Not Bombs (FNB), aided by FNB activists from around the western United States, who were to some degree reenacting the old IWW tactic of rushing to the city of a conflict over rights to put their bodies—their numbers—on the line, challenged the law directly by continuing to set up tables and ladle out free food in city parks. "I wouldn't call this civil disobedience," one FNB activist said. "It's not civil disobedience when you've been doing something for years and someone suddenly passes an ordinance that says it is illegal."[37]

In a well-publicized event, a local radio personality also challenged the law. "Back-Seat Beth," as she was known, brought donuts and water to Frank Wright Plaza near City Hall one morning in late July. She was cited for breaking the law. Knowing there was going to be a well-organized protest of the law that morning, a local television crew showed up at four thirty to set up. At six forty-five, fifteen minutes before the park officially opened and the time at which "Back-Seat Beth" was expected to start her protest, the television crew and a photojournalist were ordered to leave. The crew, which had been there without interference for more than two hours, refused. The TV reporter and cameraperson were cited for trespassing and thus not able to film and broadcast the event.[38]

Ten days later, in another act of organized resistance, protesters, including FNB activists who had driven in from Northern California, gathered again in Frank Wright Plaza. Television and other media stood by. Despite the distribution of food to a number of homeless people, the police did nothing. The protesters moved on to Huntridge Circle Park. The TV crew did not follow (though a print reporter did). Now out of view of the cameras, the police moved, arresting the Californians who were giving out food, but not a local activist (Gail Sacco's son) who was also "providing food for free . . . to indigents." Neither the officers nor police spokespeople would comment on this selective enforcement.[39] Clearly what was at stake was the visibility of both homeless people and protesters. As the mayor made so clear, "able-bodied" homeless people simply had no right to be in the public spaces of the city; he had vowed, after all, to "run" them "out of our community."

He was not entirely to get his way. In tandem with direct resistance to the law (which drew a great deal of national attention),[40] the ACLU, joined by numerous advocacy groups, sued the city in hopes of getting the food law overturned. In January 2007 a judge granted a temporary injunction that barred Las Vegas from enforcing the law; the following August the injunction was made permanent. However, the judge specifically allowed the city to retain its requirement that gatherings of twenty-five or more receive a permit, upheld the city's no-trespassing ordinances (which allowed parks to be closed at night or altogether), and allowed the city to set aside some parks for children and their parents or guardians exclusively (which many activists saw as another way of prohibiting homeless people from using them).[41]

But what is crucial here is the trend that the Las Vegas law exemplifies—a trend that, after a decade of financial crisis and putative recovery, shows little sign of fading.[42] Bans on giving out food—and even, explicitly, *sharing* it*—in public have been implemented in numerous cities. Over the course of the whole homelessness "crisis," beginning in the 1980s, FNB has been especially targeted, in part because its basic raison d'être is to provide "food for free or at a nominal fee" to indigent people. Like squatters' movements, FNB seeks to directly alter the geography of survival. Dedicated to a radical ethos of both direct action and food decommodification, FNB has been a frequent target of police action, most famously, perhaps, in San Francisco in the 1980s and 1990s, but also in cities as far flung as Orlando and Manila. And because of their seeming radicalism, FNB collectives have been infiltrated by both the FBI and local police.[43]

Founded in Boston as part of the antinuclear movement, FNB is radically decentralized, linked by the idea that by "working today to create sustainable living that prefigures the kind of society we want to live in . . . we build a caring movement for progressive change." At the end of the 1990s, the East Bay (California) FNB collective described its work this way:

> Food Not Bombs is different in many ways from all the other organizations that run food programs. First, our meals are vegetarian, usually vegan. Second, our meals are served outdoors. This is for a number of reasons: to show the larger public that hunger is a daily problem that people must deal with, and [in their case] to fulfill the mission of People's Park [Berkeley] as a place where people can go to meet the

---

* In 2007 the city of Wilmington, North Carolina, passed an ordinance that made it illegal to "share" food on city streets or sidewalks; Orlando, Florida, outlaws "sharing" food with twenty-five or more people without a permit and restricts organizations to no more than two 1-day permits per year. NLCHP, *Feeding Intolerance*, 2.

needs of the body. The weekday meals in People's Park where most folks sit in little groups on the grass encourage an open, community spirit. It runs counter to the usual practice of hiding poor people away in church basements while they get a meal.[44]

This last point is the crucial one: FNB seeks to make the geography of survival for homeless and hungry people a visible one—and it was just this visibility that made FNB activists (as well as Sacco and Bartholomae) such prominent targets in Las Vegas.

Visibility, FNB avers, is vital both to show "the larger public" the contours of the world within which they live and to foster a sense of "community" among people of different classes. This is not the same as the exclusive "our community" the Las Vegas mayor hoped to create by running the homeless out of town, but rather one that sees cross-class interaction and involvement as a vital step in the annihilation not of homeless people, but of class itself and the creation of a city that all may inhabit. For FNB serving food in public thus reconfirms one of the basic functions of public space, a function that continually expresses the limits to capital: public space as a space for representation, a space in which "others" can be seen and recognized.[45]

Such goals often run up against more settled notions of what proper uses of public space are meant to be. In Boston in 1993, for instance, numerous FNB activists were cited for trespassing when they refused to stop serving food for free in Copley Square. Supported by nearby churches, who agreed that "we don't think the homeless should be fed in a basement where nobody will know because they are out of sight" (in the words of the chairwoman of the social action committee of the Boston Community Church), FNB activists insisted on "feeding people in the most public way, keeping the problem of homeless people in the public eye." However, as the *Boston Globe* editorialized, while providing food in the relatively spacious Boston Common might be alright (as long as proper permits were obtained), doing so in Copley Square was not: "The Square is a single open space with few trees. A stand offering free food, if it draws a crowd, could affect the atmosphere of the entire park. Food Not Bombs would do well to go elsewhere." That is to say, too much visibility is apparently not good for "a place where people of all classes meet as equals," as the *Globe* described the square.[46]

Unremarked on in the *Globe*'s editorial was a keen irony: not only was Copley Square a place where "all classes meet as equals," it was also where, on weekends, the city sponsored a highly successful farmer's market. Apparently drawing a crowd through the distribution of food was a *good* use of the square after all, one that *confirmed* rather than altered the "atmosphere of the entire park," *just so long as that food was bought and paid for.* Equality here takes on a new meaning: one is equal to the degree one can buy into society. Lacking that ability subjects one to expulsion at best and, as bans on sharing food intersect with in-novations in surveillance and trespass law, an inability to survive at worst. Here, then, is capital once again reasserting *its* limits, its limits on how—and by what means—one may survive.

Between Boston and Vegas: Survival, Anyway

Making visible in public space the inequalities—and oppressions—homeless people face is a key tactic of FNB and innumerable other activist groups, in-cluding perhaps especially homeless-led groups, around the country.* In his preface to an FNB handbook, the radical historian Howard Zinn suggested that "this slogan requires no complicated analysis. Those three words 'say it all.' They point unerringly to the double challenge: to feed immediately people who are without adequate food, and to replace a system whose priorities are power and profit with one meeting the needs of all human beings."[47] Of course (and as no doubt Zinn knew) feeding people immediately is no simple process, and doing it in public is not only doubly hard but getting harder.

That is why FNB so obviously targets the existing geography of survival—and its criminalization—and through direct action seeks to transform it. In this sense it is not only that organizations like FNB threaten the smooth functioning of the capitalist city—the circulation and accumulation of capital through and in the built environment—with their effort to decommodify food but also that they challenge the structures of visibility and invisibility that construct such a re-strictive geography of survival. Closed-circuit monitoring of dumpsters behind restaurants, closing off alleys to "strangers," eliminating regulations that require there actually to be a complaint of trespassing before a citation is issued, arrest-ing the media covering demonstrations, criminalizing free food in public—all these are just so many desperate attempts to construct a structure of visibility that will secure urban space for specific classes (as the Las Vegas edict against providing food to indigents made so clear), and thus for specific patterns of the circulation and accumulation of capital through the built environment. In doing so, however, such efforts necessarily imperil the geography of survival for oth-ers, especially the homeless and hungry who are now a seemingly permanent part of the American cityscape. As Kurt Iveson has argued, "The visibility asso-ciated with being 'in public' has another set of effects beyond enabling participa-tion" in public life. "Most importantly, fields of visibility are bound up with the techniques and technologies of discipline through which . . . some ways of being (in) public are normalized. To be 'in public' is to have one's conduct exposed to

* Perhaps the best-known cases of homeless-led activism are New York's Picture the Homeless and Los Angeles's LA-CAN. For a lesser known but just as important example, see the discussion of Boul-der, Colorado's, homeless-led organization HOME in Mitchell, Attoh, and Staeheli, "Whose City? What Politics?"

the normative gaze of others, and exposure to this gaze is one of the technologies of governance which incite[s] us to regulate our own conduct with regard to what is 'appropriate' when in public."[48] If subjection to the normalizing gaze is in fact what many of us want (CCTV is enormously popular), the costs of such a desire should not be underestimated. The costs include not only exclusion from collective involvement in being part of the public (a serious enough problem) but also banishment from the right to *inhabit* and to *make* the city—to not have to live beyond the limits of capital.

Homelessness, Public Space, and the Limits to Capital

San Francisco has one of the largest homeless populations in America, and it is an expensive problem to have. Once the cost of policing and medical services is taken into account, each chronically homeless person is estimated to cost the city $80,000 annually. Bus tickets cost a few hundred dollars.

—*Guardian* (2017)

Just before Christmas 2017, the *Guardian* published a long, important examination of city programs, common across the United States, that provide free or deeply discounted bus (and sometimes plane) tickets out of town to homeless people. Often run by nonprofit homeless service agencies (though with considerable public funding), such programs are sometimes credited by recipients of tickets as saving their lives, or at least with having provided them a way out of homelessness, by allowing them to move hundreds or thousands of miles to reunite with relatives or friends who can offer housing and other support. Perhaps as often, however, such tickets just move homeless people around (and it is not uncommon for transported homeless people to eventually return to the city they were sent from). And sometimes, they move homeless people into harm's way: the *Guardian* tracked one family of four sent semivoluntarily from New York City to Puerto Rico in July 2017. They were four of 2,350 people sent to the island that the *Guardian* found data for. There they rode out devastating Hurricane Maria in September—or maybe not, as the *Guardian* had not been able to contact them since the storm.[1]

Beneficial or not, life-saving or deadly, such programs merely recapitulate, in a modern form, the old American practice of "warning out" the (putatively) nonlocal homeless, the undeserving by definition. Yet it is easy to see why such programs (called Greyhound therapy by their opponents) are popular. In its exposé, the *Guardian* was able to gain data on thirty-four thousand separate transportations, with more than twenty-one thousand of them occurring since 2011. Since there is no national accounting of such programs, and since many jurisdictions and agencies refused to provide data (much of what the *Guardian* gathered came from

Freedom of Information Act requests), it is uncertain what percentage of transported homeless people this represents. What is certain is that cities see them as cost-effective interventions into the problem of homelessness—and at least some social service agencies see them as ways to attract money from donors. Key West, like many cities, makes receipt of a bus ticket contingent on the recipient agreeing to be banned for life from further services in the city, a policy that a local shelter operator describes as popular. This operator "asks residents to contribute to a fund that will buy homeless people one-way tickets to relocate elsewhere. He makes clear that they will not be allowed to come back. 'That, I figured, was the easiest "sell,"' Miller said. 'Give us money and we'll ship our homeless problem to somebody else.'"[2] According to the *Guardian*'s research, San Francisco was able to "ship" more than 10,500 homeless people out of the city over twelve years (it received perhaps 150 from other cities). Though the data are partial (and the *Guardian* is very clear on its limits), a decent estimate is that San Francisco's official homeless population would be more than twice as large (18,000) as it currently is (7,600). With San Francisco estimating that each "chronically homeless" person in the city costs eighty thousand dollars per year, there is every incentive to just buy a bus ticket for tens or hundreds of dollars. According to the police officer in charge of the San Francisco program when it started in 2005, "Giving free bus tickets was considered a 'win-win'

because each homeless person that left was 'one less call for services.'"[3]

But these direct savings are not the only reason such programs are popular.* "Warning out" is, despite whatever humanitarian aspects it may have (and these can indeed be quite important to individuals), a homeless removal program, a simple form of banishment (as the Key West example makes clear), and one with significant political-economic consequences. As the *Guardian*'s analysis shows, the vast majority (88 percent) of those bussed and flown out of cities are transported to lower income places. Rich cities are shipping the poor out to poor places.

> "The folks who so often fall into homelessness come from communities that have been experiencing a Great Recession for decades, living in neighborhoods with broken or absent support systems, enervated public schools, and little or no economic prospects to lift themselves up beyond their current circumstances," said Arnold Cohen, president and CEO of The Partnership for the Homeless in New York. "Moving them out to other struggling neighborhoods is just another way of neglecting the root issues that continue to drive the problem."[4]

The root issues include, as we have seen, the wrenching transformation of the American political economy in the last two generations: the "Great U-turn" in the United States manufacturing economy, the rising power of financial capital, the squeeze on urban space that these have produced,

---

* As the *Guardian* additionally reports, cities also like the programs because they allow for a certain statistical legerdemain: by counting transported homeless people as having "exited" homelessness, cities can claim higher records of success in "combatting" homelessness than is actually the case. In San Francisco, fully half of the seven thousand people the city claims it helped "exit" homelessness were simply given bus tickets to exit the city instead.

and urban space's deepening commodification as city space—the built environment itself—has come to be a, if not the, central locus of capital accumulation in the contemporary economy.

A closer examination of this last point—that space is a key locus of capital accumulation—is now in order because it will help us better understand why America's increasingly mean streets—and the shifting practices of public space regulation that is part and parcel of them—is a phenomenon that affects not only homeless people, but also those of us who are housed as well, the subject of the second part of this book. To reiterate, I have been arguing so far (mostly through example rather than theoretical exegesis) that homelessness is best understood *not* as a problem of individuals (as something rooted in their characteristics and their characters) and *not* in the first instance as a problem of housing (though this is a phenomenal form that it takes), but rather as rooted in how capital circulates and is accumulated, and of the limits to capital itself. I have further been arguing—again by example more than by theory—that the very meanness of the streets, what Neil Smith influentially labeled the "revanchism" of neoliberal cities, is not just some phenomenon of social psychology, but instead directly tied to these very same processes of capital circulation and accumulation in the built environments: it is a very material reaction to the very material problems such circulation presents to cities, their investors, and their residents.[5] It is now time to make the argument—and the theory behind it—more explicit. Doing so will allow for a slightly different analysis of cities' bus transport programs (and by extension their broader programs concerning homelessness and public space) than is apparent in the *Guardian*'s invaluable reporting.

□ □ □

America's, and more broadly the Global North's, "great U-turn" reset the value of labor power in the capitalist core countries driving it down in ways that far exceeded what could have been accomplished through the further socialization of social reproduction (which was the strategy of the Keynesian era, when effective costs of labor to individual firms were lowered through socializing pensions, medicine, education, and the like, while purchasing power for large portions of the working class was propped up). Simultaneously, the U-turn freed up a significant portion of accumulated surplus to stalk the globe looking for productive sites of investment. Beginning in the 1970s, competitive, now global, pressure on capital by *capitals* was sharply increased. Higher rates of accumulation were consequently accomplished both through (1) increased absolute surplus value production (lengthening the working day: after a period of shortening in the first three-quarters of the twentieth century, the length of working days has been steadily increasing, and is now coupled with a growing use of precarious, "zero-hour"—that is, totally flexible—contracts, which effectively stretch the working day beyond the physical limits of any human being) and (2) increased relative surplus value production (increasing the intensity of the work day, largely through the use of machines, to which workers become mere appendages). This double intensification of production has, near-constant economic crisis notwithstanding, reinvigorated capitalism, now in its neoliberal form.[6]

Near-constant economic crisis is, however, *not ever* notwithstanding. Crisis is a central, indispensable, if intermittent (or rather punctuated) part of the process.* Capitalism is in a permanent crisis of over-accumulation, which means it has massive realization and absorption problems: too much stuff is being produced for all the surplus value in it to be "realized" in consumption (that is, for the capital trapped in it to be turned back into money and returned to the capitalists who fronted it) and, even so, too much surplus capital is being realized for it to be productively reabsorbed (reinvested) in production or other profitable endeavors, at least without a great deal of ingenuity and effort, and, as we will see, crisis. Capitalist growth, as David Harvey has insisted, is and must be compound growth. At historical rates of growth (about 2.2 percent globally), the size of the capitalist economy doubles every thirty years.[7] Something like double the amount of capitalist value must be realized and something like double the amount of capitalist value must find productive outlets for investment today compared to the late 1980s. And double the current amount again will have to be realized and find productive outlets at the end of the 2040s.[†]

The first thing to remember in relation to this fact is that the general law of capitalist accumulation never stops operating. The growth of capital at one pole is the immiseration of ever growing numbers of people at the other pole, if now in highly complex global patterns. This is a logical—and historical—outcome of the capitalist process. Capital accumulation *must* produce misery.[‡] Some portion of that misery has always been lived by the reserve army of labor, both permanent and latent, both homeless and housed, which itself is always tending toward growth. With the rising organic composition of capital (in essence, the replacement of human labor by machines), which has been the purpose of, and accelerated by, the tech revolution we are all living through, more and more people are simply made redundant. Capital accumulation *necessarily* produces unemployment, poverty, and homelessness. If these were ameliorated (not eliminated) through the housing, make-work, education, welfare, and health care policies of the Keynesian era, then this is no longer the case.

The result is a massive problem of management as the necessary, and necessarily growing by-product of capitalist accumulation litters city streets, seeks out housing by

* On the semantics of using "crisis" to describe the ongoing turbulence of the contemporary global economy (and especially its financial aspects), see Christophers, Leyshon, and Mann, "Money and Finance after the Crisis." As they point out, crisis is "both foreground and background," "endemic, even constitutive." If, during the Keynesian period, crises were exceptional moments, then in the post-Keynesian period of neoliberal capitalism (and indeed in the pre-Keynesian period of liberal capitalism) crisis is the norm, only occasionally punctuated by seemingly "normal" periods of economic stability. At the same time, as I have argued elsewhere, it *is* something of an abuse of language to call something that is a permanent state (like the "crisis" of homelessness) a "crisis." We need a better language, but we do not yet have it.

† Of course there are all kinds of countervailing processes, including innovation itself, which means that this is in no way a straight-line process of accumulation, realization, and reinvestment—that double the capital means double the stuff to be sold or (as we will see) destroyed. But the general tendency is correct and the estimate is likely within an order of magnitude.

‡ That some of this misery is "relative" (as measured in increasing levels of inequality even in places where standards of living appear to be rising across the board) even as some is "absolute" (the total abjection of some people, populations, and regions) is no argument against the validity of the law.

building up favelas, tent cities, or squatting abandoned buildings, participates in black market survivalism, wastes outs its days hanging out by the corner stores or abandoned schoolyards, or takes over city centers in indignation. Vigorous policing is one management solution.[8] Anti-homeless laws, antisocial behavior orders, area bans, stop-and-frisk policing, anti-squatting laws and policies, and innovation in protest policing all continue as (frequently ineffectual) attempts at management. A second solution, since social housing, universal education (formerly an important place to park a portion of the reserve army), or wage support seem unthinkable in an age of austerity, is to rely on the charitable sector to succor those spit out by the great capitalist maw.* A third solution is Greyhound therapy: the expedient of "warning out."

The second thing to remember about capitalism's necessarily compound growth is that all that new-made surplus capital must go *somewhere*. Rising organic compositions of capital do not just make people redundant; they also diminish the *rate*, if not the mass, of return on invested capital. Competitive pressures (within the financial sector as well as beyond it) to continually increase the *rate* of return on capital thus means that capital must continually seek out new sectors for investment. Commodity markets and production systems are thus notoriously volatile, especially as the realization problem—the problem of selling all the stuff that is produced—never disappears. Investment in

production, or for that matter retail, and now even services, can quickly lose its luster. But the built environment might be different story. As indicated in chapter 1, capital must construct a landscape broadly suitable to its own needs, a landscape that itself is created from and as commodities. In order for some capital to circulate, other capital must be fixed in place, so new built environments must always be produced (especially since the needs of capital as it circulates are continually shifting). Chances to make money abound. Not only are there delicious possibilities of rent, but also and perhaps especially (if counterintuitively) the relatively slow turn-over times of capital fixed in the built environment make urban landscapes an enticing site for investment.

All this is, however, deeply contradictory. To extend our discussion from chapter 1, fixed capital (that is, capital frozen in buildings or machinery), while an absolute necessity for the circulation and accumulation of capital, is also capital *at risk*. Production needs can and do shift, innovations in transportation and communication make landscapes redundant. Hurricanes and earthquakes hit. Wars are launched. Landscapes are destroyed along with the investments in them. Destruction is a primary means of devaluation, but also, then, a primary means for creating opportunities for new investment, new patterns of accumulation, since, in a finite world, a world where, as Neil Smith long ago detailed, absolute geographical expansion of capital is

* The ever-growing reliance on charity to fill in for state support, freeing up public money, as in LA, to use on policing instead has led some geographers to argue that contemporary cities are not "mean" or "revanchist" but rather *defined* by care, which is a difficult argument to square with reality. This is especially true in austerity-era Britain, but it was no less so before 2010, when a supposedly more compassionate Labour government reigned. See esp. Cloke, May, and Johnsen, *Swept Up Lives?*

no longer possible (there are no new lands and peoples to conquer), a world where uneven development is thus now fundamental to the circulation and accumulation of capital, such destruction is also a necessary part of the dynamic.[9] Destruction of capital is vital to the accumulation of capital—and capitalism can in no way just wait for the accidents of nature and the depredations of war to do the job. Compound capitalist growth requires compound capitalist destruction, destruction that prepares the ground for another round of accumulation. Such a dynamic is, of course, right at the root of not only Smith's theory of uneven development but also his related theory of gentrification (which at base is a process of capital *circulation*): the rent gap—that difference between potential land values after "upgrading" and actual values given current use—is a phenomenal form of compound capitalist destruction in particular places, given here the deceptively passive name, "disinvestment."[10]

Compound capitalist destruction—disinvestment, the rent gap—is not some sort of deus ex machina but is rather fully and inescapably *social*. It is *lived*. Obviously, first, this is true for those living at the blunt end of the bulldozers or those living in housing being asset-stripped by its landlords (which are increasingly disembodied investors organized into real estate investment trusts or various other exotic instruments of finance capital), those who toiled in abandoned factories, those in the paths of the leveling bombs, and those flooded out by unmaintained levees. No matter how disinvested, how seemingly abandoned, how ruined, these are landscapes of home, of life and memory, and people will defend them while seeking to make and remake

their lives in them anyway. This is especially true for those urban landscapes targeted for what Ruth Wilson Gilmore has identified as "organized abandonment" by capital and the state—planned devaluation—but within which this abandonment has not been fully realized.[11]

Second, capital is fractionalized.[12] Different capitals have different social and economic needs, desires, and logics. While it is tempting to think of capital as fully mobile, or fully footloose, as we saw in chapter 2, only a fraction of capital is mobile in that way. Some capital is rooted in place: the preservation of *its* values—and its ability to spin off surplus value (or at least revenue)—requires the building up, rather than the destruction, of values all around it. It is in the interest of some fractions of capital to ensure that the asset-stripping private equity fund does *not* land in their neighborhoods. Intra-capitalist struggle is a vital part of the dynamic of capital circulation through the built environment. Place-bound capital seeks inward investment of capital perceived and hoped to be relatively stable, and hence all manner of inducements might be offered to attract it, from free land to tax breaks to the provision of elaborate, state-funded infrastructure. Mobile capital, to this fraction, is something to be deeply desired—and an existential threat.

What this looks like socially can be seen in any local development authority or chamber of commerce meeting, or at the mayor's office as she figures out how to attract the latest starchitect *and* repair the aging sewer infrastructure, or to manage homeless people who seem to be hanging around in ever-greater numbers and scaring residents, tourists, and footloose capital away from the newly gentrified warehouse district or former skid row. For, third, the threat to local fractions of capital, and thus to local economies and lives, is not only existential and not only applied to certain fractions of society. Rather, it hunkers down and makes its presence felt in the tax coffers. As the neoliberal revolution rolled back taxes on high-income and high-wealth individuals and especially on corporations (and despite this being a total failure as social and economic policy continues to do so), localities have become even more dependent on revenues from sales and property taxes. Both are in turn dependent on the "success" of the urban landscape—on its development and redevelopment rather than its abandonment. The latter—property tax—is especially so dependent, not only because property values are relational, a function of the overall rent surface,* but also because increasingly the development tool of choice, in American cities at least, is tax-increment financing. With tax-increment financing, eventual repayment for public investment in preparatory infrastructure in a district—creating the conditions for inward investment—is derived solely from that portion of the property value that is an *increase* over the values that had prevailed before redevelopment, not the total value of the district's properties. City revenues are dependent on continually increasing exchange values in the built environment. Anything that threatens such increases in exchange value must be confronted and neutralized.[13]

Fourth, and perhaps by now quite obvious, the dynamics of investment and disinvestment in (in other words, the dynam-ics of capital circulation in and through) the built environment is a multifaceted struggle. Yet what this struggle is really about needs now to be specified.

□ □ □

The struggle over investment and disinvestment, over compound growth and compound destruction, is a struggle over how *abstract space*—that is, *space made commensurable or exchangeable*—is to be produced. Abstract space is like Marx's notion of abstract labor.[14] In order to be useful labor must be highly differentiated, but in order to be purchasable labor must be commensurate. Marx's category of abstract labor helps us see the dialectic between difference and commensurability, and turns our attention to the question of how (through what sorts of social struggles and processes) differentiated labor is made exchangeable, how we know that X amount of janitorial labor is equal to Y amount of construction labor and Z amount of engineering labor. Henri Lefebvre developed the concept of abstract space to perform the same function. In both cases these are concrete abstractions, which is to say, they are not just concepts, but describe real material processes.

"We already know several things about abstract space," Lefebvre wrote. "As a product of violence and war, it is political; instituted by the state, it is institutional. On first inspection it appears homogenous; and indeed it serves those forces which make a *tabula rasa* of whatever stands in their way, of whatever threatens them—in short of differences. These forces seem to grind down and crush everything be-

---

* Actually it is property *prices* that are reflected in rent surfaces, but it is conventional in both everyday language and political economy to talk about property *values*.

fore them, with space performing the function of a plane, a bulldozer or a tank. The notion of the instrumental homogeneity of space, however, is illusory." Instead, "abstract space is *not* homogenous; it simply *has* homogeneity as its goal; its orientation, its 'lens.' . . . But in itself it is multiform."[15]

Though abstract space predates capitalism (as Lefebvre's references to war and the state indicate), *capitalist* abstract space is "a medium of *exchange* (with the necessary implication of interchangeability) tending to absorb use."[16] The production of abstract space—or the constant attempt to produce abstract space despite all the spatial practices that will seek to produce it otherwise—is a capitalist necessity. In capitalism, space *must* be made exchangeable. Use must be "absorbed" into exchange, with the latter dominant.* Lefebvre no doubt overstated the case, but his general point is correct: "Existing property and production relations . . . shatter conceptions of space that tend to form in dreams, in imaginings, in utopias or in science fiction."[17] Alternative *conceptions* are not enough. Only alternative *practice*—practice that remakes space against, or in spite of, or within, capitalist abstract space—can create a different kind of space (and must do so if life, or, for that matter, capitalism, is to survive).† In this sense, Lefebvre argued,

> Today more than ever, the class struggle is inscribed in space. Indeed, it is that struggle alone which prevents abstract

space from taking over the whole planet and papering over all differences. Only the class struggle has the capacity to differentiate, to generate differences which are not intrinsic to economic growth *qua* strategy, "logic," or "system"—that is to say, differences which are neither induced by nor acceptable to that growth. The forms of class struggle are now more varied than formerly. Naturally, they include the political action of minorities.[18]

In other words, while the constant differentiation of space is necessary to the very survival of capitalism (space must be both abstract *and* differentiated), such struggles for difference, which include struggles against the capitalist production of space, must be contained and made productive. Here, then, we can begin to see why so much effort and money are put into policing and managing unruly populations including, especially, the homeless. The homeless, by their very act of being in public space, differentiate space in ways that are *not* "intrinsic to economic growth." They must, at minimum, be corralled and controlled. If their role in the reserve army were not so vital (if still contradictory, problematic, and even at times far in excess of the real needs of capital), then surely they would simply be eliminated.

Yet, unfortunately for capitalism and for capitalist cities (and their managers), it is not only the homeless who differentiate space in unruly, unpredictable, and

---

*Of course "abstract space" no more wears a label marking its presence than does "value" (the material form of abstract labor). Value—abstract labor congealed—takes form in specific (commensurable) commodities; abstract space takes form in specific—potentially commensurable—*places*.

† As Smith showed more broadly in *Uneven Development*, capitalism must always negotiate between two competing tendencies: toward equalization on the one hand and differentiation on the other. This negotiation is the fulcrum of uneven capitalist development. The tendency toward abstract space and the struggle for differential space are material instances of these broader tendencies.

"unproductive" ways. So too do many of the housed, who also use space in ways that can be counterproductive to the political-economic order: hanging out, protesting and other "political activities of the minorities," expropriating seemingly disused space for gardens or ballfields, engaging in petty (perhaps black market) trading, and maybe just behaving in ways not fully visible or legible to official society. All these activities differentiate space—produce "differential space" in Lefebvre's terms—and *thereby* set a limit to capital and its total conquest of our social spaces and social lives.

These limits matter because the built environment, it bears repeating, possesses value and this value is a function of the degree to which it is *realized* (a process in which differentiation is both necessary and a problem), thus returning capital to investors and revenues to cities and states. Realization is itself a relational process, since the value to be realized in any component of the built environment is partially a function of the values incorporated in the surrounding components. In this sense, there is nothing abstract about the struggle over abstract space, either to those who are involved in it or those who stand to benefit from it. Precisely how these struggles get worked out and values are (or are not) realized is never assured and never clear in advance. The struggles must be fought, and someone must win, or some sort of compromise or ceasefire must be struck (perhaps negotiated by the courts, as we

will see in the next part, or perhaps negotiated in the courts of public opinion, as we will also see) that properly resets the value of labor power, preserves the commensurability of space, and creates appropriate conditions for the realization value more generally, and which therefore does not threaten but advances the continued accumulation of capital—together with its associated cycles of destruction.

◻ ◻ ◻

Public space (what it precisely is, what can be done in it, who owns and manages it, and what role it plays in the political economy) is frequently the focus of such compromises. Public space is a particular kind of space in the political economy of the urban built environment, at once a commodity like any other capitalist space and a commodity like no other. Because public space is part of the built environment, it has value (and thus an exchange value—a certain worth on the market), but its *use* is always complex and, by definition, never merely confined to private consumption. This is obvious enough, for example, in the case of streets and sidewalks, given both their public accessibility and their multifarious uses, from promoting the flow of traffic, people, and goods, to hosting advertising, making room for street furniture, and creating social life. Urban think tank reports, planning journals, and city newspaper columns alike are full these days of the importance of creating lively streets for the economic success of a city.* Streets

*Sacramento, California, has been at the forefront of such innovation in recent years, engaging in a broad-based public-private effort to build a fancy new basketball arena and a lively streetscape outside it as a means of revitalizing the city's downtown. In the reporting on these efforts I have seen, no mention of Sacramento's ongoing crisis of homelessness is made. The two are *always* reported separately, as if they bear no relation to each other. See Keith Schneider, "Welcome to the Neighborhood: America's Sports Stadiums Are Moving Downtown," *New York Times*, January 19, 2018.

are functionally necessary: the movement of goods, people, and vehicles is simply a sine qua non of social life, in whatever its political-economic form. But since the street is at once part of the physical infrastructure of the city, the social infrastructure of the city, and *property* (and thus subject to all the dynamics of rent, even when publicly owned), its uses are frequently in conflict with each other. The promotion of movement or flow might conflict with the street as a space for advertising, café tables, or political action, to say nothing of homeless people's tents or shopping carts.[19] Though flow or circulation might not be as vital a function in plazas and parks, the same point nonetheless holds true: public space is *necessarily* a space of conflicting uses—unless or until, that is, such uses are regulated (some ceasefire or compromise is negotiated or imposed).[20]

Because it is necessarily conflictual, and because its uses always significantly exceed its function within the circulation and accumulation of capital, public space poses significant management, regulation, and policing problems. Public space can thus be scary—seemingly out of control, and therefore *dysfunctional*. Cities are forced to invent and try out new tactics of policing and regulation. We've already seen how this is the case in relation to homeless people and their uses of urban space, and the very particular contradictions this gives rise to. But our analysis should not be confined only to that issue, as important as it is, for the problem of public space—its position at the limits of capital and its sometimes role as a limit to capital—reaches well into housed society. None of us lives outside the contradictions of public space in capitalist societies, and

none of us is free from the effects (often deleterious) of regulating space in favor of capital accumulation and the creation of a social order amenable to this, no matter how devoutly we may desire, and fight for, such regulation—regulation that continually seeks to turn the differentiated spaces we are constantly producing through our differentiated desires and uses, into the abstract space that is so vitally necessary to the survival of capitalism.[21]

□ □ □

If San Francisco and other cities are developing new ways to engage in the age-old practice of "warning out" the poor and homeless—offering them bus tickets, for example—it is not simply because San Franciscans despise or fear homeless people. It is not merely because of some sort of sociopsychological feeling of revulsion. Nor is it merely that homeless people are seemingly unproductive in the capitalist economy. But, rather, and as the police overseers of San Francisco's budding program were so happy to admit, providing a bus ticket is far *cheaper* than actually addressing homelessness. And that is just thinking about costs in the shallowest of ways: the cost of housing and emergency services, of shelter and sustenance for those deemed to be useless to society. But, as now must seem obvious, it is also the case the homeless people in public space represent a very *deep* cost: homeless people, existing right at the limits of capital, are in fact an existential threat to capital circulation and accumulation altogether (even as they remain a necessary part of the processes of circulation and accumulation). And getting rid of homeless people (or at least trying to) is certainly far cheaper, socially, politically, and economically, than transforming the very means by which, *and for which*, capital circulates.

Yet that is only part of the story. The next part shows that the homeless are not alone in representing this sort of an existential threat. A lot of other people, too, are destined to get a one-way bus ticket, at least metaphorically. That is to say, most of the rest of us—though some people, like young black men a lot more than others—present a regulatory problem right at the limits to capital. With the contra-dictory dynamics of the political economy of public space now more firmly in mind, then, the three chapters of part 2 turn to these broader issues (beyond homelessness itself) of public space and the limits to capital. In each chapter we will see that the streets of the modern capitalist city are only marginally less mean for a broad swath of urban residents than they are for homeless people themselves, including some of those who are beneficiaries of such meanness. Homeless people are not the only ones being "warned out."

PART 2

Mean Streets Metastasized

Somewhere, a society must say that this is now enough. These are conditions
that we would never ever accept in other contexts. Now for several years
we have had a debate about this [Roma beggars and homeless people
in public space] and have found that we make an exception regarding
our principal stance concerning the equality of all human beings.

—Eskilstuna, Sweden County Council leader Jimmy Jansson (2018)

Mean Streets Metastasized

CHAPTER 5

The SUV Model of Citizenship

> In the form of society now under consideration, the behavior of men
> in the social process of production is purely atomic. Hence their
> relations to each other in production assume a material character
> independent of their control and conscious individual action.
>
> —Karl Marx, *Capital* (1867)

It is not only in the sphere of production, and it is not only for men, that social relations have become "purely atomic." Increasingly this is also so in the realm of social reproduction, especially as this realm is worked out in public. Such atomic individuality is a fundamental requirement of capitalist production and reproduction. While there is no doubt that cooperation between workers can pay unremunerated dividends to capital in the form of increased productivity and is thus vitally important (indeed, Marx argued in the midst of his analysis of relative surplus value production that "cooperation ever constitutes the fundamental form of the capitalist mode of production"),[1] and while there is no doubt that human instincts and perhaps especially desires for comradery are vital to social cohesion (to say nothing of such things as child rearing and education), maybe even more fundamental to successful capitalism is competition between workers, and now, increasingly, between people fulfilling the other roles of their everyday lives. Capitalism thrives—at least in good part—on the construction and reinforcement of a kind of radical individualism, a form of comparative, competitive, commodity-defined isolationism that older sociologists described as the "lonely crowd," and more recent geographers like Kafui Attoh describe as a sort of idiocy of urban life.[2] Capitalism has torn sociality and cooperation from their traditional moorings in historically sedimented community and reconstituted them as a "money relation," in which "the ties of personal dependence, of distinctions of blood, of education, etc. are in fact exploded, ripped up . . . and individuals *seem* independent . . . free to collide with one another and to engage in exchange within this freedom."[3] Laws of property, coupled with ideologies of individualism and freedom, have combined to construct *economic* subjects who are "free agents," equal before the law, stripped bare of mutual obligation and dependency, left to sink or swim, apparently, on the basis of their own merits and their own talents (which is why the distinction between deserving and undeserving poor is so ideologically important).

This ongoing reconstruction of sociality as purely atomic has never been natural or easy, and it has always been contested, sometimes in quite retrograde ways as people seek, for example, to reclaim their "distinctions of blood." Other times such contestation is quite progressive as people struggle, against the odds, to construct what Raymond Williams described as a "new kind of community" that "only became a reality when economic and political rights were fought for and partially gained, in recognition of unions, in the extension of the franchise, and in the possibility of entry into new representative and democratic institutions."[4] Or, increasingly, it is something in between as the economic, atomic relation between individuals is *policed*, since, without a doubt, such an abject sense of loneliness is frightening and, for many, deeply insecure. Law has responded to this insecurity, and in the process has worked to *reinforce* the primacy of what might be called the juridical individual, in part to forestall exactly the sort of community Williams describes. What is being created, as this chapter shows, is a new kind of individual who is not just autonomous in her or his own body, but who is in fact surrounded by a moving zone of autonomy—something like a personal bubble of inviolable private property, which is to say a bubble of *abstract space*—that putatively will protect her or him from "collisions," or that will ensure that such "collisions" are either voluntary or, more importantly, winnable.*

The Right to Be Left Alone

On the legal front, and to a certain extent on the streets (though not in the legislative chambers), the last ten years have been relatively quiet ones in the long war over women's reproductive freedom in the United States.† Where the streets and sidewalks outside women's health centers used to be sites of continual confrontations between anti-choice activists, many of them highly militant, and women and allies seeking to either use the service of the health center or defend women's rights to access reproductive health care, now, while protest is hardly absent, the

---

*As with all tendencies and movements discussed in this book, the push toward the purely atomic, autonomous individual is contradictory and also constantly transgressed in ideology and law, as any woman hoping to maintain her rights to reproductive choice knows (to take the example at the heart of this chapter).

† As I write during the summer of 2018, President Trump has nominated his second virulently anti-abortion and anti-woman Supreme Court justice. No doubt the era of legal quietude is coming to a rapid end. And as I make copyediting corrections in the summer of 2019, this prediction has been borne out as states across the country compete with each other to write the most draconian anti-abortion—that is, anti-woman—laws.

intensity of the threat of violence has lessened, at least a bit. Many attribute this to the Supreme Court finally, and fairly firmly, laying out a legal compromise in 2000—an almost literal ceasefire—between the rights of anti-abortion protesters on the one hand and women seeking abortions (or other reproductive health care), doctors, nurses, and other health care staff on the other hand.*

At stake in the case—called *Hill v. Colorado*—was a "bubble law" passed by the Colorado state legislature in 1999. Seeking to protect citizens' "access to health care facilities for the purpose of obtaining medical counseling and treatment," this law not only made it illegal to "knowingly obstruct, detain, hinder, impede, or block another person's entry or exit from a health care facility," it also held that "no person shall knowingly approach another person within eight feet of such a person, unless such other person consents, for the purpose of passing a leaflet or handbill to, displaying a sign to, or engaging in oral protest, education, or counseling with such other person in the public way or sidewalk area within a radius of one hundred feet from any entrance door to a health care facility."[5] The law created two kinds of bubbles. First, it established a one-hundred-foot radius buffer zone around health clinic entrances. Second, within that buffer zone, it established an eight-foot floating bubble around each person who enters, a bubble that cannot be pierced for the purposes of politically charged conversation, leafletting, "education," and so forth.

The legislative history of the bill (or even just the most basic awareness of abortion politics in the United States) makes it clear that the Colorado law was designed as a means to regulate militant, sometimes violent protest outside health care facilities where abortions are performed. A key tactic of anti-abortion activists in the years since abortion was legalized in 1973 has been to engage in what they call "sidewalk counseling," which usually entails rushing up to women entering clinics (and sometimes just passing by), pleading with and shouting at them, shoving photographs of what they claim to be aborted fetuses into their hands and faces, and so forth. But the Colorado law did not outlaw *anti-abortion* protesters from approaching any person in a bubble. Instead it outlawed approach by *all* protesters. If it had done the former, it surely would have been struck down as a "content-specific" ban, which, as the Supreme Court has ruled in a string of cases, can be done only in the most extreme of circumstances and in the most limited way.† Rather, restrictions on protest in

---

*The battle has hardly abated on other fronts. Anti-choice, anti-woman legislators have, for example, had considerable success in defunding and hobbling the operations of Planned Parenthood in the United States and creating ridiculous requirements on health centers that perform abortions that are not required of any other outpatient surgery centers in a fairly successful attempt to drive them out of business, and now, in the Trump administration, blocking funding to global health NGOs that also perform abortions (even though U.S. money does not, by law, go toward funding abortions).

†As we saw in chapter 4, not only are laws aimed at specific ideas subject to sharp judicial scrutiny, but so too are laws aimed at specific *classes* of people. There is, in American law, an apparent interest in formal equality, an interest, as we will see in the next chapter, that can often have the perverse, if not entirely unexpected, advantage of making it possible to target specific *kinds* of people.

the "public forum" must be "content neutral."* The broad reach of the Colorado law was meant to achieve that content neutrality. Yet that broad reach was also why the law was opposed not only by anti-abortion activists but also by the AFL-CIO, which was worried about its effects on striking health care workers, and by People for the Ethical Treatment of Animals, which sometimes protests against medical research conducted in health care facilities.[6]

In terms of earlier Supreme Court jurisprudence on protest in the public forum, however, "the statute's breadth was its *saving feature*."[7] Because it was content neutral, the law was seen by the court to be a reasonable, narrowly tailored "time, place, and manner" restriction on free speech.[8] And, the court ruled, the law served a compelling state interest in that it sought to "protect those who enter a health care facility from the harassment, the nuisance, the persistent importuning, the following, the dogging, and the implied threat of physical touching that can accompany an unwelcome approach within eight feet of a patient by a person wishing to argue vociferously face-to-face and perhaps thrust an undesired handbill upon her."[9]

The dissenters in the case (Justice Anthony Kennedy and Justice Antonin Scalia, who was joined by Justice Clarence Thomas), together with legal scholars from across the political spectrum, questioned the majority's decision in *Hill* on a number of grounds. Scalia argued that the decision's breadth was less its saving grace than its Achilles' heel because it outlawed so much speech.[10] Kennedy complained that "protest," "counseling," and "education" were imprecise terms and that "no custom, tradition, or legal authority gives these terms the specificity required to sustain a criminal prohibition on speech." Kennedy further argued that the eight-foot floating bubble was unworkable in practice and therefore vague.[11] But especially both Scalia and Kennedy (joined later by a chorus of law scholars) complained that in *Hill* the court radically expanded the doctrine of "the unwilling listener," and thereby created a whole new kind of privacy in public space, a kind of privacy that might have profound effects on the possibilities for political discourse in the public forum.[12]

Before *Hill*, the court had fairly consistently held that in a public forum it was the responsibility of the *listeners* to avoid unwanted messages: it was up to them to avert their eyes or step out of earshot.[13] By contrast, when listeners were "trapped," for example in their own homes, they did not have to be subject to

*The court defines a "public forum" as publicly accessible property on which free speech, petitioning, leafletting, demonstrations, and so forth have "traditionally" taken place. The prime examples are streets, sidewalks, and parks. Governments may regulate the time, place, and manner in such forums, but only if such regulation is "content neutral" and "narrowly tailored" to serve a specific and "compelling" government interest. In traditional public forums, the presumption is that regulation is likely to be unconstitutional, and therefore courts are required to subject any regulation to "strict scrutiny," meaning that the burden of proof of constitutionality rests with the government and not those being regulated. I explore the evolution of public forum doctrine—and the spatial practices it licenses or bars—in detail in "Political Violence," *Right to the City*, chap. 2, and "Liberalization of Free Speech."

unwanted messages. "Captive audiences" had the "right to be left alone."[14] The quintessential case (called *Frisby*) concerned picketing on a street—a public forum—outside a private residence. Here the court held that such picketing could be regulated because the message it imparted could not be avoided. The audience was captive since it was "figuratively, and perhaps literally, trapped within the home, and because of the unique and subtle impact such picketing [it is] left with no ready means of avoiding the unwanted speech." Protesters had "no right to force speech into the home of an unwilling listener."[15]

In other words, before *Hill* the court's jurisprudence made it clear that protecting the rights of "unwilling listeners" was a significant state interest *when those listeners were in their own homes.* They had a reasonable expectation of privacy. However, in public, no such expectation of privacy existed, and it was up to the unwilling listener to avoid speech that bothered her or him. The distinction it made between the public forum and the private home "was one of the few fairly 'bright lines' in the Court's 'captive audience' analysis."[16] With *Hill* individuals could now carry this "right to be left alone" as they traveled through public space. The "bright line" no longer existed. Indeed, the majority was explicit on this point. It argued that the right to be left alone was one of the "most comprehensive of rights and the right most valued by civilized men."* Further, the court ruled that "while the freedom to communicate is substantial, 'the right of every person to be left alone' must be placed in the scales with the right of others to communicate."[17] "It is that right" to be left alone, the court argued, "as well as the right of 'passage without obstruction' that the Colorado statute legitimately seeks to protect."[18]

In fact, in its brief before the court, Colorado had specifically denied that the state was seeking to protect the "right to be left alone," prompting Justice Scalia to complain, with some justification, that the right to be left alone the court said the state sought to protect "is not only completely *different* from the interest that the statute specifically sets forth; it was explicitly *declaimed* by the State in its brief before this Court, and characterized as a 'straw interest' *petitioners* served up in the hope of discrediting the State's case."[19] Scalia therefore argued that in *Hill* the court once again revved up what he called the "ad hoc nullification machine" that, in his view, operates to annul the rights of anti-abortion protesters whenever the laws and injunctions restricting their actions come before the court.[20]

*This line is from a famous dissent in the 1920s by Justice Louis Brandeis. After quoting Brandeis on how important the right to be left alone was, however, the majority immediately muddied the waters with a footnote that read, "This common law 'right' is more accurately characterized as an 'interest' that States can choose to protect in certain situations" (717n24, citing *Katz v. United States*, 387 U.S. 347 [1967]). It is unclear what function this note plays in the court's decision other than to provide clear insight into how the court thinks about rights, and their mutability, in general. The main quotation from above is from *Hill*, 716, quoting *Olmstead v. United States*, 277 U.S. 438 (1928), Brandeis dissenting.

While Scalia may have been correct, it is more plausible to argue instead that the majority was beginning to craft a new standard for protest and other political engagement in public space, a standard for which the proximate cause may be violence and potential violence outside health centers that provide abortions, but which in fact codifies a new expectation for all *civic* space.* This new standard suggests not so much that there can be no expectation of *privacy* in public space (though elsewhere the court does continue down this avenue too), but rather that there can be no expectation of *publicity* there. In *Hill*, the court argues that the Colorado statute is constitutional because "instead of drawing distinctions based on the subject that the approaching speaker may wish to address, the statue applies equally to used car salesmen, animal rights activists, fundraisers, environmentalists, and missionaries. Each can attempt to educate unwilling listeners on any subject, but without consent may not approach within eight feet to do so."[21] Within the hundred-foot buffer zone, then, individuals are surrounded by an eight-foot floating bubble that another may enter for purposes of communication (political, commercial, or otherwise) only at the individuals' behest: in public space, people can now travel in an eight-foot bubble of privacy.

This is a striking legal innovation, and one of potentially limitless expansiveness, as I suggest below. But to see how it may be expansive, and why it is plausible to suggest, as I will soon do, that it establishes a new kind of citizenship (a citizenship based on and protective of the fully privatized juridical individual— the perfect person for abstract space), it is important to delve a bit more deeply into the logic of the court's reasoning in *Hill*.

During the 1990s the court decided two cases that were similar but concerned injunctions against protesters rather than statutory laws. In *Madsen v. Women's Health Center* in 1994, the court upheld the validity of no-protest "buffer zones" but restricted their size so that they did not burden "too much" speech. The court recognized that women patients and employees *inside* a health center or their homes were, by circumstances, a "captive audience" and so found limits on noise levels and appropriately sized buffer zones outside residences and clinic entrances (in the latter case, thirty-six feet) to be reasonable "time, place, and manner" restrictions on protest activity. At the same time, the court specifically invalidated a three-hundred-foot "no approach zone" arguing that it was impossible "to justify a prohibition on *all* uninvited approaches" and that "the 'consent' requirement"—the requirement that protesters could approach an individual only with that individual's explicit consent—"alone invalidates this provision" since "it burdens more speech than is necessary to prevent intimidation and to ensure access to the clinic." A large "no approach" zone was unconstitutional.[22]

---

*The plausibility of this argument is given added force by the court's decision three years later in *Virginia v. Hicks*, which is the subject of the next chapter.

Three years later, in *Schenck v. Pro-Choice Networks of W. New York*, the court again sustained the use of stationary buffer zones and again invalidated the portion of an injunction that created a fifteen-foot floating bubble around clinic employees and patients. An injunction had banned protest "within fifteen feet of any person or vehicle seeking access or leaving" four health clinics in the Buffalo area. The court said of the floating bubble, "We hold here that because this broad prohibition 'floats' it cannot be sustained."[23] Moreover, the fifteen-foot floating bubble made *any* protest practically impossible because (1) the sidewalk outside one of the clinics was only seventeen feet wide and (2) the movement of two or more persons entering or leaving a clinic could make it impossible for a protester to comply with the injunction even if she or he tried, since by remaining fifteen feet from one person, the protester might inadvertently enter the bubble of another. And, further, the court suggested (in its review of lower court decisions on the case) that when a District Court upheld the fifteen-foot floating bubble, its reasoning—"to protect the right of the people approaching and entering the facilities to be left alone"—did not "accurately reflect our First Amendment jurisprudence in this area," since "as we said in Madsen . . . 'as a general matter, we have indicated that in public debate our citizens must tolerate insulting, even outrageous, speech in order to provide adequate breathing space to the freedoms protected by the First Amendment.'"[24]

Why then—or, as importantly, *how*—did the court uphold just such a "float" and just such a "right to be left alone" in *Hill*, given its earlier dismissal of exactly these practices? First, the court noted that the Colorado law was a statute, not an injunction. Injunctions need to be more carefully examined than statutes because they are made by fiat, involve only one branch of government, and are necessarily directed at specific individuals or groups rather than the population as a whole. Statutes, by contrast, express the will of the majority, which should be accorded some deference.[25] Second, the court placed special emphasis on the phrase "no person shall *knowingly* approach another person within eight feet."[26] This clause, presumably, indemnified protesters from accidently entering an individual's floating bubble: protesters could not be held responsible if they *unknowingly* moved only seven feet away (thinking it was eight and thus trying to abide by the law); and they could not be held responsible if while trying to stay eight feet from one person, they accidently moved within eight feet of another. This clause distinguished *Hill* from *Schenck*, since under the terms of the injunction at issue in the latter, the protesters *could* be held responsible for such inadvertent transgressions.[27]

Third, the court held that at eight feet, under normal circumstances, a person could speak to another in a normal tone of voice and still be heard. In fact, the authors of the Colorado law experimented on just this issue, moving around a hearing room at the capitol, measuring distances and checking on audibility, finally determining that eight feet was the proper distance.[28] Whereas in *Madsen* and *Schenck* the court had found fifteen-foot floating bubbles to be too large, in *Hill* they agreed with the Colorado legislature that eight feet was just right. Though the eight-foot bubble made it impossible to approach a person and hand her or him a leaflet (without permission), the court declared that nothing in the statute "prevent[s] a leafletter from simply standing near the path of on-coming pedestrians an proffering his or her material, which the pedestrians can easily accept."[29] In fact, fourth, the court noted more generally that there was nothing in the statute that disallowed *stationary* protesters from carrying out their protest. Protesters could not "knowingly approach" others without permission. But they did not have to move if an individual seeking access to a health center entered *their* eight-foot bubble. In *Schenck* that was not the case: protesters were liable no matter who approached whom.

Finally, whereas *Madsen* and *Schenck* targeted specific—anti-abortion—protesters, as noted already the Colorado statute regulated *all* political speech. For the court, "The fact that coverage of a statute is broader than the specific concerns that led to its enactment is of no constitutional significance. What is important is that all persons entering or leaving health care facilities share the interests served by the statute.... Here, the comprehensiveness of the statute is a virtue, not a vice, because it is evidence against there being a discriminatory government motive."[30] This is where matters get truly interesting: what the court validated, with only some hesitancy, was a truly broad-based reconfiguration of civic interaction, one that covers "used car salesmen, animal rights activists, fundraisers, environmentalists, and missionaries"—anyone with a message to impart or a cause to fight for. Against all these, the court has declared, individuals in public space have an essential right to be left alone.

Legal scholar Robert Nauman has argued that the court's decision can be interpreted to have quite broad or much narrower implications. The broad implications are scary; the more narrow ones are still troubling. Interpreted broadly, Nauman suggests, the court's recognition that individuals have an enforceable "right to be left alone in a public forum . . . broadens where this interest is applied" by taking the private (the rights of the home) public. In particular, the court "substantially lessen[ed] the burden on unwilling listeners to avoid unwanted speech in a public forum" and moved that burden to speakers, making them responsible for helping "unwilling listeners" avoid their speech. As such, the decision "runs the . . . risk of establishing a 'heckler's veto,' in which the audience possesses the power to prohibit speech that it does not want to hear simply by being present." The Colorado statute was merely the specific regulatory means by which this new right to be left alone in public was accomplished.[31]

More narrowly, the decision can be interpreted as a refinement (rather than an outright expansion) of the "captive audience" doctrine. "In this sense, the statute merely requires demonstrators . . . not to behave in a manner that makes it impossible for the listener to avoid the speech unless this listener consents. Thus, by standing still and not 'forcing' speech on an unwilling listener, a protest will not violate the statute."[32] In this regard, Nauman suggests, *Hill* represents a reasonable balancing act between the rights of protesters and the rights of others not to be bothered by the protesters. While he notes that "if the government truly has the ability to protect unwilling listeners in a public forum to the same extent that the government may protect the home from verbal and visual assault, there is left a broad government power to restrict speech that may have few limits," Nauman nonetheless argued (based on two lower court decisions) that in fact what the court had done was give better direction to how governments should tailor floating bubble laws:

> For states wishing to draft statutes using the "floater buffer zone" concept, these opinions seem to establish some fundamental guidelines. First, the size of the zone cannot be too great, and probably eight feet is the most appropriate distance. However, narrowing the size of the zone does not alone guarantee constitutionality. Second, the statute must only restrict affirmative acts of the speaker, such as approaching a patient. Punishing speakers who merely stand still and continue to communicate their message will be seen as impermissible, as it will put too much power in the hands of the listener to cut off speech. Thirdly, the government must apply reasonable standards with which one can measure their compliance with the statute, which is best accomplished by providing an element of *scienter* [i.e., a "knowingly" clause].[33]

This more narrow result remains troubling because the court made it clear that establishing such "floating buffer zones" is not limited to instances of controlling anti-abortion protest.

Indeed, the majority in *Hill* is clear that the right to be left alone "can also be protected in [other] confrontational settings." It supports this point by quoting extensively from a 1921 case concerning labor picketing:

> In going to and from work, men have a right to as free a passage without obstruction as the streets can afford, consistent with the rights of others to enjoy the same privilege. We are a social people, and the accosting by one another in an inoffensive way and an offer by one to communicate and discuss information with a view of influencing the other's action, are not regarded as a violation of the other's rights. If, however, the offer is declined, as it may rightfully be, then persistence, importuning, following and dogging, become unjustified annoyance and obstruction which is likely soon to savor of intimidation.[34]

The "right to be left alone" is thus coupled with "the right of free passage," and together they can be advanced by even narrowly drawn "floating bubbles." As we shall shortly see, such bubbles have indeed been extended outward from the doors of health care facilities in ways that make clear just how amenable this sort of regulation is to the production of abstract space in the city, since, as numerous commentators have noted, the court expends no effort on saying what makes medical facilities necessarily different from other, potentially confrontational settings. And as its reliance on the 1921 labor picketing case indicates (which in any event was not decided on explicitly First Amendment grounds), it presumably does not think it should be so limited.

While legal scholars have seized on this issue, the related question of "overbreadth" (that the regulations are not "narrowly tailored" enough), and a set of technical issues about how the "right to be left alone" might now legally be defined and enforced, there remains to be better understood the issue of the form of citizenship—and *therefore* the nature of public space—that *Hill* both presupposes and reinforces.

Public Space, Private Property

The nature of public space in part defines the nature of citizenship—which is the term used to indicate where and how people sit in relation to, are subject to, and seek to gain some degree of sovereignty within or against the state as well as the broader social relations (including economic relations) that determine their lives. Public space provides a "space of engagement" within which not only individuals but especially various publics come to recognize themselves and act collectively. It provides a material basis for the public sphere.[35] By definition, while individuals populate public space, public space is both collectively produced and productive of the collective. Its very point is to bring people together and to provide a literal, material foundation for the formation of collective *publics*, in all their diversity. They are where the dialectic between differentiated and common interests is given form and struggled over, as Iris Marion Young long ago argued: "Because by definition public space is a place accessible to anyone, where anyone can participate and witness, in entering the public one always risks encounter with those who are different, those who identify with different groups and have different forms of life. The group diversity of the city is most often apparent in public space." Furthermore, "politics, the critical activity of raising issues and deciding how institutional and social relations should be organized, crucially depends on the existence of spaces and forums to which everyone has access."[36] There is little room, in this way of thinking, for an expansive "right to be left alone." When the right to be left alone takes the form of buffer zones and floating bubbles, it militates against not just this *ideal* but the very practice of agonistic politics by promoting a form of *access* to public space (for "everyone") that radically transforms the possibilities for *association* in it.

Of course this phenomenon—of promoting access to public space while transforming the nature of association in it—is not restricted to the legal process. For more than a quarter of a century geographers and others have been debating "the end of public space," through privatization processes ranging from the development of malls and festival marketplaces to the creation of business improvement districts and park conservancies that outsource everything from maintenance to policing and the rise of gated suburbs, all of which shape interaction—association—through an ethos of commodification and privacy, tying the right to be left alone closely to both the ability to spend and the need to preserve property values.[37] The result, as Darrell Crilley rightly put it back in the early 1990s, helps create an "illusion of a homogenized public" by minimizing or otherwise controlling "the social heterogeneity of the crowd, [and] substituting in its place a flawless fabric of white, middle class work, play and consumption."[38] Closed-circuit television and other sophisticated surveillance technologies coupled with the generalized "revanchism" Neil Smith saw as animating much urban policy and practice, as well as continued "zero-tolerance" policing, have reinforced this trend toward promoting access to public space (for some) while closely regulating the form that association may take—as we will abundantly see in the next two chapters.[39]

But what sets the legal innovations typified by the *Hill* case apart from these other moves toward reconstructing publicly accessible space is that the courts seem to be legitimating what are in essence personal, traveling zones of autonomy. We can now take our privacy with us into public space in ways we could not before; we retain a *legal* right to be left alone even in the most public of spaces. Or to put the matter in different terms, what seems to be happening, through the expansion and refinement of the right to be left alone, is an important—and startling—innovation in *private property* that significantly amplifies the sorts of transformations of property uncovered in the privatization research just mentioned.

In its geographical sense, private property is a parcel of territory over which the property holder possesses a "right to exclude."[40] This is why it matters deeply when key spaces of public access and association are on private property, like a mall or festival marketplace:* the rules of exclusion are different than they are on public property.[41] Private property—privately held geographical space—is more than mere possession; it is a bundle of rights that imply some set of *duties* on the part of others, like the duty to stay out of private property without the property holder's permission to enter.[42] The liberal philosopher and legal scholar Jeremy Waldron suggests that "in a private property system, a rule is laid down that, in the case of each object, the individual whose name is attached to that object is to determine how that object is to be used and by whom. His decision is to be upheld by society as final."[43] This notion of control over how an object, privately held, is to be used is behind the "right to be left alone" that the Supreme Court long ago declared was essential for people "trapped" in their own residences. The

---

*That much association now takes place in virtual space owned by Facebook, Twitter, and the like only doubles down on the proposition. Ownership matters—deeply.

court's promotion of this right to be left alone functioned precisely to ensure that a property owner's "decision is . . . upheld by society as final." By contrast, public property is organized on a different basis. Commonly accessible public (that is, state-owned) property, like streets, sidewalks, and parks, in urban capitalist societies, functions somewhere between what Waldron calls "collective" property and what he calls "common" property. Collective property is governed "by a sovereign authority, which determines the rules of property, . . . retain[s] control of . . . resource[s] . . . , and [does not] allow . . . resource[s] to be controlled exclusively by any private organization."[44] What is crucial here, of course, is what kind of sovereign the state is and how it makes its decisions: indeed, there is a rather long litany of cases debating the degree to which a state's activities as a sovereign can be separated from its actions as a landlord (as we will discuss in the next chapter). In common property, on the other hand, "rules are organized on the basis that each resource is in principle available for the use of every member [of a collectivity] alike. In principle, the needs and wants of every person are considered, and when allocative decisions are made, they are made on a basis that is in some sense fair to all."[45] Rules of publicly accessible property are made by a sovereign presumably beholden to democratic decisions and vetted, often, through a process of judicial review. Much First Amendment jurisprudence centers precisely on the issue of how well the sovereign does at ensuring that the "wants and needs of every person" are taken into account. The Supreme Court calls this "balancing."

Such balancing is in part based on common law precedent. When the Supreme Court first recognized the right to protest in public space, it did so by basing its decision on common law and arguing, in effect, that the streets and parks functioned *as if* they were common property for which the state was no more than a "trustee." "Wherever the title of the streets and parks may rest," the court argued in *Hague v. CIO* in 1939, "they have immemorially been held in trust for use of the public and, time out of mind, have been used for purposes of assembly, communicating thoughts between citizens, and discussing public questions."[46] The question for authorities—the representative of the sovereign—then, was how to balance competing claims to public space held in trust as a common resource. But by now promoting a right to be left alone in public space, the state is simultaneously promoting the privatization of a common resource: it is changing the relationship between public space as collective and common property, in Waldron's terms. It is promoting a new property regime in which common property—public space—is no longer so much held in trust for assembly, communicating thoughts, and so forth, but instead parceled out, albeit temporarily, to individual "owners" as they move through it.[47] To the degree I have a right to be left alone, then to that degree I can exclude you from the space around me (up to eight feet, say). "One of the functions of private property rules, particularly so far as land is concerned," Waldron has also argued, "is to provide a basis for determining who is allowed to be where. . . . The rules of property give a way of determining, in each case, who is allowed to be in [a] place, and who is not. . . . An individual who is in a place where he is not allowed to be may be removed, and he may be subject to civil or criminal sanctions for trespass or some other offence."[48] It matters greatly, therefore, whether the "organizing idea" (as Waldron calls it) of a property system in general, and of specific properties in particular, is one of private or common property—or something else altogether.[49] It matters because it determines not only the rules of *access* to property, but also the forms of *association* that may take place on it. It determines the quality of civic engagement, the nature of social, including class, struggle, and therefore the content of citizenship.[50]

Where much normative, progressive political theory seeks out a form of association based on solidarity—or at least in which difference is valued for its own sake because it is the root of any nonoppressive collective—civic engagement based on social practices defined primarily by private property (the right to be left alone) is, at root, fundamentally individualistic, privatizing, indeed libertarian. As Alan Ryan explains, libertarianism holds that "we are essentially self-owning creatures; our bodies, our thoughts, our actions, and whatever we can create by employing our efforts on things we have either acquired in an unowned state or have acquired from their previous owner are ours outright. . . . The only restraint upon our ownership of ourselves is that which stems from everyone else's proprietorship in themselves."[51] We have full sovereignty over ourselves and what is ours. This is a libertarianism appropriate to a neoliberal world order in which property ownership is the base for all other, superstructural, social relations.[52] There is no such thing as society, as per Margaret Thatcher, only individuals and families—and also property titles and the entitlements that property titles confer on individuals. "Since all persons are the sole proprietors and outright owners of themselves," Ryan continues, "there is one legitimate form of social cooperation and many illegitimate forms. The legitimate form is based on voluntary exchange; the illegitimate forms are in one way or another extractive."[53]

Under a private property regime, and the legal rules (and thus state-sanctioned violence) that support it, civic engagement should always be entirely voluntary (and hence the right to be left alone truly is the "most comprehensive of rights and the right most valued by civilized men"). Thus the right to exclude becomes paramount, even in what are putatively commonly held properties. Waldron has made a withering argument about how in a "libertarian paradise" where all property is private, the result will necessarily be *un*freedom for some.[54] This is because in fact territorial property is finite and public property is the only place for those without ownership of (or use rights to, in the case of renters) some piece of private property to perform necessary actions—the root of the U.S. Department of Justice's intervention in Boise that featured in chapter 1.

But it also promotes unfreedom because it eliminates the possibility for *chance*, which must be at the root of any true freedom. Under the guise of complete liberty, it eliminates the possibility of agency—the possibility of being swayed or transformed by that which one does not want or expect.*

It does so by eroding the necessary distinction between public and private. Some theorists of citizenship argue that "insisting" on a public-private divide creates an emaciated form of citizenship (by, for example, excluding emotions from forms of behavior deemed "public"), but this concern misses the point.[55] The problem is not that the divide exists, but rather the conditions under which it exists, and what happens when it disappears. What happens when the private *becomes* the public, when the right to exclude expands from the home to commonly accessible space, or when that right exists as a new spatial practice that allows you to always and everywhere keep those you do not want to encounter out of your own personal "bubble" of privacy? What does it mean when a public space comes to be governed by rules formerly reserved for private property?

Bubble Laws, Inflated

These questions are being raised regularly in city councils and state capitols around the United States and answered daily on the streets of American cities. The answers come in the form of what can best be described as a kind of regulatory experimentation within which, unsurprisingly, homeless people are the guinea pigs. Given the foregoing analysis of *Hill*, however, it should be clear that homeless people are not the only ones targeted for new modes of management. But they are a primary one—and one in which the creation zones of privacy in public space as well as the right to be left alone seem like just so much common sense.

In the wake of a series of court decisions that for the most part upheld beggars' panhandling as a form of either political or commercial speech, and thus protected by the First Amendment, cities have turned instead to limiting behaviors associated with panhandling rather than begging itself. In cities both small (Palo Alto, California, and Evanston, Illinois, for example) and large (San Francisco, Miami, Chicago), a wave of legislation swept over the urban landscape beginning in the mid-1990s that still has not receded (as the National Law Center on Homelessness and Poverty reports cited throughout this book document)— legislation that has been given further impetus, and cover, by decisions like *Hill*. Typically this legislation outlaws "aggressive" panhandling. In Evanston, for example, legislation passed in 2001 made it illegal to "impede" the progress of a person when asking for a handout; unlike with the anti-abortion protesters in

* Here, then, is one way in which experiments in regulating the homeless redound on all of us.

Hill, however, it is up to the beggar to stay out of the way of an oncoming pedestrian that she or he wants to communicate with. As the pedestrian passes, the beggar can ask for a handout once; asking twice is considered aggressive. In addition, begging is outlawed near bus stops, on buses or trains, within ten feet of an ATM or bank entrance, or "near" outdoor cafés (whose tables are often, though not always, on public property).[56] Unlike in several other cities, though, the Evanston City Council did not outlaw all begging, in any form, after dark.

The Evanston law, like many passed around the country, was based on model laws developed by right-wing policy consortiums like the Center for the Community Interest (CCI) (formerly called the American Alliance for Rights and Responsibilities, an important proponent of anti-homeless laws in the late 1980s and early 1990s, but now apparently defunct),* which by the mid-2000s was boasting that it had advised more than fifty cities on "quality-of-life" issues and in the drafting of anti-panhandling legislation. CCI argued that its model aggressive panhandling law merely regulated the time, place, and manner of begging. But as with the Colorado law at stake in *Hill*, the importance lies in the implications of such regulation. CCI's model ordinance defined "aggressive" as follows:

1. Approaching, speaking to, or following a person in a manner to cause fear of bodily harm, or to actually cause harm to a person or property.
2. Asking for a handout a second time.
3. Touching a person without consent "in the course of soliciting."
4. Blocking or interfering with a person or a vehicle in any way "including unreasonably causing a pedestrian or vehicle to take evasive action to avoid physical contact."
5. Making threatening gestures.
6. Following a person "with the intent of asking that person for money or other thing of value."
7. "Speaking in a volume unreasonably loud under the circumstances."
8. Begging from people who are waiting in line.

In addition, the model code held that no person should:

1. Beg within 20 feet of public toilets, payphones, ATMs, banks, check-cashing businesses, any "valid vendor location," or within six feet of the entrance of any other building.

* In the 1990s and well into the 2000s CCI received considerable funding from conservative foundations like the Olin and Bradley foundations as well as from major law firms and boasted a board of directors that included such luminaries as George L. Kelling, one of the architects of the broken-windows policing theory, Fred Siegel, a longtime editor of the Manhattan Institute's *City Journal*, and Allison Stern, the president of the A. M. Stern Foundation. The web pages for the American Alliance and CCI no longer exist. The quotations here were accessed from www.communityinterest.org in 2004 and are quoted in my article "S.U.V. Model of Citizenship." CCI's web domain seems to now be a Japanese blog site.

2. Solicit an operator of a motor vehicle for the sale of goods or performance of a service (purveyors of requested emergency services excepted).
3. Offer to reserve a parking place or direct people to a public parking space.
4. Beg while under the influence of alcohol.
5. "... solicit by stating that funds are needed to meet a specific need" when that need does not exist, the beggar has funds to cover the cost of the need, of the beggar doesn't "intend" to use money for that need.
6. Beg on any public transportation vehicle, at any stop or station, or in any public parking lot.
7. Beg "in a group of two or more persons."

Every city already has laws against harassment, intimidation, and assault, so that is not what is at stake here (those parts of the aggressive panhandling laws are merely redundant). Rather, the anti-aggressive panhandling laws are designed to create a public geography in which nonindigent people can move unhindered by panhandlers, and therefore in which they can experience a kind of urban freedom that is "greatest in an empty volume" as the sociologist Richard Sennett has put it: "The ability to move anywhere, to move without obstruction, to circulate freely."[57] Through law, CCI and other like-minded advocates seek to create the sort of frictionless cityscape that in practice city engineers are expected to design: a city of flows wherein beggars, like bus stops, hot dog stands, book stalls, picketing workers, political demonstrators, and hanging-out youth, are hindrances, obstacles like stones in a river that do little more than create turbulence, and that must be minimized ("neutralized" in Peter Marcuse's apt language) if not eliminated altogether.[58]

This empty volume, this frictionless cityscape, this *abstract space*, is, of course, quiet: now not just outside homes or health clinics, where an audience might be "captive," but even on bustling city streets, where laws may now require some people on the street—beggars—to not speak "in a volume unreasonably loud for the circumstances." It is not the listener's responsibility to avoid unwanted speech: it is the speaker's responsibility to ensure that avoidance is easy. The Colorado health care law had a *scienter* clause that clearly increased its constitutional legitimacy in the eyes of the court and legal commentators: a protester could not "knowingly" enter the space of another, and so the responsibility for helping unwilling listeners to avoid one's speech could not be held hostage to fortune. But the model aggressive panhandling law makes it illegal to only *unreasonably* cause a pedestrian or vehicle to "take evasive action." But these are extremely slippery terms: What is unreasonable? Who decides? What constitutes evasive action? Having to step a foot or two out of the way? Having to roll up a window? And just how does a beggar impart to a passer-by the message that she or he would like a handout? The beggar cannot stand in front of an oncoming pedestrian and ask, cannot follow once the pedestrian has passed, and cannot speak "unreasonably" loudly as the pedestrian goes by. The answer, according to CCI and city councils that followed its lead, is that beggars must always be passive.[59] And what about a beggar approaching a person sitting on a low wall eating lunch? Can a beggar approach that person without permission? The answer from CCI was a solid no: it broke the rule of passivity. The right to be left alone in public space, in other words, means that *some people* must repress their (otherwise perfectly legal) agency. It means that any (nonindigent) pedestrian can travel the city in his or her own bubble of privacy.

Or, more accurately, a (nonbegging) person in the city can exercise something like private property control over public space as she or he moves through the city. Beggars, like protesters, must be invited into the private space of the individual, even when that individual is in public space. What is new is that this property right, this right to exclude, is no longer rooted in specific, clearly demarcated spaces (as with traditional private property), but instead "travels." We can carry it with us wherever we go.* Individuals in public space now resemble a spaceship reentering the atmosphere or a speed boat plowing through a lake: the spaceship or boat creates a bow wave that pushes the air or water out of its way, and travels in something like a vacuum; and for some distance behind it, the wake keeps the vacuum from being filled. Similarly, armed with new anti-aggressive panhandling laws, (nonindigent) people plowing through the streets of the city can push beggars out of the way (it is *they* who must not hinder *your* progress; *they* who must take evasive action), and provisions in the laws against "following" ensure that the vacuum thereby created will not be immediately filled.

For many cities, of course, this is not enough. The second part of the model ordinance in effect zones public space into a series of "begging" and "no begging" zones, just as the Colorado ordinance creates specific "protest" and "no protest" ones around health clinic entrances.[60] Such zoning of public space ensures that encounters with those with whom we may disagree, be different from, not like, or not want to meet, are kept at a distance, and all our interactions come to seem entirely voluntary: *we* must seek out protesters; *we* must approach panhandlers; *we* can spend all our lives without encountering the unpredictable. We can—and indeed many of us seem very much to want to—live in a world quite at odds with the image of public space and democracy that animates much political theory (including the important work of Iris Marion Young). For such volun-

---

*Perhaps yet even more accurately, what is new here is the *degree* to which such autonomous zones exist. The *American Steel Foundries* case discussed above created severe restrictions on the actions of labor picketers, restrictions that over the course of the twentieth century were in fact severely eroded, to the degree that a congressional investigating committee in the 1940s could suggest, not entirely accurately, but not entirely inaccurately either, that even by then courts would strike down similar restrictions on picketing as unconstitutional. To the degree that these restrictions existed, and to the degree they are being revived, they do not yet create a "bubble" around passersby, pedestrians, or other citizens. See Mitchell, "Scales of Justice" and "Liberalization of Free Speech."

teerism, and the law that is bringing it into being, is anti-urban and anti-public.* It is a private ethos writ large that makes social relations, as Marx put it, "purely atomic."[61] Purely atomic social relations mark the eclipse of civic, *differentiated* space; civic space becomes an illusion, little more than a representation of public life that no longer exists. Abstract space does not in this sense "paper over," difference, as Lefebvre put it, but rather through law, spaces of difference—of dissensus—are *made over* into abstract space. Purely atomic relations, reinforced through bubble laws, represent the apotheosis of abstract space—*and of the individual.*

Between the Individual and the World

And here we get to the nub of the issue. The apotheosis of the individual is the victory—however temporary, however tenuous—of abstract space for, as Raymond Williams reminded us long ago, "individual originally meant indivisible," and implied a "necessary connection," but through "an extraordinary social and political history" of which the development of bubble laws is merely a recent moment, "the phrase 'an individual'—a single example of a group— was joined and overtaken by 'the individual': a fundamental order of being."[62] But this fundamental order of being is *ideological*, because just as fundamental, and always pushing against the idiocy of individualization is exactly this need for connection, for communion, for *class*, and for the common struggles that bring these into being. Laws like those discussed in this chapter, then, are a form of class struggle, designed precisely to break apart and make ever more difficult common action, if through no other means than creating the very material conditions whereby "the individual," alone in her or his bubble, is all there is. That these processes, struggles, and experiments in regulation are deeply contradictory—and we will see even better just how deeply contradictory in the next chapter—merely makes clear that what is being described here is an ongoing history, not an "end of public space" (or of collective action and collective life) but rather the new material conditions of its very possibility, however constrained. And public spaces are deeply constrained, now. Instead of understanding public space—differentiated space—to be "agonistic" and "associational" and the citizenship that forms it as being a product of the collective actions of people, the American courts, led by the Supreme Court, are codifying a model of public life that is the antithesis of public space. We are, each and every one of us, radically individual, completely "free agents" to use Marx's term. As free agents, we are "free to collide with one another and engage in exchange." But we *do not want to collide with one another*. We might want to join together. Yet

---

*And both the fact of its existence and its popularity should make us leery, at least, of calls to build a new radical politics on the chance of a chance encounter, as, for example, Andy Merrifield seeks to do in his otherwise insightful polemic in favor of city life and urban struggle: *Politics of the Encounter*.

when the possibilities for that are blocked, many of us just want to move freely through public space, and, absent any kind of collective, solidaristic modes of shaping the urban order, we are increasingly happy to be encased in an impregnable bubble of property (made real through law, and given force by the police), and watched over by a network of surveillance cameras, their operators, and the state. We want—and expect—to feel safe at all times, and if, absent other options, bubble laws are what is on offer, then we'll take them.

What we'll take, what U.S. courts are pushing us toward, is a model of citizenship and urban life that matches the cars we drive. The rise of the SUV over the past two decades has been attributed to any number of factors (and cannot be explained only in terms of consumer choice), but a central factor has been the sense of inviolability that a couple of tons of steel and fiberglass can instill. Cocooned in a sealed chamber, behind tinted glass, with the temperature fully controlled, and the GPS system tracking, and sometimes dictating, our every turn, our every stop and start, we are radically isolated from each other, able to communicate only through the false connectedness of our cell phones. We ride high and sovereign; we are masters of space; we are safe against all who might intrude, all who might stand in our way (and against the weather too). That this is a false security has been amply shown in traffic accident statistics; that this is a false (or rather deeply regressive) isolationism has been proven in the way that the large consumption of raw materials and fuel the SUV society requires makes us, through the gas tank if in no other way, even more radically connected to others in the world. But never mind: *that* kind of connectedness (where "individuals *seem* independent" but aren't) is a connectedness only of the most abstract and distant kind (the deployment of troops and starting of wars notwithstanding). In our SUVs and with our SUV citizenship, *that* kind of connectedness can always be banished beyond the shell of the Nissan Armada, Ford Expedition, Toyota Sequoia, or the eight-foot bubble we now carry with us when we climb down out of the driver's seat and are forced to walk. We are now, truly, the liberal, autonomous subject. We own ourselves and no one can intrude on us without our permission.

Developing an argument by the libertarian political philosopher Robert Nozick, Jeremy Waldron writes, "To say I own myself is to say that nobody but me has the right to dispose of me or to direct my actions. *I* have rights to do these things (though I must not harm others in doing so; that is, I must not exercise my self-ownership in a way that violates theirs), and those rights are exclusive of anyone else's privilege in this regard, for they are correlative to others' duties to refrain from interfering with what, in this sense, I own."[63] The sort of bubble laws legitimated in *Hill* coupled with the push toward aggressive panhandling laws like the ones pushed by conservative think tanks like CCI, seek to protect just this kind of self-ownership. The "right to be left alone" is at the heart of this kind of self-ownership. It imposes on *others* a set of duties (not to approach within eight feet without being invited in; not to "impede" another's progress by asking for a handout; not to attempt to wash the windshield of my Armada [!] while I am idling at a stoplight).

Just as SUVs have transformed the conditions of accessibility to country and city, opening up at least the possibility of going "off road" while also making white middle- and upper-class citizens feel comfortable in the city (the role of the SUV in gentrifying the city should not be discounted), so too do aggressive panhandling laws and decisions like *Hill* (and as we will see in the next chapter a decision made soon after *Hill* in a case called *Hicks*) transform accessibility to— but especially association in—public space and therefore transform both what it is and what kinds of struggle and citizenship can develop within it. As attractive as is the vision of associational and agonistic citizenship that progressive scholars seek to theorize, any such theorizing must be set against the kind of reality of *this* purely atomic citizenship now in formation. Such theorizing must take seriously the degree to which laws and court decisions—the frameworks through which modes of being citizens and being politically engaged are pounded into shape—are tending away from associative, agonistic, differentiating forms of interaction and more toward constructing Sennett's "empty volume"—the very essence of abstract space. Or really, what the courts seem to be constructing, and thus what needs close and sustained attention, is a dual empty volume: the empty volume immediately surrounding the individual defined by either law or a couple tons of steel; and the empty volume that this law- and steel-encased individual can now travel through, a space made empty on the one hand by the scurrying, fleeing dance of those who might see a need to impede your progress (to make a political point—whether about women's reproductive rights or the "rights" of capital to take and remake the city to suit its own needs alone—or to ask for a handout) but who now can't, and on the other by those who—we are about to see—have simply been banned altogether from the space.

CHAPTER 6

Judicial Anti-Urbanism

The ruling gives the poor a right the rich have long had: to keep
loiterers, and potential criminals, out of their homes.

—*New York Times* (2003)

In 1997, the city of Richmond, Virginia, transferred the deed to the streets in
and surrounding all city housing projects to the Richmond Redevelopment and
Housing Authority (RRHA). The ordinance deeding the streets to the RRHA
ordered that agency—which is a public entity—to close the streets to "public
use and travel, and to post signs at 100-foot intervals announcing 'NO TRES-
PASSING PRIVATE PROPERTY.'"[1] No gates, barriers, or other impediments to
travels were constructed at any project, nor were other alterations made to the
landscape that might signal the streets were no longer public (the signs were neither large nor conspicuous). Indeed, despite the city council's order to bar "public use and travel," the RRHA still permitted automobile through traffic on the
newly privatized streets. Instead of barriers or landscape alterations, the RRHA
enforced its new property rights by writing rules that made it illegal for any person, other than a resident or employee of the housing projects, to enter beyond
the new trespassing signs if she or he did not have a "legitimate business or social
purpose." If a person without a legitimate business or social purpose was found
on the new RRHA property by either a police officer or an employee of the housing authority, she or he could be served with a "barment notice" either orally or
in writing. This barment notice said that if the person receiving it were ever to
enter onto any RRHA property anywhere in the city—*for any reason whatsoever*—then she or he could be arrested for trespassing. In other words, once a
barment notice was served, its recipient could not enter RRHA property, even if
this time she or he had a perfectly legitimate business or social purpose.[2]

There were no guidelines given to employees or to police as to what consti-
tuted "legitimate" purposes: the issuance of a barment notice was entirely at the
discretion of the issuer. No notice was given as to how such barments could be

appealed, and once issued they lasted forever. A person could be barred from RRHA property, in other words, on purely capricious grounds, and for the rest of her or his life be forever banished from a significant number of city streets—streets that had formerly been like any other streets, streets that looked and performed the same functions as they had before, but streets that were now private property because of a deed transfer between two public agencies.

The use of such trespass-barment rules became common in American public housing projects during the 1990s. Public housing authorities (PHAs) saw them as "a crucial . . . tool . . . to prevent wrong doers from gaining access to public housing grounds." They were a tool that allowed PHAs to "act as landlords" and better control who could and could not be on their property.[3] Such rules typically covered the grounds and buildings, but not the streets, of housing projects.[4] In Richmond, housing officials and police worried that such standard trespass-barment rules were ineffective "because the sidewalks and streets of RRHA projects remained public property" and "intruders could avoid arrest and prosecution by simply stepping onto an adjacent street or sidewalk."[5] In late 1996 the manager of Richmond's Whitcomb Court housing project therefore suggested that all the streets in and around that complex be privatized and subject to trespass-barment rules. On August 1, 1997, after negotiations between the RRHA and the city and the passage of the ordinance, city streets in and around all public housing projects in the city became property of RRHA.

The city of Richmond and the RRHA were concerned about street crime, especially drug-related crime, and on that front the privatization and trespass-barment policies seemed effective. In the year before the streets were privatized, violent and property crimes averaged 8.0 per month at Whitcomb Court. In the year and a half after, they dropped to 6.2 a month.* The RRHA and the city of Richmond argued that the privatization of the streets and the trespass-barment rule were behind this decrease and that the "notable reduction" in crime "was a contributing cause to a general trend in Richmond, where the number of homicides dropped . . . [to] the lowest total in the city since 1983."[6] The RRHA did not entertain the idea that the local drop in crime at Whitcomb might have instead been a function of the secular, citywide drop in crime rather than vice versa.

People Like Hicks

Kevin Hicks was not a resident of Whitcomb Court. His mother and his aunt were, however, as were his girlfriend and their two children. In late 1997 and

---

*Violent crimes dropped from 2.4 to 2.1, property crimes from 5.6 to 4.1. In the forty-two months the policies were in effect before the case under discussion was decided, violent crime dropped to 1.9, but property crimes inched back up. But these numbers are misleading because a "systems error" meant that crimes were not tallied on Deforrest Street, one of the key entry points to Whitcomb Court from the surrounding neighborhood. Brief of the City of Richmond, 12.

early 1998, Hicks was twice arrested for trespassing at Whitcomb Court.* In court for the second of these arrests, Hicks was served with a trespass-barment notice, which he duly signed. One of the peculiarities of all that followed is that it is clear from the record that (1) Hicks was considered (by police and RRHA employees) to be banned from the streets of Whitcomb Court for all of 1998; (2) his two arrests for trespassing were for breaking the trespass-barment rule; but (3) he was actually never formally notified of his barment until after his second arrest; and (4) this inconsistency never came up in all the appeals to his arrests— appeals that eventually reached the Supreme Court.

Hicks was arrested for a *third* time in January 1999. Hicks had entered the streets of Whitcomb Court on his way to visit his family and particularly to deliver diapers to his younger child who lived there with her mother. A police officer recognized him, knew that he had been served a barment notice when he had been in court before, and arrested him for trespassing.[7] Hicks was caught in a tight catch-22. As nonresidents, by merely setting foot on the (formerly public) streets and sidewalks of Whitcomb Court, people like Hicks were liable to be barred for any arbitrary reason—even if they had done nothing wrong—just so long as they could not prove a "legitimate business or social purpose" to the satisfaction of a RRHA employee or police officer. Once barred (or, as Hicks's second arrest indicates, even *before* being officially barred), such people could be arrested for trespassing even if they *did* have a perfectly "legitimate business or social purpose," like delivering diapers to one's baby and visiting with one's relatives. By seeking to visit his family, by visiting in public with friends, or even by walking to his polling place, which was located in the Whitcomb Court recreation center, Hicks could be—and was—made a criminal, made a criminal simply because he set foot on streets now deemed "private" by a public agency.

Hicks, perhaps, saw things more simply, less concerned with the vagaries of property and the inconsistencies in the barment procedures, and more concerned with his family and staying out of jail. "Judge," he said at sentencing for his third arrest,

> I'd like to say prior to all the trespassing charges that I have, it was all due to the fact of me trying my best to take care of my children and make sure my girl gets everything that she needed. I know that by me catching trespass charge, I did wrong, but all I can say is I did it for my kids. . . . Your honor, I never got in no kind of trouble. Never. Every time it seems like as far as the trespassing charge, it always be because of my kid. I mean she [his girlfriend] don't have no phone, so I be back and forth to the house to make sure she have everything. And if I can get any slack off this right now, I promise you I will never trespass on RRHA property again, because right now, I have an eight-month-old girl and four-year-old son that I'm really trying to be with.[8]

* The first of these arrests was made in November 1997, just over three months after the privatization took effect. See the statement of S. Benjamin in the *Joint Appendix*, found in 371 U.S. (2002), 65.

The judge was unsympathetic and tightened the catch-22 further. "Son," he intoned from the bench, "don't you recognize by doing this [walking on the streets of Whitcomb Court, it] is the worst thing you could do for your child. . . . I know one thing, he's [Hicks] my number one candidate for hard headedness. Keeps going back time and time again. He's the Coolhand Luke of the projects over there. . . . Mr. Hicks, you need to understand the world does not revolve around you."[9] The world may not revolve around Kevin Hicks, but the case did, and it raises innumerable issues about the relationship between property and other rights, as well as the growing importance of banishment through trespass law as a policing strategy against not only homeless or other street people but many of the rest of us (especially those who are not white), that are best understood by paying attention to the details of the case and the arguments that framed it as it worked its ways through the courts.

The case revolved around Hicks because through changes in how space—that is, property—was classified, Hicks was made a persona non grata on streets and sidewalks in and around every housing project in Richmond. It did not matter that he needed to traverse the streets to see his family. It did not matter that until the first time he was arrested for trespassing—on streets that used to be public and that he used to have full access to—he had never been arrested for any other crime. And perhaps, most importantly, it did not matter that the privatization of the streets that made him a criminal was not aimed at *him*.

News articles at the time the streets were privatized, and lawyers' arguments later, made much of how the streets in and around Whitcomb Court were an "open-air drug market." In its brief before the U.S. Supreme Court, the Commonwealth of Virginia began with exactly this assertion and then went on to argue that the arrest of people like Hicks was necessary because the "open-air drug market" was an outsiders', rather than a residents', operation. "The root of the problem," the commonwealth averred, "was not the people living there, but those who came from outside." Quoting the Virginia Supreme Court, the commonwealth continued, "The majority of the persons who had been arrested for drug crimes at the Whitcomb Court housing development were individuals who did not reside there."[10]

This may have been true, but while it was true Hicks did not reside at Whitcomb Court, it was also the case that he was never arrested, charged, or convicted of drug use or trafficking crimes. There is no evidence anywhere in the record that Hicks was in any way involved in the drug trade. So this was a case about Hicks because it was a case about how particular individuals *like* Kevin Hicks can be removed from streets for what are, in essence, arbitrary reasons.*

---

*Kevin Hicks was a young black man, and we know enough about racist policing to know that young black men are targeted by the police, so his arrests were likely not arbitrary in the colloquial sense of the term. But I am using "arbitrary" more formally: the term means, among other things (and according to the *Shorter Oxford English Dictionary*), "Dependent on will or pleasure; dependent

But while the *case* was about Hicks, the *law*—or really the legal discourses within which the law is contested, ratified, and given force—was not. Instead, and perhaps surprisingly, the law in this case was about the constitutional limits to free speech when that speech runs up against the rights of property.

Contesting Privatization

To understand why—or rather how—the case ended up being about free speech, it is important to raise a set of more general questions. How, in America, can one contest one's arbitrary removal from public space, one's arbitrary banishment from streets that must be traversed to see family, or streets that are simply a place to hang out with friends? How, to put this differently, can one contest a privatization of space—a perfectly legal deed transfer—that makes what one used to do legally, now illegal? In a society where property is highly valued, even held sacrosanct, does one contest the privatization of the streets itself? In a country presumably organized around the rule of law, does one instead contest what appears to be arbitrary use of police power? In a country where the urban is, by contrast, not so highly valued, does one make a more abstract argument about the need for public space in city life?

For Hicks, the argument about property turned out to be irrefutable—literally—with significant costs not only to Hicks but also to the residents of public housing in general (as we will see) and thus has a deep significance for what city streets are not just at the limits of capital, but in the very heart of capitalism. The argument about property—about what kind of property it was that was transferred to the RRHA—hinged on just what sort of agency the RRHA was. By law, the RRHA was not a *governing* body, in the sense of being a lawmaker and thus directly accountable to the democratic process. Rather, it was a special "political subdivision of the Commonwealth" chartered to "operate housing projects" among other things.[11] RRHA, therefore, acts "like a landlord" rather than as a "sovereign." Once the deed was transferred from the city of Richmond (the sovereign) to RRHA (a landlord), the property needed to be considered, according to the commonwealth, like any other privately held property. According to the commonwealth (joined by the city), the real issue, therefore, was that Kevin Hicks "had been arrested *inside* Whitcomb Court, on property owned by the Housing Authority, where he had been told not to return."[12] Thus, a key question when the case reached the U.S. Supreme Court was, "Does the Constitution recognize a distinction between actions taken by government as landlord and actions taken by government as sovereign?"[13] Virginia's position was that the case revolved around arrest for trespass, and if the Supreme Court invalidated the ar-

---

on the decision of a legally recognized authority . . . based more on mere preference as opposed to the real nature of things; capricious . . . unrestrained in the exercise of will or authority; despotic; tyrannical." On the nonarbitrariness (in the other sense) of racist policing, see Kelley, "Thug Nation."

rest, then it would threaten every government agency that performed the function of landlord, from the military wishing to restrict access to bombing ranges to state universities seeking to restrict the general public's access to dormitories, to the Supreme Court itself seeking to regulate behavior in its galleries or keep people out of its private chambers, a point made explicitly by the solicitor general of the United States who worried that U.S. "ownership and other interests" in property would be undermined if Hicks's conviction were overturned.[14]

A bit more narrowly, the Commonwealth of Virginia argued that "as landlord, government may take measures that it could not take as sovereign. The need to protect the safety of public housing tenants justified such a distinction."[15] And keeping loiterers, drug dealers, and everyone else without a "legitimate social or business purpose" off RRHA property was thus both legitimate and necessary. The Council of Large Public Housing Authorities agreed, arguing in its brief that "public housing developments are not public fora. Where PHAs take steps to exercise dominion over the streets and sidewalks within public housing developments to which they hold title, those streets and sidewalks are likewise nonpublic fora, and PHAs are entitled to use trespass-barment policies to limit access to these areas."[16] In other words, title conferred responsibility on PHAs and limiting access to streets and sidewalks, the Large PHAs argued, was vital if they were to be able to prevent wrongdoers from gaining access to public housing grounds.[17]

Yet such an argument—common to a number of briefs filed in the Hicks case, and a point of much discussion during oral arguments—missed (or perhaps simply avoided) a key point. What was at stake was not whether housing authorities can act like landlords or not, but whether it is legitimate for one part of the government to transfer a deed to another part, simply for the purpose of renouncing its function as a sovereign and *thereby* to act solely like a landlord and bar people for any or no reason from historically open property.* For its part, the U.S. Supreme Court studiously avoided addressing this issue, except to say that Virginia's trespass statute was "unquestionably valid" and "Hicks unquestionably violated it."[18] That is to say, once the streets were privatized, accord-

---

*A brief filed by several states argued that "schools, libraries, and courthouses have strict restrictions on unauthorized persons entering all or portions of their property," but this argument seems to forget that there are significant differences between streets and the property of schools and libraries, and that the Supreme Court has frequently made a point of distinguishing between the interiors of buildings and open, exterior courtyards, nearby sidewalks, and so forth. Similar issues, in a case decided the year before Hicks, were resolved in a very different way by a lower court. The city of Salt Lake City deeded the boulevard in front of the Mormon Tabernacle of the Mormon Church, which turned it into a park and then closed it to political activity. The Tenth Circuit Court of Appeals held that when Salt Lake City deeded the street to the church, the space's public forum status remained unchanged and so First Amendment activities of free association, free speech, and right of access had to be protected, even though the park was now private property. The Supreme Court refused to review the Tenth Court's decision, allowing it to stand; nor has it commented on that decision's inconsistency with its own ruling in Hicks. See States Brief, 2; First Unitarian Church v. Salt Lake City, 308 F3d 1114 (2002); Sjoblom, "Case Note."

ing to the court, then *of course* the RRHA was a landlord and had both a right and a duty to regulate who entered and stayed on its property, even though the city of Richmond, in its deed transfer, explicitly declared the streets to be "public highways for law enforcement purposes."[19] And since the streets were private property (though public highways), then the RRHA as a landlord not only could but *should* act arbitrarily. In other words, by not addressing it the court denied Hicks's argument that "the Housing Authority is no more 'landlord' of the streets and sidewalks around public housing than the city is 'landlord' of the rest of the streets and sidewalks in Richmond."[20]

Or, perhaps more accurately, the Supreme Court agreed that the RRHA was no more and no less a landlord than other government agencies since it explicitly held that it is legitimate to ban people from public spaces like parks (e.g., for engaging in vandalism at some point in the past) and then using that barment to prevent them from attending even a "political demonstration."* What is at stake in such cases, according to the court, is "nonexpressive conduct"—trespassing—not political action or speech. Agents of the government have not just the right but the duty to prevent such nonexpressive conduct as trespassing even if it makes constitutionally protected political activity impossible.

Through such means, the justness or otherwise of the original act—the privatizing of public property, conducted by a governmental body for the express purpose of removing some people, or some classes of people from public space—is rendered moot. The very question of whether such privatization—and if it really was a privatization, given that the deed transfer was between two public bodies—is good, bad, or indifferent quickly faded from the case. And with it went something else, something even more intriguing: the property rights of the *tenants* of Whitcomb Court (and other housing projects across the United States). While the Council of Large Public Housing Authorities, the U.S. attorney general, RRHA and the city of Richmond, the Commonwealth of Virginia, and a consortium of state governments all made much in their court briefs of their rights as landlords and their duties to protect public housing residents from "wrong-doers," the tenants themselves saw things rather differently. The Richmond Tenants Organization, "whose membership consists of all the residents of public housing in the City of Richmond," joined by tenants associations from around the United States, argued in its brief against the privatization and barment policy because it undermined tenants' rights "to associate with and invite others into their homes," especially since the policies at stake did not require those serving a barment notice to notify any tenants the barred visitor may

---

* It gets worse. As Katherine Beckett and Steve Herbert detail in *Banished*, the growing use of SOAP (stay out of areas of prostitution) and SODA (stay out of drug areas) orders, served to individuals, barring them from setting foot in designated areas—often dozens of blocks in size—can have the perverse effect of preventing people from getting to work, seeing their drug counselors or parole officers, or even, sometimes, getting from their apartments to any stores. See *Virginia v. Hicks*, 2199.

have been attempting to see.[21] If, as we know, property rights can be defined as the "right to exclude," then by upholding such rights for the RRHA, the Supreme Court simultaneously undermined them for tenants (who no longer have the power to determine who is welcome and who is not).[22]

In American legal culture the language of disputation is the language of rights, and many progressives see the development and expansion of rights as a key means and object of struggle. But as the arguments about property rights in the *Hicks* case make clear, and as the Supreme Court's siding with the Housing Authority over tenants reinforces, rights, and especially property rights, can also be a means of limiting the possibilities for justice. This is not because rights are dysfunctional, as some radical legal scholars and many activists have long argued, but rather because what much political and legal theory too often forgets is that rights are always in conflict, and thus it is the *power* and *interests* behind rights, not rights in the abstract, that matter.[23] In *Hicks*, and in terms of property rights then, the Supreme Court came down on the side of power—hardly a startling result and one the lawyers for Hicks seemed to anticipate: they did not work very hard at contesting either the privatization or the exercise of property rights per se in their arguments before either the lower courts or the Supreme Court.

Contesting Arbitrary Banishment

A second line of argumentation in this case concerned the arbitrary use of police power, and perhaps especially its role in supporting shifting regimes of property rights.

As we have already seen, the RRHA, the Commonwealth of Virginia, and their supporters made much of the fact that public housing developments are often sites of crime, including crimes related to drug trafficking. They argued that privatizing the streets and arresting trespassers were appropriate means for combatting crime. The city of Richmond and the RRHA together argued that since most families who live in public housing "do not have the capability to locate to a safer neighborhood," extraordinary measures were needed to fight "the crime brought to their streets, sidewalks, and playgrounds from without."[24] Indeed, earlier trespass policies of the RRHA were a result of just this desire to fight crime. In 1990 the authority implemented rules that barred unauthorized people from the actual buildings and grounds of RRHA projects. But by the end of the decade it feared that those it deemed "criminals" or "unwanted" could just step onto the street (off RRHA property) to avoid arrest for trespassing. Hence the plan to privatize the streets and sidewalks.

While it might seem the height of arbitrariness to arrest people for merely *being* in (formerly) public space, the city of Richmond and RRHA reminded the

Supreme Court that the court itself had already sanctioned the arbitrary punishment of people if it might have the effect of lessening drug use and drug crime. In a 2002 case called *HUD v. Rucker*, the court held, once again without dissent, that it is perfectly legitimate to evict public housing tenants if a household member or guest was *even suspected* of being engaged in "drug-related activity" and *even if that tenant was unaware of the suspected activities.*[25]

That is to say, the Supreme Court sees nothing wrong with the arbitrary use of police power, with in essence punishing the innocent for the *suspected* crimes of others just so long as that punishment appears to serve some legitimate state end. In the *Hicks* case, several U.S. states submitted a brief to the court that specifically supported this theory of punishment by driving home what, from their perspective, was at stake: "In a society where we have guns at schools and bombs and anthrax at courthouses, trespass laws are a major tool for law enforcement officials. These laws are not typically 'keep off the grass' regulations enacted to make property maintenance easier. Invalidating them poses a much greater threat than does invalidating speech-restriction laws or expressive-conduct-restriction laws."[26] For the states, in other words, reinforcing the arbitrary rights of property—of property owners, even if those owners are state bodies—is a crucial tool in the fight against crime and even terrorism. Trespass-barment policies are thus designed to protect public order and safety, and, seemingly, the net must be cast so broadly that it ensnares even those *not* involved in crime (or terrorism). This is the same logic that drove the development (and persistence) of the "terrorist" prison in Guantanamo Bay, only writ small and reinforced as a *right of property*. Indeed, it is exactly the rights of property ownership that make arbitrary banishment—of Kevin Hicks or of the relative of someone suspected of engaging in drug-related activity—possible. If, in the case of Guantanamo, the Supreme Court evinced at least a degree of discomfort with arbitrarily punishing innocents, when the issue revolves around public housing, the rights of agencies to act like landlords, and drugs, the court's decisions in *HUD* and *Hicks* seem to indicate that any such discomfort is easily allayed.[27] To be effective, the decision in *HUD* declared, police power had to be arbitrary. If innocent people were caught up in the dragnet, that could be excused by the fact that a compelling state interest—the war against drugs—was being served.

As the American Civil Liberties Union complained in its brief in the *Hicks* case, "RRHA officials have taken the position that Hicks can be barred for any and no reason."[28] Police power was, as the ACLU put it in its summary of the findings of a related Richmond public housing case that did not make it as far up the ladder of appeals, "unfettered."[29] As an official of RRHA testified in that case, arbitrariness was exactly the point. Though they would arrest anyone without a "legitimate" purpose on the streets, he said, "it has never been our intent to deny anyone from using the sidewalks and streets for their intended purpose"

and therefore the streets in Richmond housing projects "remained open to joggers, drive-through traffic, pedestrian 'walk-through' traffic, and all public use
and travel"[30]—a point that wasn't just ignored by the Supreme Court but was instead, as we will see, turned radically on its head.

Testimony in cases related to Hicks's made it clear that police power was indeed used arbitrarily in Richmond. Police in the projects typically approached
a person they did not recognize. If such a person was not in the presence of a
resident of the housing project, the police would order the individual to leave
the property, including the privatized streets (which nonetheless remained open
to joggers, pedestrian traffic, and cars), and often serve barment notices. This
was the case even if the person in question was on the way to see someone who
lived in the projects. Just as frequently, police would proceed directly to arrest
for trespass—without warning and without banning (as was apparently the case
in Kevin Hicks's first two arrests). This was sometimes true even if an "unrec-
ognized" person was in the presence of a resident, at least if that person refused
to answer police questions. In addition, according to testimony, police would
disperse or arrest any and all people found loitering or hanging out on project
streets and sidewalks, whether they were residents or not, dealing drugs or not,
or merely enjoying the summer air.[31]

Though the ACLU and others raised these issues of arbitrariness in their
briefs, though counsel for Hicks tried to introduce them in their oral arguments,
and though they seemed to suggest that important Fourth Amendment issues
were at stake in this case, they were simply ignored by the court.* They seem to
have been ignored because the Supreme Court found that the streets in question were indeed the private property of the RRHA and thus the RRHA had every right to act like a landlord and to act as capriciously as it wished: RRHA possessed the right to exclude even on the streets and sidewalks, and it had the right
to call on the police (or its own employees who had been handed police power by
policy fiat) to enforce this right. But its path to this finding—that the RRHA could
and should act capriciously—was not direct. Rather, it traveled through the First
Amendment, where the crucial issue was not whether the arbitrary use of police
power was in and of itself unconstitutional, but whether that arbitrary use inter-
fered with people's ability to engage in political speech—a question that might
seem quite far removed from the *Hicks* case. Kevin Hicks was, after all, seeking to
bring diapers to his family, not engage in a protest, circulate a petition, or climb
up on a soapbox like IWW speakers did in Denver back in 1913. To see why First
Amendment issues loomed so large in this case, it is worth examining the third
question I raised earlier: could Hicks's barment and arrest have been contested
through arguments related to the value of public space in human life?

* The Fourth Amendment guarantees the "right of the people to be secure in their persons ... against
unreasonable searches and seizures" and that "probable cause" be present for any warrants, searches,
or seizures.

Contesting the Right to Hang Out

Where—if anywhere—does the right to simply be in public space exist within the American discourse and practice of rights? And if it can be found, does that right to be in public have any chance at all of trumping the right to property, especially now since so much of the political economy (the very ability to circulate and accumulate capital) is based in property itself?

Perhaps the right to be in public resides in circulation itself since the Supreme Court has in fact recognized a fundamental right to travel, seeing it as one of the foundational rights of individual liberty (and finding support for it both in the body of the Constitution and in several amendments). The ability to move from place to place is fundamental to liberty, the court has made clear, but it is not unlimited. Indeed, private property limits it (you do not have an unrestricted right to travel through my property; I have the right to exclude you). Additionally, as several cases have made clear, the right to travel poses no duty on the state to provide a *means* to travel. Hence, what is foundational to liberty is also tenuous: in a world defined by private property and privatized transportation there is, in essence, a means test for travel.

Yet tenuous as it is, it is important, for the right to travel implies a right not to be forced to travel (a right *against* the sort of Greyhound therapy described in the interlude), the right to hold one's ground, the right to stay put.* Given this, one might expect that anti-loitering ordinances might have a difficult constitutional time, both for this reason, and because of the right to assembly enshrined in the First Amendment. And, indeed, in 1999, just as Kevin Hicks was being arrested for the third time for entering the newly privatized streets of Richmond, the Supreme Court struck down Chicago's anti-loitering law.[32] In this case, the majority of the court ruled against a law that made it illegal for two or more persons to loiter together in any public place, if one of the group was reasonably suspected of being a "criminal street gang member." But the majority decision turned not on questions related to the rights of travel or assembly, but rather on the vagueness of the ordinance and the failure of the legislation to establish minimal guidelines for the police. The proposition that the freedom to hang out, to loiter, to have *no* "legitimate social or business purpose" but still have a right to *be* in a public space—that is, the proposition that the right to be in public is fun-

*The right to stay put is usually invoked in relation to gentrification—a right not to be displaced. But it can, or ought, to operate more immediately, on the streets—a right not to be moved along. The New York Right to the City homeless-based organization Picture the Homeless, assisted by the American Civil Liberties Union, has recently filed a legal complaint against the New York City Police Department, contesting its policies of "moving along" homeless people who had committed no crimes. The complaint, however, is that the NYPD is violating §14–151 of the Administrative Code of the City of New York, which, among other things, bans profiling suspects on the basis of status, in this case perceived housing status, rather than constitutional issues. See *Picture the Homeless, Inc. v. New York City Police Department*, available at http://picturethehomeless.org/fighting-illegal-move-along-orders/. See also Newman and Wyly, "Right to Stay Put, Revisited."

damental to the liberties protected by the due process clause of the Fourteenth Amendment, the assembly clause of the First Amendment, or the doctrine of the right to travel—was unable to attract even a bare majority of the court.

As the ACLU recognized in its brief in *Hicks*, the U.S. Supreme Court "has not expressly recognized a fundamental right to move at will on the streets and sidewalks in the city where one resides." But the court *has* recognized the importance of the right to assembly. As the ACLU put it, "Streets and sidewalks cannot retain their traditional function of 'assembly, communicating thoughts between citizens, and discussing public questions,' if individuals may be arbitrarily excluded from them."[33] The ACLU was driving right at the heart of one of the most well-developed areas of Supreme Court doctrine: First Amendment questions of political speech and assembly. In doing so, however, it was conceding what seems to be the case as far as constitutional law is concerned: the right to public space—the right to be *in* public space—does not exist in and of itself, but rather exists only to the degree that it serves some other end (some "legitimate" purpose). That end is, primarily and most forcefully, the end of engaging in political speech.

Therefore, and perhaps inevitably since after all the primary goal of Hicks's lawyers was to keep him out of jail, Hicks's case was made to turn on issues of free speech—to disastrous results not only for Hicks, but for public life more generally. This is because speech and assembly rights, while perhaps the most constitutionally developed of any rights, are also among the most constricted.

It is obvious that Kevin Hicks was not engaged in what normally—or even extraordinarily—can be construed as political speech or activity: he was delivering diapers to his child. And even if he was just hanging out with friends, is that what the First Amendment protects when it proclaims a right to assembly? Probably not, as the language of the First Amendment is clear that what is at stake are *political* rights: it is the right of "the people" to peaceably assemble "and to petition government" that is protected, not the right of people to just be on the streets without purpose, legitimate or otherwise. Hicks was not, in any real sense, engaged in political assembly. So why did this issue become the dominant one? The answer relates to rights of property—and one of the very few ways within the American constitutional system that those rights might be attenuated.

Hicks's attorneys found the First Amendment was one of the few avenues open to contesting the arbitrary use of police power in defense of RRHA's new property rights. At trial for his trespass arrest, Hicks's attorneys sought specific records and information about two issues: first, why Hicks himself was originally banned; and second, RRHA's banning policies more generally. RRHA refused to produce any records relating to either request, arguing that they were irrelevant since what was at stake was Hicks's arrest for trespassing, not his, or anyone else's, barment. Records pertaining to barment policies were irrelevant, according to RRHA's attorney, because "a landlord can ban anyone they want for whatever reason they want and any time they want to."[34] Nevertheless, the court ordered any documents related to banning practices to be delivered to Hicks's counsel. Significantly, RRHA was unable to produce any, beyond an informational pamphlet delivered to residents, which RRHA was clear to say was not a codification of rules and regulations.

In testimony, however, RRHA admitted that there was a set of unwritten rules, including one that said that guests or visitors must be entertained on residents' "assigned" property areas—their stoops or yards, or the interiors of their apartments.[35] Because there were no written rules, there was no evidentiary record on which the justness—or otherwise—of rules leading to barment or arrest could be judged. And in any event, for the judge in this case, the issue was rather simple. Hicks was a hardheaded young man who refused to abide by his banishment, and as such was guilty of trespassing. The only issue at stake was whether Hicks had trespassed or not, not whether the trespass-barment policies were legitimate.

The question for Hicks's attorney then was *how* to appeal his conviction (since the evidentiary record was so slight), and one answer was to turn attention from Hicks himself and focus instead on the likely effects of RRHA policies, both written and unwritten, on *others*—in essence to meet the courts, which had already signaled their approval of the arbitrary use of police power, on their own grounds but to show how this arbitrary use, while perhaps serving some legitimate state end, came with severe societal costs. The surest ground on which to make this argument was the First Amendment. If the case could be made that RRHA's rules, including its enforcement of Virginia's trespass law, might have the effect of "chilling" political speech (to use the legal term of art), not necessarily of Hicks, but of others, then there was a chance that Hicks's case could be overturned because the trespass-barment policy, together with the privatization of the streets, could be shown to be invalid because it contravened the free speech provisions of the First Amendment.

In the event, Hicks appealed his conviction on three grounds. The first, quickly dismissed, related to whether the judge and venue were the appropriate ones. The second argued that Virginia's trespass statute in and of itself was overly broad and vague. The third, and most crucial, related to whether the conviction should be thrown out on First Amendment and due process grounds because the trespass-barment policy unacceptably "chilled" possibilities for political speech. A three-member panel of the Virginia Court of Appeals denied all three appeals and upheld Hicks's conviction. On the third area of appeal, however, one member of the panel vigorously dissented (this judge also held that the grounds for appeal in the second area were so tightly bound to those of the third area that there was no need to discuss it in dissent).[36]

During trial, Hicks's attorney tried to ensure that the record showed that the streets of Whitcomb Court were just like any other streets in the city (despite the deed transfer) and thus functioned as a "public forum"—a public property traditionally reserved for the communication of political ideas. Speech and other political rights are more stringently protected in public forums than on other kinds of public and private property. The argument was that the privatization and trespass-barment policies had undermined not only Hicks's ability to visit his family, but—potentially at least—others' desire to engage in political activity in a public forum.[37] The majority of the appeals court panel, however, found that the streets and sidewalks of Whitcomb Court *did not* constitute a public forum under Supreme Court doctrine because they were private property—never once addressing the issue of how the very act of privatizing the streets had transformed them from what clearly would have been recognized as a public forum into something else. Even more, the majority held that the states' "interference" in Hicks's "intimate associations"—his third conviction for trespassing—was "reasonable, limited, and justified" because he had in the past been convicted of crimes, leaving aside once again that the very reason for those convictions was because the streets had been privatized and he had been arbitrarily banned (and maybe not even that since, as we saw, it seems that no barment notice was served until after he had been arrested for violating it). What was at stake, for the majority, was the rule of law, not how changed geographies might alter the meaning, and the effects, of law. For them, geography did not matter, but property did.

For the dissenting judge, geography did matter. He noted that the streets were not physically closed, that they remained open to vehicle and pedestrian through traffic, that they continued to function like other streets in the city, and that they therefore remained, despite the deed transfer, a "traditional public forum." The city of Richmond and RRHA thus "infringed on Hicks's right to move freely and be present in a 'traditional public forum.'"[38] Use and spatial arrangement trumped property, for this judge, especially since the effect of the deed transfer was, essentially, to criminalize classes and individuals who had committed no crime. "To be barred from Whitcomb Court," the dissenting judge argued, "one does not have to be guilty of a crime in Whitcomb Court or to have done anything wrong, but rather, one simply has to fail to fit within the category of people who RRHA has deemed entitled to be on the streets and sidewalks in the public housing development."[39] The city is required, this judge averred, to make its streets safe, but it could not do so in a way that "unduly restricts or criminalizes innocent or protected behavior." Transferring the deed to the streets and thereby removing public forum protections created such an undue restriction.[40]

The decision of the three-member appeals court panel was itself appealed to the full Virginia Court of Appeals.[41] Deciding the case on First and Fourteenth Amendment grounds, the full Court of Appeals voted six to five to reverse the panel and dismiss Hicks's conviction. The full court affirmed that streets and parks are "the archetype of a traditional public forum," and trenchantly noted that in the very case that created public forum doctrine, the Supreme Court made it clear that title—actual ownership—of public space was not a key determinant of public forum status. *"Wherever the title of the streets and parks may rest,"* the Supreme Court had declared in that case (in a justifiably oft-quoted passage), "they have immemorially been held in trust for the use of the public and, time out of mind, have been used for the purposes of assembly, communicating thoughts between citizens, and discussing public questions. Such use of the streets has, from ancient times, been part of the privileges, immunities, rights, and liberties of citizens."[42] More recently, the appeals court noted, the Supreme Court had held, in a case concerning the sidewalks around the Supreme Court building itself, that "Congress may not by its own ipse dixit destroy the 'public forum' status of the streets and parks that have historically been a public forum."[43] For that reason, the majority of the full Court of Appeals held that "the City of Richmond is not permitted to transform the public streets and sidewalks of Whitcomb Court into private, nonpublic property simply by passing an ordinance declaring them closed, conveying them to another governmental entity, the RRHA, and placing signs along the streets."[44] Therefore, this court decided (over the strong objections of the minority), the streets of Whitcomb Court remained a traditional public forum and any regulations governing their use was subject to "strict scrutiny."

Strict scrutiny means that any regulation must burden no more speech than is absolutely necessary to achieve some narrowly tailored, compelling state interest. The appeals court majority found the state interest—maintaining safe public housing—to indeed be compelling but found the trespass-barment policies to be overbroad. The court held that "the barment-trespass procedure is not limited so as to encompass only those persons whose conduct the City and RHA [sic] were seeking to curtail" since it could lead to the arrest of people engaged in not only innocent, but also constitutionally protected, activities.[45] The court thus found the trespass-barment policies *and the ordinance itself that transferred the streets to RRHA* to be unconstitutional and reversed Hicks's conviction, not because Hicks was not trespassing but because of the high social costs of the rules that led to his conviction, rules that "infringe upon a citizens' First and Fourteenth Amendment rights to lawfully be present in a public place."[46]

Since the majority of the Court of Appeals did not address issues related to the fairness of the original trial or the validity of the Virginia trespass statute in and of itself, when the case was appealed to the Virginia Supreme Court, that court addressed only "the narrow issue" of whether the RRHA's trespass-barment policy was overly broad and therefore unconstitutional under the First and Fourth Amendments. The first issue the Virginia Supreme Court had to consider was whether Hicks had "standing" to make a First Amendment challenge against the trespass-barment policy. Rules of standing (which, recall, were crucial in the Boise homeless anti-camping case discussed in chapter 1) hold that "a person to whom a statute may constitutionally be applied may not challenge that statute on the grounds that it may conceivably be applied unconstitutionally to others in situations not before the Court."[47] By this rule, Hicks would seem to be out of luck: he was not engaged in constitutionally protected activity. But the U.S. Supreme Court has carved out an exception to this rule of standing, to be used sparingly, for what it calls "overbreadth" challenges. Such challenges attempted to show that the very breadth of a law will cause people to "refrain from exercising their right [to free speech and assembly] for fear of criminal sanctions."[48] In such cases the mere existence, not just the actual application, of a law might be enough to "chill" speech, and therefore a case contesting the law may never come before the court, since the chilling effect works, in effect, as a form of "prior restraint."* By a seven-to-two majority, the Virginia Supreme Court held that Hicks did indeed have standing to bring an "overbreadth" challenge to the RRHA policies.

In doing so, however, the court refused to rule on whether the streets and sidewalks in Richmond public housing projects remained "traditional public forums" and in fact expressly vacated that part of the lower court's ruling. The Virginia Supreme Court instead passed judgement only on the breadth of the trespass-barment procedures, finding that since the manager of Whitcomb Court—a government official—was given absolute discretion as to what political activities could occur on Whitcomb property (a provision of the trespass-barment policy—unwritten but used several times—required those wishing to petition or leaflet to get the manager's permission first), the trespass-barment policy was overbroad and therefore invalid.

But by refusing to rule on the question of public forum status, the Virginia Supreme Court in effect erased the geography that was truly at the heart of this case. It left aside the question of whether the government can privatize a public forum by fiat and ruled only on the degree of power a representative of the government *acting as landlord* can exercise in publicly accessible property. The question of political rights remained, but with the erasure of geography, so too was there an erasure of what could be called urban rights, and particularly the right simply to be present in public space.

Hicks in the U.S. Supreme Court

Geography—the shape, structure, and nature of urban space, as well as the social reality of the city—is right at the heart of this case, and both friends of Hicks and friends of the RRHA reasserted it repeatedly in their briefs when the case reached the U.S. Supreme Court. In numerous briefs and in oral testimony, allies

---

*Though the U.S. Supreme Court has pronounced itself as suspicious of prior restraint, it has encouraged it strongly in the context of protest through the sanctioning of protest permit systems. For an analysis, see Staeheli and Mitchell, *People's Property?*, chap. 1.

of RRHA asserted the need to maintain order and public safety in public housing projects, whose residents were said, in essence, to be trapped in a geography of poverty and potential violence. They argued for the rights of landlords, fearing what would happen to all manner of government property if Hicks's conviction was overturned. And they asserted, once again, that Hicks had no standing to bring the challenge that he did because he himself had not been engaged in constitutionally protected activity. For their part, allies of Hicks sought to ground their arguments in public forum doctrine, stressing the chilling effect and sweeping breadth of the trespass-barment policies and procedures.

Weighing arguments from both sides, the Supreme Court came down, unanimously, on the side of RRHA. Hicks's conviction for trespass had to be upheld; the Virginia Supreme Court's invalidation of the trespass-barment procedures had to be reversed. Antonin Scalia delivered the opinion of the court. He argued that the question of standing was moot because it had been accepted by the Virginia Supreme Court as a matter of state law; thus the only issue the U.S. Supreme Court could entertain was "whether the claimed overbreadth of the RRHA policy is sufficiently 'substantial' to produce facial invalidity."[49] Scalia began by summarizing the Virginia Supreme Court's findings: "The Virginia Supreme Court found that the RRHA policy . . . allowed the manager of Whitcomb Court to exercise 'unfettered discretion' in determining who may use the RRHA's property. Specifically, the court faulted an 'unwritten' rule that persons wishing to hand out flyers on the sidewalks of Whitcomb Court needed to obtain [the manager's] permission."[50] But, Scalia continued, "Hicks, of course, was not arrested for leafletting or demonstrating without permission. He violated RRHA's *written* rule that persons who receive a barment notice may not return to RRHA's property." And it was this written policy—the one that says that people without a legitimate business or social purpose could be served with a notice barring them forever from the property—that was at stake, according to Scalia. And here "Hicks has failed to demonstrate that this notice would ever be given to anyone engaged in constitutionally protected speech." Moreover, even if a barred person was arrested for returning to Whitcomb Court to engage in protected speech, according to Scalia, that would "not violate the First Amendment" since the arrest would be for conduct—trespassing—not speech.[51]

Crucially, in making this argument, Scalia went out of his way to broaden his own decision and give it an importance that stretched far beyond the precincts of public housing projects. "Most importantly, both the notice-barment rule and the 'legitimate business and social purpose' rule apply to all persons who enter the streets of Whitcomb Court, not just those seeking to engage in expression. The rules apply to strollers, loiterers, drug dealers, roller skaters, bird watchers, soccer players, and others not engaged in constitutionally protected activity—a group that would seemingly far outnumber First Amendment speakers."[52] This is an extraordinary result. By focusing on the very narrow question of whether Hicks was engaged in constitutionally protected speech, and by finding that even if he was it would not matter since it was his conduct (trespassing) that was at stake, while also refusing to consider the reason behind that trespassing (the wholesale pseudo-privatization of public property as a means to criminalize the otherwise legal activities of a suspect class of people), Scalia and the unanimous court endorsed a world in which public property can be made "private" (merely by deed transfer between two public agencies) and *all* nonconstitutionally protected activity (from bird watching and drug dealing to loitering and soccer playing) can simply be banned, and people engaged in such activity can be barred from a significant number of city streets—arbitrarily, capriciously, and forever. It is not hard to think how this decision can and will be used by those seeking to cleanse the streets of those deemed unwanted, whether young black men like Kevin Hicks, homeless people like Charly Keunang, or militant activists of all stripes who can now simply be banned (provided the streets have been pseudo-privatized first) and *then* barred from political struggle, not putatively because of what they are fighting for, but because of what they have done—at least in the eyes of some cop, security guard, or semipublic employee.

Indeed, the decision in *Hicks* makes it clear that the state has not just the power to restrict all nonprotected activity (meeting friends, riding skateboards, watching birds, delivering diapers to a baby) but *a compelling interest in doing so*. Government now can, and sometimes must, act with the full rights and arbitrariness of a landlord, though with the lonely exception that unlike most mall owners (for example), it might be required to permit leafletting and carefully regulated demonstrations on its property. The U.S. Supreme Court, that is, entered, on the most narrow of grounds, a most stunningly broad decision. The decision in *Hicks* announces a thoroughly *anti-urban* legal regime, one that places no value on constructing spaces to be present—to be visible as a member of the urban public.

While Kevin Hicks may have had little choice but to stake his appeal on First Amendment grounds, it turns out this line of appeal provided the room the Supreme Court needed to announce not an extension of rights in and to public space but their significant constriction. The First Amendment may have been seen as something of a Trojan horse by Hicks's attorneys; yet what it contained was not a means to keep Hicks out of jail and together with his family, but a force allied instead with those who seek to reinforce order at the expense of liberty, security at the expense of freedom, and the rights of property owners, including the state, at the expense of the rights of people (like the tenants of the Richmond public housing projects who opposed the trespass-barment rules).

Indeed, what the *Hicks* decision showed was how narrow arguments over free speech can be seized on and transformed into an unassailable right of property.

Between Home and Street

This was a point quickly grasped—if at the wrong end—by the *New York Times*. In one of the few commentaries in the popular press on the unanimous *Hicks* ruling, the *Times* editorialized that "the ruling gives the poor a right the rich have long had: to keep loiterers, and potential criminals out of their homes."[53] Of course, "the poor"—the tenants of Richmond public housing joined by tenants from around the country—specifically asked the Supreme Court to reverse Hicks's conviction and to declare the privatization of streets and the trespass-barment procedures to be unconstitutional. And, of course, neither the laws nor the written and unwritten policies at stake had anything at all to do with keeping loiterers and criminals out of *homes*, or even out of common areas of public housing projects. They did, however, and as the *Times* intuited, establish a legal basis for a *geographical norm* that many people find appealing—an anti-urban norm in which street life is not just demonized but actively banished. It is banished beyond the gates of exclusive suburban streets and from the streets around public housing projects.[54] As the *Times* rightly understood, while *Hicks* was decided on First Amendment grounds, it was not about the First Amendment.

So what was it about? A note in the *Harvard Law Review* suggested that because the Supreme Court failed to "address the underlying question of the streets' public forum status," the decision "enables local governments to continue curtailing constitutional rights in the guise of 'privatization.'"[55] Since the court made no effort to distinguish a redevelopment and housing authority from other government agencies, or even other quasi-governmental landholding agencies, it is easy to see how this decision will help justify, for example, the transfer of city land to a ballpark district, which can then declare the property private and ban all manner of legal activities on it, even though it remains fully open to the public. Indeed, within a year of the decision just this happened in San Diego, where the city transferred a public park to the owners of the San Diego Padres baseball team and then allowed that private organization to write the rules of use for it.[56]

But the case is also about how rules of law positively allow justices to ignore what might be most crucial in a case, like the real geography of the city. Hicks's case had nothing to do with free speech or assembly, but the rules of law together with a set of wagers about what judges might be sympathetic to led it to being argued in those terms. And when the case was narrowed to questions related to the First Amendment, the U.S. Supreme Court was able to make a sweeping and quite remarkable argument about how not speech *but social life* could be regulated on city streets, just so long as appropriate exceptions were made for overt, properly regulated, political behavior.

Perhaps the original judge was right in saying the world did not revolve around Kevin Hicks. But the case did, even (or especially) when his concerns—about seeing his family and being with his girlfriend—disappeared in a haze of legal argument about "standing," "overbreadth," and the nature of the public forum. It remained about Kevin Hicks because it was a case about him as a black man in public space in a world where black men—more than skateboarders or bird watchers—in public space are consistently seen as "wrongdoers" (to use the language of the Council of Large Public Housing Authorities), a view that has clearly only deepened in the years since the decision, as the ongoing, consistent killing of black men on city streets by police attests. Kevin Hicks, to put this another way, was a synecdoche for all other potential "wrongdoers" who seek to be in public: the homeless in gentrifying neighborhoods (like Charly Keunang), teens hanging out near a new convention center or in a back alley, or other racialized men and women seeking simply to socialize in parks or on the streets, or anywhere else that publicly held property deeds can plausibly be transferred to those semipublic agencies that can readily perform the function of landlord without being obliged to act like a sovereign.

The *Hicks* case, in other words, was one more means to resurrect the vagrancy laws struck down during the "Constitutional revolution" of the 1960s and 1970s when status crimes came under full political and judicial attack.

CHAPTER 7

Doing Antisocial Things

> An alley tends to be blocked off from view. . . . There's often not a real reason
> for people to be walking out there except to do anti-social things.
>
> —Planner Ann Forsythe (2006)

Let's return, by way of something like a conclusion, to an example first raised in chapter 4: the proposal to ban all "strangers" from the back allies of Minneapolis. The proposal was made by city councilmember Robert Lilligren at the end of May 2006, at the behest of the police as well as his constituents who were concerned about a reported rise in crimes like graffiti, vandalism, and drug use.[1] Like many American cities that grew rapidly in the early twentieth century, Minneapolis is a city of alleys. While the main roads serve the bulk of automobile traffic and houses and apartments along them present a façade of either Midwestern stolidity or almost bucolic charm, the back alley is functional. It provides access to garages for residents, serves as the place where garbage cans are placed to be picked up by trucks, and functions as a corridor for power and telephone lines. But the back alleys are also places where people walk their dogs (or themselves), where they meet up with neighbors, or where they find a shortcut to a nearby street.[2] Relatively hidden, they serve as places for youth to hang out and homeless people to scavenge or sleep—and for drug deals and drug taking, prostitution, and sometimes assault or robbery. It was the specter of these sorts of activities, including perhaps especially youth hanging out, that led Lilligren to propose the outlawing of walking through or (in fact) being in *any* of the 455 miles of back alleys in the city for everyone except people who live on the block the alley ran through, guests of those residents, police officers, garbage collectors, and others (like utility crews) who had official business there. (Vehicular traffic, however, was not targeted.) Violators would be prosecuted for trespassing.

Should it have passed (it didn't), the ordinance would have been the first of its kind: no other city in the United States had created a total ban on walking through alleys, though many had closed specific streets and alleys, and of course, as we have seen, trespass-barment procedures were becoming a tool of choice for regulating the public presence of the poor. As with the *Hicks* case, it was *presence* rather than behavior that was to be outlawed here, only now on an even grander scale and in a far less discriminating manner (the pun is fully intended, even though it is easy to surmise that any such law would of course be used in a discriminating fashion).[3] The proposal was, in other words, the logic of *Hicks*, slightly mutated and fully metastasized.

Yet this is not quite how the city saw things. Alleys in Minneapolis (as in many cities) are a particular kind of property. Like sidewalks in many jurisdictions, they are owned by the abutting property owners, but "are dedicated by plat 'to the public use' and the City has an easement on them which is dominant to all other uses."[4] To all intents and purposes, in other words, the city owns the *rights* to the use of the alleys and is expected to exercise those rights to further *public* use. A staff report prepared for the city council noted, however, that the dedication to public use could be circumscribed because the "City Charter gives the Council the authority to regulate and control the alleys." To ban "strangers" from alleys was thus "similar" to "restrict[ing] bicyclists from using Nicollet Mall [a downtown pedestrianized shopping street] during business hours" or prohibiting jaywalking.[5]

At first the proposal seemed quite popular. At a city council meeting the following August, some 80 percent of the citizens who spoke supported the ban.[6] Yet city council members also reported being "flooded with angry e-mails from residents about the proposal"—emails that presumably made it clear that many city residents were opposed to the law.[7] As one columnist for the *Minneapolis Star-Tribune* complained, the very notion of banning *strangers* was nonsensical. "Strangers" was, he said, "a useless word that covers everything from murderers to Aunt Martha from Moorhead," a small city on the prairie invoked to call up images of small-town virtue, middle-class values, and rural provincialism—the opposite, that is, of the black, hooded, teen gang members who seemed to populate the alleys in much of the popular imagination.[8]

How was seeking to ban "strangers" a mutation (and not only a metastasization) of the logic of *Hicks*? One of the problems with the trespass-barment process ratified by the Supreme Court in *Hicks* was that it required a high degree of specific knowledge about specific individuals on the part of police and Richmond Redevelopment and Housing Authority employees. First (at least in theory) a person had to be served a trespass notice, then the police and employees had to know *that* person was barred, if the person was to be arrested for trespassing. Presumably, such barments could be tracked in a database available to authorities that could be consulted during encounters, which is how gang injunctions work in many jurisdictions: cops find some pretext to stop or question someone—usually someone of color, usually young—and then look them up on a gang database (which typically are hardly discerning in who has been added, or why), or add the person to it, frequently capriciously.[9] But in Richmond, at least, no such database seemed to have been kept. Rather the practice relied on the intimate knowledge of individuals. Such intimate knowledge is time-consuming to develop and possesses obvious limits (not all cops will be aware of all individuals). Banning *strangers*, a small mutation in the procedure as it metastasizes, eliminates such limits: everyone is suspect, everyone is barred—nothing needs be known about them; they are strangers—unless they can prove they live along the alley. It eliminates the need for specialized knowledge.*

In the end, however, the city council voted down the measure ten to three, voting to not outlaw walking (or for that matter running, standing around, or simply being *present*) in the public alleys of Minneapolis. In the wake of the defeat, the *Star Tribune* editorialized that the proposed ordinance was really just a "sad and desperate solution" to the problem of urban crime and fear. But for the first time, at least in the published record, it also named the real purpose behind the law: to "give cops a pretext to break up gangs of alley-based criminals."[10] That is, the law's real purpose—the real purpose behind excluding the public from the public's space—was an excuse, a *pretext*, a concealment of real purpose (as the *Shorter Oxford Dictionary* defines "pretext"). The willing use of pretexts as a means of keeping out people the authorities (or property owners or other vested interests) simply do not want or like should give everyone pause.†

Still, the law did not pass. Couple that with the Obama administration's Department of Justice intervention in the Boise case, and (between these two events) voters in Berkeley, California, in 2012 refusing to pass a ballot initiative that would have outlawed nearly all sitting and sleeping on sidewalks, and it might seem like the relentless tide of *meanness* that has governed American streets for a generation is beginning to ebb—or that at least there might be a few islands of sanity rising above the flood. That would be a false impression.

The Berkeley case was, as we have seen through the National Law Center on Homelessness and Poverty's tracking of the continued growth of anti-homeless legislation in American cities, exceptional. Proponents of the sit-lie ordinance for Berkeley (which would have outlawed sitting or lying on sidewalks between the hours of seven in the morning and ten in the evening in districts zoned commercial, except in cases of medical emergency, people sitting in wheelchairs, on permanent benches and at bus stops, on seating at a festival for which a permit had been granted, or—of course—at café tables) claimed that such an ordinance

*Another mutation from the *Hicks* case is that RRHA still permitted walking (or roller skating!) through the streets of Whitcomb Court, just so long as one had not yet been banned.

†One of the (many) things #BlackLivesMatter has brought more fully into wider public consciousness has been the pernicious use of pretextual stops—cars stopped for some minor violation (like a burned-out turn signal) and then the trumping up of reasons for a full search and arrest—or, on more than one occasion, summary execution. New York's now partially suspended stop and frisk tactics were also largely pretextual.

was necessary to prevent the formation of what they called "street encampments" by those who "resist our help."[11] The initiative itself declared in its findings that "public spaces in commercial areas have become increasingly inhospitable due to groups of individuals, often with dogs, having created encampments on sidewalk areas of our commercial streets. These encampments obstruct pedestrian access, and result in litter, debris, and waste left on our sidewalks."[12] The new ordinance would have been enforced not only by police but also by special "ambassadors" (whom the proponents misleadingly labeled "outreach" and "social" workers) paid for by the various business improvement districts in the city, allowing supporters the pretext that the ordinance was really designed to "help people get services."[13]

Opponents of the law pointed out that the San Francisco sit-lie ordinance on which it was based had, according to a report by the San Francisco city controller, "failed 'to improve merchant corridors, serve as a useful tool for SFPD, connect services to those who violate the law, and positively contribute to public safety.'"[14] Despite being outspent ten to one by proponents of the law, the opponents prevailed: the initiative solidly lost, 48 percent in favor, 52 percent opposed. But it really was a truly exceptional outcome. It was the first time since 1994 that voters anywhere in the United States rejected an initiative "criminalizing homelessness"—and that last time was in Berkeley too. Indeed, across the Bay, despite the obvious ineffectiveness of anti-homeless laws, San Francisco voters continued to pass more of them. In November 2016, by the same 52 to 48 percent by which Berkeley voters had rejected a sit-lie law four years earlier, San Francisco voters passed an ordinance giving the city the right to remove any tents on city sidewalks provided the tent dwellers were given twenty-four hours' notice and an offer of either (unspecified) temporary housing or bus tickets out of town. (Had the voters rejected the ordinance, existing sit-lie and obstruction of sidewalks laws would have remained in place; this initiative merely added a specific prohibition of tents.) At the same time, voters passed (by 67 percent) an ordinance setting aside General Fund revenues of fifty million dollars per year (with scheduled increases) for twenty-four years to provide services to homeless people. Paired with a similar new General Fund set-aside for public transportation, the ordinance likely garnered so much support because it was, in fact, revenue neutral, according to the San Francisco controller. It created no *new* funds for homeless services, merely specified the account from which they were to be paid.[15] Indeed, two years later, in June 2018, San Francisco voters rejected—55 percent to 45 percent—an initiative that would have added a 1.7 percent tax on commercial leases (for landlords with more than a million dollars in annual gross receipts) to fund homelessness services, single room occupancy housing units, housing for poor seniors and (at varying levels) for households making up to 50 percent and 80 percent of the city's median income (plus some additional moneys for the general fund),* while candidates for mayor competed with each other to appear the most tough on the homeless.[16]

Paranoia and Pretexts

While it is abundantly clear that what *produces* homelessness in its contemporary forms is the specific structure of the political economy—the ways in which capital circulates through the built environment—and that the myriad attempts to address the problem by individualizing and criminalizing it are an utter failure, it nonetheless remains that the problems of homelessness, to say nothing of young men hanging out on streets near housing projects or in back allies, are *felt* as an existential insecurity among many, if not most, of us. This insecurity, in turn, is more and more coming to be expressed as a kind of social paranoia: the state of being "very distrustful or suspicious of others" (as the *Shorter Oxford English Dictionary* defines it), of simply assuming that "there's often not a real reason for people to be walking [or sitting, sleeping, *living*] out there except to do anti-social things."

Yet, and this is crucial, paranoia is not only social, it is, now, a *strategy* of power, control, and profit, with its own ineluctable logic. The landscape of fear in American cities is, as Richard Longstreth noted in a study of Washington, D.C., in the wake of the 2001 terrorist attacks, utterly banal, "manifesting a sense of vulnerability to unknown forces." In Washington, there was "no shortage of paranoia," but there was also "no shortage of hubris." That is, institutions of the state had latched on to fear as a means of promoting their importance and had reorganized space accordingly: "The more likely an agency is deemed to be a terrorist target, the more important it must be in a city obsessed with power."[17] The *need* to be fearful is a mark of status, and this holds for cities too: the more a city seems beset by the modern problems of the day—terrorist attacks, growing homeless populations, intractable, "wicked" problems of poverty—the more important it must be. So-called security measures and the sheer number of anti-homeless and other similar "quality-of-life" laws are a marker of status. The corollary is clear: even a hint that a space might be uncontrolled or uncontrollable—or even open for banal uses outside the gaze of organized power—is anathema. Thus is fear in, and of, the city reproduced and magnified. A metastasizing sense of "vulnerability to unknown forces," to use another definition of paranoia, predominates. And it is urban *space* that gives form to these fears.

*This initiative required a supermajority of 66.6 percent to pass. It wasn't even close. Instead, voters passed a competing measure (with under 51 percent of the vote) to create a similar commercial lease tax to fund early childhood education. See https://ballotpedia.org/San_Francisco,_California,_Proposition_D,_Commercial_Rent_Tax_for_Housing_and_Homelessness_Services_(June_2018) and https://ballotpedia.org/San_Francisco,_California,_Proposition_C,_Commercial_Rent_Tax_for_Childcare_and_Early_Education_(June_2018).

The response is clear and has been ever since the Edicts of Bern: urban space needs to be brought under control. In this regard, Minneapolis's serious consideration of banning pedestrians from alleys makes more sense. Alleys are the archetype, in many ways, of uncontrolled space. They are part of the backstage of the city, places often out of the way of prying eyes of the state and far less susceptible to redevelopment in an image of control. Just as importantly, they are often sites of unstructured play and leisure, as kids (especially) seek out their hidden corners and transform them through their imagination into something new, something great. This is a kind of play, and appropriation of space, that is not easily commodifiable. Parents perhaps understand this: as they fear for their children, they understand that something might be lost if alleys and other unscripted spaces in the city disappear altogether, and so the desire for control of access—for fences, bollards, and laws barring strangers—becomes all the stronger, as does the ingenuity with which capital finds ways to exploit that fear, by creating, for example, fee-based play zones in private shopping malls.[18] Any sense of spontaneity fades, any sense of the city as a place where children *belong*—in public and as part of the public—disappears, just as it has for homeless people. And fear becomes productive not only of order and control but of profit.

But, in this realm anyway, direct profitability may not necessarily be the crucial point. Rather it is that while paranoia is a powerful structuring force, it is not productive in and of itself. Rather, paranoia has to be organized and has to be given an object. That is, it is not just fear (in or of itself) that is crucial, but fear of some (not quite knowable) thing: that something might be people of color, or pedophiles and other sex offenders, or terrorists.[19] Or it just might be the disorderly and disheveled figure of the homeless man (or as we saw in chapter 4 the disorder*ing* figure of the server of decommodified food). In Minneapolis it was a fear of the alley (which stood in for the fear of unnamed and unseen "criminals"). In other words, the fear of black people, of homeless people, of terrorists, of criminals, and especially of what Zygmunt Bowman aptly noted is often just apprehended as an unknowable "world out there" is in fact a fear of the unknowable *within* a well-known context: the context of urban space.[20] The matter at stake, then, is less how to address specific social problems (homelessness, youth unemployment, lack of stable and supportive housing for sex offenders, racist assumptions and policing that make "strangers" necessarily people to be feared and in need of constraint, and so forth) and more about reclaiming control over space. The only question is how.

To address this issue, we have seen, cities (and other levels of the state, as well as innumerable private actors) have engaged in thoroughgoing experiments in regulation, from stepped-up trespass-barment procedures to piling on ever more anti-homeless legislation and sometimes even looking for nonpunitive ways to remove unwanted people from the public spaces of the city—like giving them one-way bus tickets. In each case, however, in an attempt to organize the paranoia that gives rise to the perceived need for regulation, urban planners, police, city officials, ballot initiative sponsors, and judges have engaged not so much in an analysis of spatial or geographical context but in a plausible resort to pretext: "a reason put forward to conceal the real purpose or object; an ostensible motive of action: an excuse, a pretense" (to quote the *Shorter Oxford* more fully).

If the diagnosis is that uncontrolled, unauthorized public spaces invite disorder, crime, and even terrorism, and that each of these often takes on an appearance that cannot be distinguished from normal life—disorder looks like men and women having a picnic in a Las Vegas park or dozing on a bench in any city, crime looks like teens and adults walking through Minneapolis alleys, terrorism looks like tourists snapping pictures (remember the craze for outlawing photography of transportation and sporting venues, public spaces, and "critical infrastructure" in the wake of the 9/11 terrorist attacks?)—then normal strategies of policing and what criminologists like to call "order maintenance" are simply no longer enough. Rather space itself has to be regimented, and behaviors all the more carefully scripted. Urban social life has to be remade. In this regard, fear of and in public space (a kind of generalized social agoraphobia that marks contemporary life) is a pretext for a larger re*ordering* of social interactions, and a hoped-for general, sometimes contested, sometimes welcomed, surrender to authority—to being authorized, like a homeless person who must always ask permission to pee, to *only* be in urban space at the sufferance, and with the explicit permission, of others.[21] The surrender to authority takes many forms. It is often expressed in polls through a simplistic assessment of how many, and what kinds of, civil liberties people are willing to trade for a greater sense of security. Sometimes it is expressed as an argument against liberty itself, with (especially) commentators on the right arguing that (excess) liberty and the "pursuit of freedom" begets "chaos."[22] It is the reinforcement of order itself that stands for the social good in such arguments, while refusing to name, yet always implying, who is to benefit from this order, this surrender, and who is not.

In a world—the world of liberal democracy—where law is supposed to be grandly neutral, law can only rarely be allowed to target certain populations for doing things that are otherwise normal and legal, which is why Supreme Court justices so frequently invoke soccer players (who in the United States are understood to be middle class and white) and bird watchers (ditto) as they justify laws and practices aimed at black men or protesters, and which is why the Las Vegas ban on handing out food to impoverished people (but not rich ones) was so startling. It, at least, did not even try to hide its class basis and for that reason was quickly struck down perhaps less because it was unjust, which it was, and more because it threatened the legitimacy of law itself. The problem with the Las Vegas law was that its pretext was just too plain. It was not the handing out of food but *poor people* that the city found offensive, and the intent of the law was

not to eliminate poverty but to eliminate poor people who scare us, who are dis-
ordering public space, who threaten property values, and who are, in any case,
assumed to have no right to the spaces of the contemporary city. The Las Vegas
law was not a bad law because it used a pretext—handing out food—to target a
class or people; it was a bad law because it targeted those people poorly.

In this regard, the proposed Minneapolis alley law was a "better" one. It was
better because it banned all "strangers" from all alleys. It accorded exactly with
what the Supreme Court legitimated in the *Hicks* case. The pretext in *Hicks* was
drug dealing—and also the war against terrorism (at least if we believe the arguments of the U.S. solicitor general)—but the bid was to gain authoritarian control over city streets. In its decision the court could not have been clearer that
trespass and banishment procedures were a ruse, but a good one, precisely because they were not, on their face, geared at a certain class of people. Roller skaters and strollers as well as soccer players and bird watchers were targeted (at
least in the court's imagination) along with loiterers and drug dealers. Of course
the Minneapolis law did not pass. But, then, neither have trespass-barment procedures ever been used against bird watchers and soccer players. They have
been reserved almost exclusively for young black men (and, increasingly, other
people of color) who like to walk and hang out in city streets. The *blanket* prohibition in the use of space (unless you have a legitimate purpose as determined
by some authority) is really just a pretext for removing those who are suspect.
Hicks had been barred and arrested for merely *being* on streets he used to have
full access to, not for drug dealing or involvement in any other sort of crime. But
the city of Richmond and its housing authority banned him because he, or especially others *like* him, *might* do something illegal. For that reason, he had to be
removed. Paranoia spurred the drive for pretexts. The result was a metastasization of exactly the sort of prohibitions on the use of space that have long shaped
the lives of homeless people, now given their fullest expression not so much in
specific anti-camping or anti-food-sharing laws but, in a further metastasization, this time of trespass law.

No Trespassing

The 1990s was the decade when gentrification went global (as capital sought
out new circuits of accumulation in the built environment), anti-homelessness
non-coincidentally became entrenched in urban policy, Kevin Hicks was barred
from visiting his family in Richmond public housing or even passing through
adjacent streets, and, as the great British satirist Craig Brown noted, we all became aware of "Global Warning." "Everywhere," he said, "there was a rise in
Global Warning. Every day, there were new Global Warnings about killer vi-
ruses, killer waves, killer drugs, killer icebergs, killer vaccines, killer killers and
other possible causes of imminent death. At first these Global Warnings were

frightening, but after a while people began to enjoy them."[23] In the 2000s, after the truly paranoid but freakily fun Y2K scare, the terrorist attacks of 9/11 (and the many that followed) transformed enjoyment back into abject fear. Global Warnings came out of nowhere—out of the clear blue sky—and from every direction: aviation schools in Florida, clandestine meetings in Bangkok, the caves and killing fields of Afghanistan, the streets and laboratories of Iraq (in some people's minds at least), as well as the housing projects, homeless shelters, and tent cities of nearly every city. The only solution was to keep the "killers" *out*—out of the "homeland," out of the garages below skyscrapers, out of the sports stadiums, and out of the street and parks. Borders—of the nation, and of the street—had to be secured, or else Global Warnings would become local realities of death and mayhem.

Then came the global economic crash of 2007–2008, the violent inequalities it deepened at all geographic scales, and the global reaction, from the Arab Spring and Syrian Civil War to the mass migration of people fleeing economic catastrophe, political and social violence, and not merely Global Warning, but the increasingly dire stresses on life and livelihood caused by global warming.[24] Borders at every scale seemed under assault, and no "homeland" seemed immune from the mass influx of unknown, seemingly unknowable, but certainly desperate people. City streets, too, seemed under assault. In Europe, growing numbers of beggars, typically from Romani-speaking communities in Eastern Europe, showed up in front of nearly every store and bank in the wealthy enclaved nations of Northern Europe, forcing, in the words of a Social Democratic municipal council leader in Sweden, even countries like his to finally give up on the idea of fundamental human equality.* In America homelessness continued to grow. And on the streets, in both Europe and the United States, the tool of choice for securing local space has been, more and more, the enforcement of no trespassing laws.

To trespass is a broader sin than we often think it is. It is to "disobey, violate (a law, etc.)," as the *first* definition in the *Shorter Oxford English Dictionary* puts it. Only secondarily is it to "wrongfully enter on a person's land or property." By extension, to trespass is to "make an *unwarrantable* claim, intrude, encroach (on or upon a person's time, attention, patience, domain, etc.)."[25] In turn (and as noted in chapter 4), to be *warranted* means "permitted by law or authority; authorized; justified; sanctioned"—that is, to have a "legitimate business or social purpose" as determined by *law* or *authority*. Homeless people are, nearly by definition, not legitimate. Five hundred years of history have made that clear enough. But now neither are the rest of us, at least a priori, and at least in the eyes of the authorities and law, if not entirely yet in how we are policed (white

---

* It is important that the center-left Social Democrats—not Sweden Democrats, the increasingly popular right-wing, nationalist, racist, populist party—have taken the lead in declaring the end of a belief in human equality. Hansson and Mitchell, "Exceptional State of 'Roma Beggars' in Sweden."

people do not generally carry with them an unceasing *expectation* of being violently policed when they are in public as do people of color). There is little we can permissibly do in our everyday urban lives that is not, now, warranted. Without permission, without authorization, we are always intruders, even on our own spaces. And—crucially—so is everyone else.* Until authority can be established and shown, we are all now potential trespassers, each of us making a claim on another's attention, time, property, and sense of well-being (this is *atomic*, SUV citizenship metastasized). So it is not just *Global* Warnings that beset us everywhere, but intensely local ones too. That homeless man in the park, that darkish-skinned bearded man with a backpack, that teen slouching through an alley: they are all trespassers, all potential threats, all exactly the people we need to guard, and be guarded, against. Paranoia reigns supreme, and the only way to corral it is to reconstruct the world as one in which the no trespassing sign is one that we welcome with open arms and deeply internalize. The only way to allay such social, productive paranoia is to create a world in which trespass is foundational to *governance*. And it certainly does not hurt—indeed it does nothing but help deepen just what is at work in our cities—that this internalizing of trespass is necessarily an internalization of the goodness of private, that is, alienable, property. The warrant of trespass is, also and essentially, the warrant to accumulate.

Between Warranted and Warned Out

Here we arrive at the perverse nub of the matter. The creation and reinforcement of a kind of anti-urbanism rooted in a metastasization of trespass law and based in the fundamental idea that some people just aren't worth it and always need to be warned *out*—by judges, cops, property developers, city council leaders, and often we ourselves in our everyday practices—is essential to creating the conditions of possibility for capital to successfully circulate through, and accumulate in, the built environment. It is the means by which abstract space is produced and protected, even if—or rather, especially because—in the realities of everyday life on the streets and in the courts, this production and protection is constantly being challenged, constantly being threatened with differentiation *anyway*. It also makes clear who, or rather what, is "doing antisocial things."

---

*A range of Supreme Court decisions has actually upheld the right of people to go about city streets without, for example, being asked for identification or to otherwise account for themselves by the police. But as we know, these rulings are not followed in practice, and even more changes in immigration and terrorism law have made it legal for both immigration police and local (or state) police to stop for any or no reason *anyone* within one hundred miles of a border or a coastline—all of Florida, most of New York State, nearly all of California, most of New England, and so forth. Within thirty miles, immigration police can enter private property without a warrant on the mere assumption that undocumented aliens might be present.

From their very beginnings efforts to produce capitalist abstract space (as we have been defining it in this book) have relied on destroying "social" things: the commons of precapitalist England, communities of workers and their unions,[26] militant workers' abilities to speak on the street or march to Washington to press their demands, encampments of homeless people, families (especially if you are a black man living near a public housing project), food giveaways, public space itself, and lives. Those who insist on being social anyway, the lucky ones anyway, are "warned out"—given bus tickets out of town, served with trespass-barment procedures, jailed for speaking on the streets, banned altogether, or subject to the "chase 'em, chase 'em, chase 'em" paranoia of demagogues and bureaucrats alike—or, if deemed worthy, provided a tent, shed, or metal container in a heavily guarded, regimented "homelessness services area" in some out-of-the-way patch of scrub. The unworthy ones, the ones who *deserve* it, the ones like Charly Keunang, are shot. There is little that is more antisocial than capital's drive to create a landscape "suitable to its own needs." To the degree that landscape must be composed of commensurable, exchangeable, abstract space—space that contains some quantum of *equality*—it does so by forcing us to come to the realization that any principled "stance concerning the equality of all human beings" simply cannot be sustained.

But it does so imperfectly. That is why struggle in the realm of legislation and the law more generally is so intense, and why seemingly minor matters like Robert Martin and Robert Anderson getting cited for sleeping in public in Boise or Kevin Hicks getting arrested for trying to visit his family in Richmond are so important. We are in a moment of intense capitalist reorganization (globally, nationally, and locally), and so we are once again in an era of "feverish legislative activity." And the stakes are high. The outcome of struggles over the shape and form of this legislation—and, of course, its always uneven implementation—will determine the possibilities (or impossibilities) for compound capitalist accumulation *and* destruction in the built environment and thus in just what ways the streets are mean. Law remains at every *bloody* level, and it remains a central arena of class struggle. In the arena of law, as in the arena of capitalist circulation, homelessness remains a central problem to be reckoned with. Whether such reckoning is brutal or not might be an open question; that it *must* be reckoned with is not.

To determine is to set limits and exert pressures. The outcomes of these struggles in the arena of law (and the way they will ramify into and transform social relation at every bloody level) will set a limit to capital, a limit that capital will always have to strive to overcome, just as it has to overcome the limits set by its own past landscape, its own built environment that may now no longer be appropriate to its needs. As it does so, it will necessarily produce homelessness, further setting limits to itself. These limits are often most clearly seen in public space because public space, like homelessness, is both a necessity and a problem for capitalism, both indispensable and something that must be dispensed with.

The specific form that class struggle in the arena of law might take is hardly predictable. Surely labor unionists in Colorado would not have freely chosen to fight for the right to organize and picket in public space in a case concerning abortion protest, nor might advocates for homeless people immediately see how the arrest of a man like Kevin Hicks could be fully decisive for their right to *be* in public space, though neither should they be surprised, given the growing importance of area bans as a poverty management strategy.[27] Indeed, none of us should be surprised. Mean streets are metastasizing, and so their malignancy should be expected everywhere. But if that is the case, then "warning out" has reached its limit too. As all space becomes commensurable, as the primary function of all space is to now accrue value (not necessarily to support life), as abstract space continues to try to paper over the world, there is no place to be warned out *to*. Wherever the homeless and the rest of us are warned to, we become a new, bigger problem. In the short run, this might be horrible as locales seek to preserve whatever values they can, often violently, always with even more feverish legislative activity. In the longer run it presents capital—and capitalism—with its ultimate limit. Our only hope is to continue to take space, make it public, and do *social* things (sleep, protest, hang out, speak) in it—to refuse the idea that we must somehow give up on "our principal stance concerning the equality of human beings," some of whom must live in that space and thus to refuse to dignify the "smaller, meaner" question of what a man like Charly "Africa" Keunang did to "deserve" to die—no matter how much capital *must* make public space antisocial.

AFTERWORD

Thirty years ago my initial interest in homelessness was driven by pure rage. Growing up in the San Francisco Bay Area in the 1970s and attending college and university there and in San Diego in the 1980s meant confronting homelessness every step of the way.

My hometown, Moraga, was cloistered, wealthy, and overwhelmingly white.[1] But even there, toward the end of the 1970s, there was a growing population of street people, or what we called, with typical teenage meanness, "Canyon Critters," since, in our imagination at least, they lived like animals in the woods of nearby Canyon, a "hippie" town nestled in the Oakland hills. For the most part, we thought they were weird, maybe messed up, but overall pretty benign. And while that did not change much as the 1970s shaded into the 1980s, over the hills in Oakland, Berkeley, and San Francisco the population of visible street people exploded. In Berkeley's People's Park, where I would sometimes hang out while in high school, a permanent homeless encampment formed. Encampments also grew in the sunken plaza of San Francisco's Powell Street BART Station and in the UN Plaza at the next station along. One could not walk through the city's Financial District without having to step around homeless people, of all races but disproportionately black, sprawled on the ground. By even the first years of the 1980s this had become *normal*. I had a job during school breaks and summers delivering alcohol for a fancy liquor store located at the edge of the wealthy neighborhood of Presidio Heights that sent me driving all over San Francisco. Except in super-exclusive enclaves like Sea Cliff, beggars on sidewalks or holding signs in median strips near traffic lights were common sights, *normal* sights, unexceptional sights.

Down in San Diego I had a job shuttling old folks to adult day care. Most of those I picked up lived in the old working-class towns of Lemon Grove and Spring Valley, but as in San Francisco, that job and one doing dial-a-ride for the local transit authority took me all over town. All through the southeastern parts of San Diego, from Spring Valley west almost to the ocean, foreclosure notices started appearing on doors of small cottages and bungalows, and they were particularly thick in the African American neighborhoods. All up and down the poorly maintained streets of these impoverished neighborhoods men and women pushed heavily laden shopping carts or stood in line with them in vast parking lots waiting their turn to get some surplus cheese that the federal government had started doling out of the back of semi trucks.* Where they went at night, I had no idea.

They too became normal, as normal as the growing number of older men and woman, white and black, Asian and Latino, hanging out on the streets of San Diego's skyscraper downtown and its newly gentrified Gaslamp Quarter. These latter had been forced onto the streets by the steady destruction of single room occupancy hotels in San Diego's old Skid Row and the successive redevelopment of Horton Plaza so as to make it ever more inhospitable to the poor who had long hung out there and more welcoming to the growing number of shoppers heading into the private precincts of the Horton Plaza Shopping Center festival marketplace.[2]

At San Diego State University I had a professor, Larry Ford, who implored those of us in his urban geography course to just go outside and *look*. He was a forceful advocate of the idea that by looking and learning to *see* the landscape one could learn a lot about American culture. What I learned to actually see was just that which I had already been seeing, but perhaps not really appreciating all along: the growing evidence of extreme poverty and homelessness and especially its *normalness*. If, as Larry insisted, the landscape helped us know who we are, and if growing street homelessness and other forms of extreme poverty were a central part of that landscape, then that spoke volumes. It enraged me. I intuited, but did not at all have the knowledge or vocabulary to explain, even to myself, that there was no way homelessness like this could be accidental. The rapidity with which it became normal belied that. I knew I had to study homelessness.

What I did not know, then, was that to study homelessness, I could not study the homeless. This has taken me a long time to learn. But the evidence is everywhere, and always has been. When I moved east to Pennsylvania for graduate school, determined to study the landscape of homelessness, it was impossible to escape the primary question everyone seemed to be asking in the newspapers as well as in the scholarly literature: who are the homeless? The question was everywhere and almost impossible to break away from. I remember becoming particularly incensed by an op-ed piece (in the *New York Times*, I believe, though

---

* By the 1980s the federal government had stockpiled an incredible mass of surplus cheese, taken off the market or bought up in order to bolster dairy prices. The 1981 Farm Bill authorized the government to distribute much of this cheese to people eligible for food stamps. Since receipt of the cheese cost recipients no food stamps, the program was quite popular (despite regular reports of moldy cheese) even as it gave rise to the spectacle of long lines of destitute people forming, especially in California (the wealthiest state in the country and also the first to take advantage of the program), unlike any seen since the Great Depression. In the 1980s, the dawn of the Reagan era, unlike the 2000s, it seems, it was acceptable to give out food for free or at a nominal cost to indigent people.

I may not be recalling correctly, as I cannot now find it) that sought to explain what homelessness was by telling us who the homeless were, and especially what sorts of characteristics put them at risk of becoming homeless, becoming an answer to the question, who are the homeless? One of the key findings was that a significant risk factor for becoming homeless—that is, a significant characteristic of homeless people—was age. That's right. Growing old in America put one at risk of becoming homeless. Let's assume this is correct. If it is, it says *nothing* about homeless people and *everything* about the world we have made, about what homeless*ness* is.

Living then in the midst of the great industrial U-turn and seeing its devastating effects on the old industrial towns of Pennsylvania, it became increasingly clear to me that to ask, who are the homeless? was to ask exactly the wrong question. As I sought to understand the historical geography of homelessness in the recently deindustrialized city of Johnstown, Pennsylvania, it quickly became apparent instead that the much better question was, what is homelessness? For it had shifted shape, drastically, over Johnstown's history (though it had never gone away). And what became even more apparent was that a further question, which was rarely asked, desperately needed to be asked: what does homelessness *do* in society? My answer in relation to Johnstown's historical geography was largely a Foucauldian one, focusing on how homelessness continually required the invention of new forms of discipline (which I called "control," and which a couple of friends helped me understand was perfected through a geography of "sequestration").[3] My argument was, in part, that the push for social order in the spaces of the city produced forms of marginality, of which one was homelessness. In turn, homelessness required ongoing experimentation in the production of new forms of order. Obviously, such analyses remain central to my own thinking (and figuring some of this out has been central in turning my own at times inchoate rage at a world that so ruthlessly produces homelessness into something more productive than just raging on about it). But even then I was not wholly satisfied with this approach to homelessness, at least on its own, for it could not explain, really, either what homelessness *is* (and was) or *why* it is so ruthlessly produced.

Figuring that out—to the degree that I have done so—has taken these past thirty years. For my PhD studies I turned my direct attention away from homelessness (or so I thought) to examine the struggle between capital, the state, and migratory labor in producing the California agribusiness landscape.[4] But, as we have seen, migratory workers were the homeless of their day, and so understanding how and why has required reckoning directly with the labor-capital relationship and particularly coming to terms with the general law of capitalist accumulation (that the production of wealth at one pole necessarily produces misery at the other pole) *as it has been historically-geographically determined and transformed.* In other words, it has required understanding homelessness not at the margins (or even outside) of capitalism but right at its heart, not a "byproduct" but a constituting part, and *then* figuring out what homelessness *does* in society. The preceding pages have sought to work out both how homelessness is at the center of capitalist society and what it does in capitalist society, and, in my view, what it does is manifold and ramifies out to encompass all the rest of us.

The so-called crisis of homelessness has not abated, and it can't. So, therefore, has my sense of rage not abated, and *it* can't. Just as with the problem of working-class housing, capitalism has no solution to homelessness but to push it about—and to change its form. For all the myriad ways in which people have intervened in the problem of homelessness and into homeless people's lives, and for all the homeless organizing there is, and always has been, only, really, has the IWW (and scattered other radical movements of homeless people) been right in their prescription: if we want to abolish homelessness, we must abolish capitalism. This means neither that all manner of interventions into homelessness (creating shelter, defending encampments, providing real, needed, psychological support, abolishing the prison system) are not necessary—they are—nor that we must imagine a world of widespread deprivation (as many political discourses around "privilege" do). Rather it means imagining and working toward a world of abundance in which the general law of *capitalist* accumulation simply does not operate. This will entail decommodifying housing and undoing the built environment as a primary means for capital accumulation. It will entail a new collective *determination* of the historical geographies within which we live—new limits and pressures that make the limits to capital absolute.

Such collective determinations require public space, which is why—beyond its importance for homeless people to meet their needs for survival, companionship, and pleasure—struggle over the legal construction and policing of public space is so vitally important. It is why it is so vitally important to fight against the purely atomic forms of citizenship capitalism both instills and requires, however the drive toward such forms of citizenship is configured (in law, in property, or elsewhere). And it is why it is so vitally important to understand not just how, but why, the policing of homeless people in public space, up to and including the killing of homeless people like Charly Keunang, is intricately linked to the policing of housed people, like Kevin Hicks—and especially how it is the sinews of capital circulation that bind them together, however disguised in the discourses of the formal equality and impartiality of law these sinews may be.[5]

I said in the preface that this is not a politically optimistic book, and it isn't. I do hope, however, that it is an enraging and infuriating book, and out of that rage and fury comes not only further, deep analyses, as these are always needed, but especially glimpses of new political struggles worth engaging in. The Obama-era Department of Justice intervention in Boise may have been limited in both design and effect, but it remains worth paying attention to. In the first place, the intervention itself marked a (not the) culmination of thirty years of activist engagement, by homeless people's organizations, legal scholars, social scientists, public interest lawyers, and so many more fighting forcefully simply for the basic right of homeless people to *live*, to not *deserve* to die. In the second place, to the degree that high courts are now agreeing, the ground has been cleared for a new stage in the battle, or rather for the intensification of two old battles: the battle against the brutal murder of homeless people, people of color, and working people at the hands of the police as they are charged with making the city safe for the circulation and accumulation of capital, and the battle against the premature death of so many people (from exposure, lack of medical care, uncontrolled addictions, assault, and more) who are simultaneously necessary to capitalism's compound growth *and* forever being "warned out." The ground has also been cleared, perhaps, for a revival of such class struggle *toward* a new world, not only defensive struggles against the world as it now is. Homelessness *is* class struggle, but this is a struggle that extends well beyond the precincts of homelessness and homeless people themselves as I trust this book has made clear.

I have also said that to call homelessness a crisis is to abuse language, since it is a permanent and necessary part of capitalist society.[6] And yet there can be no doubt that capitalism itself is in crisis. The contemporary form of homelessness arose with the end of the Keynesian global order and the rise of the neoliberal one. The economic crisis of 2007–2008 sounded the death knell for neoliberalism, at least in the form it then took. What is arising to take its place is hard to see in its totality, but some of its political structure, at least, is becoming clear: a new form of populist authoritarianism that would perhaps make even Stuart Hall nostalgic for the relatively more benign authoritarian populism of the Thatcher years, of neoliberalism in the making.[7] That's at the level of politics and law, though. And as much as neither politics nor law keep to their own bloody levels, the rise of populist authoritarianism, which of course is poised to make public spaces and public spheres more brutal than ever, is more a symptom of the crisis of capitalism than its cure. And most symptomatic of this symptom is the targeting of surplus populations: the rapid spread across Europe, for example, of anti-homeless laws based on the American model,[8] the exceptionally brutal policing of homeless people in Hungary, and the declaration by even social democratic politicians in putatively social democratic Sweden that it is time to give up on the dream of equality and (presumably) just let surplus people get what they "deserve."

And yet, as Ruth Wilson Gilmore has reminded us, "Crisis is not objectively bad or good, rather, it signals systemic change whose outcome is determined through struggle. Struggle occurs at all levels of society as a people try to figure out, through trial and error, what to make of idled capacities," *including* especially the idled capacities of surplused people.[9] Homelessness, one phenomenal form that surplused people take, *is* class struggle.

So do as Larry Ford implored me to do all those years ago. Go outside and really look. Look at the mean streets. You'll see: Homelessness is what class struggle looks like in public space. Homelessness *is* the limit to capital. Homelessness *forces* the crisis of capitalism—and has always done so.

ACKNOWLEDGMENTS

Larry Ford taught me to look. Neil Smith taught me to think. In between Deryck Holdsworth taught me to dig down and dig in. They were abetted by Stu Aitken, Peter Gould, Bria Holcomb, and Bob Lake. That I remain so much in their debt so many years later is, I hope, clearly evident in the preceding pages.

Happily, over the long years of researching homelessness and public space, those debts were hugely compounded. I have learned and continue to learn from Matt Hannah and Ulf Strohmayer; Matt Huber, Jamie Winders, Bob Wilson, Jonnell Robinson, and Tom Perreault; and most especially Lynn Staeheli. All who know her—and me—will see just how influential Lynn remains in my thinking, even if I often turn in directions she might not.

My thinking has been pushed hard by—and in the process I have developed lifelong friendships with—Scott Kirsch, Bruce D'Arcus, Carrie Breitbach, Clayton Rosati, Jim Ketchum, Laam Hae, Bob Ross, Reecia Orzeck, Jacob Shell, Joaquín Villanueva, Kafui Attoh, Katie Wells, Jessie Speer, Ben Gerlofs, and now Brian Hennigan, Stephen Przybylinski, Maddy Hamlin, Marcus Mohall, Karolina Wallin-Fernqvist, and Sebastian Djup.

Special thanks to Nik Heynen, not only for his constant support and good advice, but also for so graciously allowing me to rework and reuse a paper we wrote together. Thanks also to all the editors and reviewers, both known and unknown, who critiqued, challenged, and—just enough—encouraged my arguments as I worked them out in the pages of journals and books. More immediately, University of Georgia Press found a couple of deeply encouraging, and—just enough—challenging readers for the whole manuscript. One was Elvin Wyly, and his review still makes me smile from ear to ear. The other was Nick Blomley, whose lead I am always happy to follow and whose advice I always cherish, even though, but especially because, we do not always fully agree.

Once again, the crew at the University of Georgia Press has been wonderful: Mick Gussinde-Duffy, Bethany Snead, Jon Davies, and Joseph Dahm, who had the unenviable task of copyediting my manuscript.

Since moving to Sweden, I have lucked into a fabulous nest of Nordic co-conspirators and colleagues who have made my new life bearable or a joy, as needed: Tom Mels in Visby; Brett Chistophers, David Jansson, Miguel Martínez, Gunnar Olsson, Micheline van Riemsdjik, Ismael Yrigoy, Maja Lagerqvist, Kevin Durand, Erik Hansson, Irene Molina, Ståle Holgersen, Thomas Oles, Adele Lebano, Pamela Tipmanoworn, and Lena Dahlborg in Uppsala; Päivi Rannila in Turku; Kristian Stokke, Karen O'Brien, and David Jordhus-Lier in Oslo; Catharina Thörn and Håken Thörn in Göteborg; Ken Olwig in Copenhagen; and Erik Clark, Tomas Germundsson, and the lovely Mustafa Dikeç in Skåne.

But the one person who (still!) makes all the difference is Susan.

□ □ □

Mean Streets is based on previously published work, much of it thoroughly updated and revised. A special thank-you to Patricia Zline at Rowman & Littlefield/Lexington Books for her immediate and gracious response to my request for permission to republish. It's so nice to correspond with a human being. Thanks also to Sage Publications for bucking the corporate trends and remembering that we authors actually own the rights to our own work and for making it easy to exercise those rights.

Portions of chapter 1 are based on, and considerably revised, arguments first made in "Homelessness, American Style," *Urban Geography* 32 (2011): 933–955 and "From Boise to Budapest: Capital Circulation, Compound Capitalist Destruction, and the Persistence of Homelessness," in *Gentrification and Global Strategy: Neil Smith and Beyond*, edited by Abel Albet and Núria Benach (London: Routledge, 2017), 99–111.

Chapter 2 is a reorganized and slightly revised version of "Controlling Space, Controlling Scale: Migrant Labor, Free Speech, and Regional Development in the American West in the Early 20th Century," *Journal of Historical Geography* 28 (2002): 63–84.

Chapter 3 is revised from "Tent Cities: Interstitial Spaces of Survival," in *Urban Interstices: The Aesthetics and Politics of Spatial In-Betweens*, edited by Andrea Mubi-Brighenti (Farnham, UK: Ashgate, 2013), 65–85.

Chapter 4 revises a large portion of Don Mitchell and Nik Heynen, "The Geography of Survival and the Right to the City: Speculations on Surveillance, Legal Innovation, and the Criminalization of Intervention," *Urban Geography* 30 (2009): 611–632.

The interlude is partially based on some arguments first made in "From Boise to Budapest: Capital Circulation, Compound Capitalist Destruction, and the Persistence of Homelessness," in *Gentrification and Global Strategy: Neil Smith and Beyond*, edited by Abel Albet and Núria Benach (London: Routledge, 2017), 99–111 and "People's Park Again: On the End and Ends of Public Space," *Environment and Planning A* 49 (2017): 503–518.

Chapter 5 is a revision of "The S.U.V. Model of Citizenship: Floating Bubbles, Buffer Zones, and the Rise of 'Purely Atomic' Individual," *Political Geography* 25 (2005): 77–100.

Chapter 6 updates and revises "Property Rights, the First Amendment, and Judicial Anti-Urbanism: The Strange Case of *Hicks v. Virginia*," *Urban Geography* 26 (2005): 565–586.

Portions of chapter 7 draw on parts of "People's Park Again: On the End and Ends of Public Space," *Environment and Planning A* 49 (2017): 503–518 and "Pretexts, Paranoia, and Public Space," in *Urban Spaces: Planning and Struggles for Land and Community*, edited by James Jennings and J. S. Jordan-Zachary (Lanham, Md.: Lexington Books, 2010), 19–38.

NOTES

PREFACE

1. My own takes on how best to theorize public spaces—and publicity—can be found in *The Right to the City*, "People's Park Again" (some arguments from which are reworked in the pages that follow), and, in collaboration in Lynn Staeheli, *People's Property?*

2. For just one account, see Gowan, *Hobos, Hustlers, and Backsliders.*

3. See the discussion and bibliography in Speer, "Losing Home."

4. Anyone curious about what the commons has been, is, and can be should consult Blackmar, "Appropriating 'the Commons.'" In a remarkably small number of pages, Blackmar lays out a remarkably complete history of the commons (and its appropriation by the propertied classes, both physically and intellectually).

5. Thompson, *Poverty of Theory*, 96.

6. Lefebvre, *Production of Space*; Lefebvre, *Survival of Capitalism.*

CHAPTER 1. BOISE, "AFRICA," AND THE LIMITS TO CAPITAL

1. Press Release, "Justice Department Files Brief to Address Criminalization of Homelessness," Office of Public Affairs, Department of Justice, August 6, 2015. See "Statement of Interest of the United States," *Bell et al v. City of Boise et al*, Civil Action No 1:09-cv-540REB, August 6, 2015. For a history of the case as well as an analysis of the limits to the DOJ's legal reasoning, see Anonymous, "Recent Court Filing."

2. National Law Center on Homelessness and Poverty, *No Safe Place.*

3. For an analysis of early attempts to establish Eighth Amendment protections for homeless people that points to much of the legal scholarship of the late 1980s and early 1990s, see Mitchell, "Anti-homeless Laws."

4. The story appeared on July 11, 2015.

5. Ginia Bellafante, "Rudolph Giuliani's Outrage on Homelessness, and Richard Gere's," *New York Times*, August 20, 2015, MB1; M. Flagenheimer, N. Stewart, and M. Navarro, "After Playing Down a Homeless Crisis, Mayor De Blasio Changes His Tune," *New York Times*, September 2, 2015.

6. Lipsitz, "Policing Place and Taxing Time," 126 (citing Los Angeles Community Action Network, "Community-Based Rights Assessment: Skid Row's Safer Cities

Initiative," December 2010, and Timmons, "Fatal Police Shooting"). See also Camp and Heatherton, "Asset Stripping," esp. 142.

7. Morin, Holland, and Parvini, "Skid Row Shooting," A1. In Los Angeles as a whole, more than three-quarters of the estimated 2013 homeless population of 82,000 lacked access to a shelter bed or other housing. Lipsitz, "Policing Place and Taxing Time," 128.

8. Gale Holland, Jack Dolan, and Kate Mather, "Police Kill Man on Skid Row: Homeless Person Is Fatally Shot in a Frantic Altercation with Four LAPD Officers," *Los Angeles Times*, March 2, 2015, A1.

9. Jeff Sharlet, " Invisible Man."

10. Ibid.

11. Morin, Holland, and Parvini, "Skid Row Shooting."

12. *Robert Martin and Robert Anderson v. City of Boise*, Case No. 1:09-cv-00540-REB, 2015 U.S. Dist. LEXIS 134129.

13. Ibid.

14. *Jones v. City of Los Angeles*, 444 F3d 1118 (9th Cir. 2006). This decision led to the settlement that currently governs policing on LA's Skid Row.

15. Boise City Code §§ 6-01-05(A), 9-10-02, emphasis added; *Martin and Anderson v. City of Boise*, 15n14.

16. *Martin et al v. City of Boise*, D.C. No. 1:09-cv.00540-REB, September 4, 2018.

17. Ibid., 17–18.

18. Ibid., 19.

19. Ibid., 28–31, 33, 34.

20. Ibid., 32, quoting *Jones v. City of Los Angeles*, 1138 (*vacated*).

21. See Hennigan, "From Madonna to Marx."

22. For just one example of this taken-for-granted discourse in full flower, see Thomas Fuller, "San Francisco's Homeless Crisis Tests Mayor Candidates' Liberal Ideas," *New York Times*, May 30, 2018.

23. See, perhaps especially, Gladwell, "Million-Dollar Murray," 96.

24. For a thorough and nuanced appraisal, see Hennigan, "House Broken."

25. Cresswell, "Vagrant/Vagabond," esp. 240.

26. Beier, *Masterless Men*; Ribton-Turner, *History of Vagrants and Vagrancy*.

27. Bauman, *Legislators and Interpreters*, 43; Cresswell, "Vagrant/Vagabond," 249.

28. DePastino, *Citizen Hobo*, 6, quoting Jones, "Strolling Poor," in Monkkonen, *Walking to Work*, 39; Rothman, "First Shelters"; Kusmer, *Down and Out*.

29. On just how ignoble, see Schweik, *Ugly Laws*.

30. On the distinction between logics of capital and the logics of the larger social formation that is capitalism, see Thompson, *Poverty of Theory*, esp. 55–70, and more recently (though less convincingly) Harvey, *Seventeen Contradictions*.

31. *Papachristou v. City of Jacksonville*, 405 U.S. 156 (1972), 161.

32. For a compelling account that brings the argument into the present and exposes to light its geopolitical implications, see Fields, *Enclosure*.

33. Marx, *Capital*, 1:668–674; Bauman, *Legislators and Interpreters*.

34. Marx, *Capital*, 1:686. Engels returned to this point, after a fashion, in *The Housing Question* when he argued that the bourgeoisie has no solution to the problem of housing

the working class except to push it about; only with the supercession of capitalism would the housing question be solved.

35. On Fort Lauderdale, see *Time*, March 11, 1985, 68, quoted in Snow and Anderson, *Down on Their Luck*, 342n21. The *Chicago Tribune* is quoted in Cresswell, *Tramp in America*, 9. Of course, there is more than a whiff of Swift's *A Modest Proposal* here, but as with Swift, the *Tribune* is pointing to something real: the real fear of tramps that had gripped the land.

36. Monkkonen, *Police in Urban America*.

37. DePastino, *Citizen Hobo*, 8.

38. Liebman, *California Farmland*; McWilliams, *Factories in the Field*; Igler, *Industrial Cowboys*; Cresswell, *Tramp in America*, 36–37.

39. Higbie, *Indispensable Outcasts*; Mitchell, *Lie of the Land*.

40. DePastino, *Citizen Hobo*, pt. 1.

41. Kusmer, "Underclass in Historical Perspective," 27.

42. Schneider, "Skid Row"; Groth, *Living Downtown*; Parker, *Casual Laborer*. The name "Skid Row" is generally thought to derive from Seattle's "Skid Road," a street down which logs were skidded to the harbor. However, geographer Kenneth Olwig (personal communication) suggests that it might also be derived from various Scandinavian words for "shit" that are cognate with "skid," including the Swedish *skit*, given both the number of Scandinavians who ended up working in the timber and shipping industries in the Northwest and the conditions of the streets in what became Skid Row districts.

43. Solenberger, *One Thousand Homeless Men*; Anderson, *Hobo*.

44. Harvey, *Limits to Capital*, 233.

45. Ibid., 165–166, 381–382, quoting Marx, *Capital*, 1:269, 642. On the surplusing and abandoning of people of color, see Gilmore, *Golden Gulag* and "Forgotten Places"; Camp, *Incarcerating the Crisis*.

46. The classic text on the policing of Skid Row is Bittner, "Police on Skid Row."

47. On the sense of fear such places, including labor camps, engendered, see Parker, *Casual Laborer*.

48. Anderson, *Hobo*; Solenberger, *One Thousand Homeless Men*; see also Cresswell, *Tramp in America*; Hopper, *Reckoning with Homelessness*; Hopper, Susser, and Conover, "Economies of Makeshift."

49. DePastino, *Citizen Hobo*, 219.

50. Mitchell, *Lie of the Land*; Stein, *California*; Gregory, *American Exodus*. On tramping labor and homelessness elsewhere during the Depression, see Crouse, *Homeless Transient*.

51. On the structural rationale for, effects of, and contradictions of the bracero program in California, see Mitchell, *They Saved the Crops*.

52. Cayo Sexton, "Life of the Homeless."

53. Dear and Wolch, *Landscapes of Despair*; Lamb, "Deinstitutionalization." On the struggle for deinstitutionalization, see Taylor, *Acts of Conscience*.

54. DePastino, *Citizen Hobo*, 231. A couple of representative works are Bahr, *Skid Row*; and Bahr and Caplow, *Old Men, Drunk and Sober*.

55. Hopper, *Reckoning with Homelessness*, 45.

56. Especially influential was the remarkable Caleb Foote's "Vagrancy-Type Law and Its Administration."

57. *Papachristou v. City of Jacksonville*, 405 U.S. 156 (1972).

58. Wolch and Dear, in *Malign Neglect*, 4, report that the U.S. economy lost some ten million jobs between 1979 and 1985.

59. Harvey, *Brief History of Neoliberalism*.

60. Hopper, *Reckoning with Homelessness*, 46.

61. Sugrue, *Origins of the Urban Crisis*. In some cases, such as in Manhattan, deindustrialization was being planned for as early as the 1920s. See Shell, *Transportation and Revolt*.

62. Laska and Spain, *Back to the City*; Smith, "Toward a Theory of Gentrification." On the circuits of capital and "capital switching," see inter alia, Harvey, *Limits to Capital* and *Urban Experience*, esp. chaps. 1 and 2.

63. Smith, "Toward a Theory of Gentrification," and *New Urban Frontier*. A good, accessible review of the dynamics and debates over gentrification is Lees, Slater, and Wyly, *Gentrification*.

64. Harvey, *Urban Experience*, 97. "Fictitious capital" is value that circulates "ahead of itself" in the form of debt; in recent decades, the invention of collateralized debt obligations and the like has brought fictitious capital to something of an apogee.

65. The Stewart B. McKinney Homeless Assistance Act was later renamed the McKinney-Vento Homeless Assistance Act.

66. Foscarinis, "Federal Response."

67. See esp. Baum and Burnes, *Nation in Denial*. Though Baum and Burnes expressed a good deal of sympathy for many homeless people, their book did as much as any to reinvigorate the deserving/undeserving divide in poverty management and to provide a scholarly foundation for a new, at times quite vicious politics that thoroughly demonized the poor and homeless for being poor and homeless.

68. Davis, *City of Quartz*; Flusty, "Banality of Interdiction"; Staeheli and Mitchell, *People's Property?*, esp. chap. 3.

69. Blomley, "How to Turn a Beggar"; Blomley, "Civil Rights Meets Civil Engineering"; Blomley, *Rights of Passage*.

70. Hamill, "How to Save the Homeless." For his legitimation, Hamill draws on Baum and Burnes, *Nation in Denial*, to assure readers that the homeless are *not* like the rest of us.

71. Indeed, the sweeping of homeless encampments and destruction of homeless people's belongings are frequently ruled unconstitutional seizures of property. See, e.g., Associated Press, "Sweeps of Homeless Camps in Washington State Violated Rights, Judge Ruled," *New York Times*, September 18, 2016, A18. In this case advocates for the homeless specifically referred to the DOJ's intervention in Boise to support its arguments.

72. Tsemberis, Gulcur, and Nakae, "Housing First, Consumer Choice."

73. Graves and Sayfan, "First Things First"; Culhane, "Cost of Homelessness"; Culhane et al., *Accountability, Cost-Effectiveness, and Program Performance*.

74. V. Law, "Too Much of a Good Thing?," *Shelterforce Online*, April 23, 2007, www.nhi.org/online/issues/149/housingfirst.html.

75. Graves and Sayfan, "First Things First."

76. Harvey, *Limits to Capital*, chap. 7; and Harvey, *Enigma of Capital*.

77. Paisner, "Compassion, Politics, and the Problem."

CHAPTER 2. FOOTLOOSE REBELS

1. The standard histories remain Dubofsky, *We Shall Be All*, and Foner, *Industrial Workers of the World*.

2. On subversive mobility, see Mitchell, *Lie of the Land*; Shell, *Transportation and Revolt*.

3. Besides the sources cited in note 1, see Foner, *Fellow Workers and Friends*; Mitchell, *Right to the City*, chap. 2.

4. Creel, *Rebel at Large*, 103.

5. Brissenden, *IWW*, 264.

6. See the *Industrial Worker* for February 13, 20, and 27, 1913.

7. "Three Men Sent to Cells for Insult to Court," *Denver Post*, December 27, 1912.

8. "Denver Speakers under Arrest," *Industrial Worker*, January 9, 1913.

9. Reports of arrests appear in the *Industrial Worker* on February 13, 20, and 27 and March 6 and 27, 1913.

10. Two Wobblies involved in the fight reported that the "Chamber of Commerce forced all the daily papers . . . to stop publishing any news regarding the fight with the exception of the Denver Express." Ingler and Perry, "Denver Free Speech Fight," 155.

11. Foner, *Fellow Workers and Friends*, 12; Foner, *Industrial Workers of the World*, 172.

12. Ingler and Perry, "Denver Free Speech Fight," 155.

13. Ibid., 153. The *Industrial Worker* ("Nineteen I.W.W. Men Jailed in Denver," February 13, 1913) sets the date of these first arrests as February 7, not February 3.

14. See *Dominguez v. City of Denver*, 363 P.2d 661 (1961).

15. Kornblugh, *Rebel Voices*, 66, quoting Parker, *Casual Laborer*, 121. On tramping women, see Cresswell, "Embodiment, Power and the Politics."

16. Several migratory histories, based on depositions taken by the U.S. Army's Military Intelligence Division's records of arrested IWW workers in 1917, are mapped in Mitchell, "Land and Labor." For an excellent account of the life of the "western stiff," see Ashleigh, "Floater."

17. Ashleigh, "Floater"; see also Monkkonen, "Introduction," 11.

18. Schneider, "Tramping Workers," 225.

19. Bittner, "Police on Skid Row"; Monkkonen, *Police in Urban America*.

20. Schneider, "Tramping Workers."

21. A romanticized depiction of Skid Row can be found in Noel, *Denver's Larimer Street*.

22. "Nineteen IWW Men Jailed in Denver," *Industrial Worker*, February 13, 1913.

23. *Industrial Worker*, February 20, 1913; March 6, 1913.

24. "IWW Must Educate Denver Police Dept.," *Industrial Worker*, March 13, 1913; "On to Denver," *Industrial Worker*, April 3, 1913.

25. "Marching on Denver to Fight for Free Speech," *Industrial Worker*, March 27, 1913.

26. "500 in IWW Army Will Invade Denver," *Rocky Mountain News*, April 8, 1913.

27. "Chase 100 IWWs out of Junction," *Rocky Mountain News*, April 12, 1913; "Whip Denver's Bosses! Is Call," *Rocky Mountain News*, April 15, 1913.

28. "66 of IWW Find Denver a Barren Spot," *Rocky Mountain News*, April 15, 1913.

29. "A Letter from the Denver Battle," *Industrial Worker*, May 1, 1913.

30. E. Nolan, "From San Francisco to Denver," *Industrial Worker*, April 24, 1913, reprinted in Foner, *Fellow Workers and Friends*, 149–152.

31. "IWWs on Bread and Water Diet," *Denver Post*, April 27. 1913; Ingler and Perry, "Denver Free Speech Fight," 155.

32. "Denver Free Speech Fight Is Won," *Industrial Worker*, May 8, 1913.

33. On "spaces *for* representation," see Mitchell, "End of Public Space?"

34. *Industrial Worker*, June 12, 1913.

35. Harvey, "Labor, Capital, and Class Struggle," 9, 10.

36. Marx, *Capital*, 1:168.

37. The best theorization of the role of capital circulation in establishing the conditions for regional development remains chap. 2 of George Henderson's *California and the Fictions of Capital*.

38. Harvey, "Labor, Capital, and Class Struggle," 34.

39. Lefebvre, *Production of Space*, 55.

40. Even so, we will return to it in the interlude and in chapter 7 because it does provide some essential theoretical insights.

41. See White and Limerick, *Frontier in American Culture*; Limerick, *Legacy of Conquest*; Cronon, *Nature's Metropolis*.

42. Page, "Charting the Middle Ground", 89, 90, 93. Besides Cronon's *Nature's Metropolis*, Page's targets include Robbins, *Colony and Empire*; Worster, *Rivers of Empire*.

43. The now classic accounts are Herod, "Production of Scale"; Herod, "Labor's Spatial Praxis"; Smith, "Homeless/Global," and Marston, "Social Construction of Scale," as well as the debate it spawned. By contrast, the later evolution of scale theory into "flat ontology" that denies the possibility of scalar difference is simply impossible to square with reality. See Marston, Jones, and Woodward, "Human Geography without Scale."

44. Smith, "Homeless/Global," 101. See also Smith's afterword to the second edition of *Uneven Development* and "Contours of a Spatialized Politics."

45. Herod, "Production of Scale," 84, original emphasis; see also Crump and Merrett, "Scales of Struggle."

46. Smith, "Homeless/Global," 101.

47. See, esp., Smith, "Contours of a Spatialized Politics."

48. Cronon, *Nature's Metropolis*, 52, 309, 340.

49. This is a point that gets obscured in Cronon's account, in large part, I think, because he is anxious to dismiss the labor theory of value. For a fuller critique, see Mitchell, "Writing the Western."

50. This is, of course, a main theme of David Harvey's work. For a recent explication, see *Seventeen Contradictions*; on capital fixed in workers' bodies, see Henderson, *California and the Fictions of Capital*.

51. Monkkonen, "Introduction," 2.

52. Ibid., 6.

53. Peck, *Work-Place*, 232.

54. Mitchell, "Scales of Justice."

55. Quoted in Noel, *Denver's Larimer Street*, 1; see also Leonard and Noel, *Denver*.

56. Brundage, *Making of Western Labor Radicalism*, 11, citing Pred, "Industrialization, Initial Advantage." Though transportation and banking were the initial advantages, Denver rapidly diversified, developing vibrant manufacturing (especially of mining equipment) and smelting industries. See chap. 4 of Wyckoff, *Creating Colorado*.

57. Wyckoff, *Creating Colorado*, 110–111; Brundage, *Making of Western Labor Radicalism*, 14; on the role, and power, of the railroads in producing space and shaping economic and social life, see Richard White, *Railroaded*.

58. White, "Tenderfoot on Thunder Mountain," quoted in Lukas, *Big Trouble*, 214.

59. Brundage, *Making of Western Labor Radicalism*, 17.

60. As Cindi Katz has made clear it is *capital* that is the true vagabond, not workers, the unemployed, and the homeless. See her "Vagabond Capitalism."

61. Tank, "Mobility and Occupational Structure."

62. Brundage, *Making of Western Labor Radicalism*, 23.

63. For a discussion, see American Social History Project, *Who Built America?*, 1:539.

64. American Social History Project, *Who Built America?*, 2:160.

65. "IWW Must Educate Denver Police Department," *Industrial Worker*, March 13, 1913.

66. Nolan, "From San Francisco to Denver."

67. "Heads of Unions Here to Prevent War on D. & R. G.," *Rocky Mountain News*, April 4, 1913.

68. Ibid.

69. "Combat I.W.W. Plan of Strike," *Rocky Mountain News*, April 5, 1913.

70. "Union Leaders Restoring Peace," *Rocky Mountain News*, April 6, 1913.

71. *Denver Democrat*, April 19, 1913.

72. "To the Rescue of Labor," *Rocky Mountain News*, April 26, 1913; "Syndicalism and Sabotage," *Rocky Mountain News*, April 28, 1913.

73. "Syndicalism and Sabotage."

74. Ibid.

75. For an incisive examination of the former—public space as the public sphere—see Said, *Culture and Imperialism*, chap. 4.

76. Ashleigh, "Floater," 81.

77. "Denver Starts Organization Work in Earnest," *Industrial Worker*, June 12, 1913.

78. Cronon, *Nature's Metropolis*, xviii.

79. Richard Brazier, interviewed by Archie Green, quoted in Kornblugh, *Rebel Voices*, 71.

80. Wyckoff, *Creating Colorado*.

81. Andrews, *Killing for Coal*.

CHAPTER 3. POWER ABHORS A TENT

1. Katz, "Vagabond Capitalism."

2. Hedges and Sacco, "City of Ruins."

3. Ibid., 17.

4. Ibid., 17.

5. A good, critical literature on homeless tent cities is at last beginning to develop. See, among others, Herring, "New Logics of Homeless Seclusion"; Herring and Lutz, "Roots

and Implications"; Sparks, "Neutralizing Homelessness"; Speer, "Right to Infrastructure"; Speer, "It's Not Like Your Home."

6. Hedges and Sacco, "City of Ruins," 17.

7. Ellickson, "Controlling Chronic Misconduct in City Spaces."

8. Duncan, "Men without Property."

9. Hopper, *Reckoning with Homelessness*.

10. Waldron, "Homelessness and the Issue of Freedom"; Kawash, "Homeless Body," 319–339. For a critique of Waldron's argument—especially the liberal acceptance of the primacy of private property at its heart—see Blomley, "Homelessness, Rights, and the Delusions."

11. Cresswell, *Tramp in America*, 41.

12. Kusmer, *Down and Out*; Hopper, *Reckoning with Homelessness*; DePastino, *Citizen Hobo*.

13. Anderson, *Hobo*, 17; quoted in Cresswell, *Tramp in America*, 43; see also DePastino, *Citizen Hobo*.

14. On the multiracial world of tramping more generally, see Higbie, *Indispensable Outcasts*, 107–116.

15. Mitchell, *Lie of the Land*; Monkkonen, *Walking to Work*. For a fairly recent appraisal of the range of contemporary discourses on homeless people and how they fit together, see Gowan, *Hobos, Hustlers, and Backsliders*.

16. Quoted in Woirol, "Observing the IWW in California."

17. Mitchell, *Lie of the Land*.

18. McMurray, "Industrial Armies and the Commonweal"; McWilliams, *Factories in the Field*; Schwantes, *Coxey's Army*; Dixon and Allen, *Bonus Army*.

19. "Troops Called Out to Halt Hobo Army," *New York Times*, March 8, 1914; "Streams of Water Rout 1,500 Hobos," *New York Times*, March 10, 1914.

20. McWilliams, *Factories in the Field*; Mitchell, *Lie of the Land*; Daniel, *Bitter Harvest*.

21. Dixon and Allen, *Bonus Army*. On Blair Mountain, see Shogan, *Battle of Blair Mountain*. On the script underlying the clearing out of homeless encampments and its deployment against Occupy, see the 2014 postscript to Don Mitchell, *Right to the City*.

22. Gregory, *American Exodus*; Starr, *Endangered Dreams*; Stein, *California*.

23. Galarza, *Farm Workers and Agri-Business*; Mitchell, *They Saved the Crops*.

24. Dear and Wolch, *Landscapes of Despair*; Wolch and Dear, *Malign Neglect*; Hopper, *Reckoning with Homelessness*.

25. For a graphic sense of the dislocations deindustrialization wrought, see Maharidge and Williamson, *Journey to Nowhere*.

26. Rowe and Wolch, "Social Networks," 200.

27. Ehrenreich, "Tales of Tent City."

28. See the Dome Village website, http://domevillage.tedhayes.us.

29. Gragg, "Guerilla City."

30. Quoted in Michal Dear and Jennifer Wolch, "Herding the Homeless Is an Unjust Answer," *Los Angeles Times*, November 14, 1994; see Takahashi, *Homelessness, AIDS, and Stigmatization*, 113.

31. Quoted in Takahashi, *Homelessness, AIDS, and Stigmatization*, 114.

32. Ibid., 114.

33. Ehrenreich, "Tales of Tent City."

34. Ibid.

35. Ibid.; see also Vollmann, "Homeless in Sacramento."

36. Marcuse, "Neutralizing Homelessness"; Harvey, *Enigma of Capital.*

37. Engels, *Housing Question.*

38. Quoted in Oliver Burkeman, "United States: Out in the Open. Recession Exposes America's Homeless Underclass," *Guardian,* March 27, 2009.

39. Ben Adler, "Sacramento's Tent Cities Still Bloom in Secret," National Public Radio, July 26, 2009; Richard Gonzalez, "Sacramento's Tent City Reflects Economy's Troubles," National Public Radio, March 16, 2009.

40. Richard Gonzalez, "In Sacramento, Hundreds of Tent Dwellers Want to Stay," National Public Radio, March 27, 2009; J. McKinley, "Homeless in Sacramento Tent City Will Be Moved to State Fairground," *New York Times,* March 26, 2009.

41. Richard Gonzalez, "Hundreds of Calif. Homeless March for Land Rights," National Public Radio, July 2, 2009.

42. Quoted in Gonzalez, "Hundreds of Calif. Homeless."

43. Quotations in Adler, "Sacramento's Tent Cities." The continuing struggles of homeless people to secure their encampments in Sacramento are detailed in Watters, "Homelessness in Sacramento," and recapitulated in Speer, "Right to Infrastructure," 1058.

44. See *Pottinger v. City of Miami,* 810 F. Supp. 1551, S.D. Fla. (1994); Simon, "Towns without Pity."

45. For analyses of contemporary struggles over officially sanctioned tent cities as safe spaces, see the citations in note 5.

46. "Local Leaders Address Homelessness," in *Tell Me More,* National Public Radio, August 17, 2009.

47. Marcuse, "Neutralizing Homelessness."

48. Speer, "Right to Infrastructure."

49. Ibid., 1063, 1061, 1064.

50. Ibid., 1061.

51. The following account has been pieced together from more than fifty news reports published between the end of 2006 and mid-2010, mostly from the *St. Petersburg Times.*

52. St. Petersburg's homeless population was estimated to be about 2,250 in early 2007; city shelters provided space for 250 people on an emergency basis, and there were 500 transitional housing slots.

53. Alisa Ulferts, "Neighbors Protest, Urge End to Tent Cities," *St. Petersburg Times,* February 4, 2007.

54. Cristina Silva, "Will Hope Fade or Stay," *St. Petersburg Times,* January 15, 2008.

55. Cristina Silva, "Tent City: Only One Thing's for Sure," *St. Petersburg Times,* May 1, 2008.

56. Cristina Silva, "Protest Gets a Cool Reception," *St. Petersburg Times,* January 21, 2008.

57. See the Pinellas Hope website, http://pinellashope.org/.

58. Adam Nagourney, "California's Deluge of Rain Washes Away a Homeless Colony," *New York Times,* April 21, 2017. The story notes that homeless people have lived along the

rivers in Sacramento since the Depression (it was actually earlier), and quotes homeless residents who have lived in the encampments for eight or ten years, but makes no reference to the earlier attention focused on Sacramento by Oprah's visit in 2008.

59. For an early statement and still helpful analysis, see Wright, *Out of Place*.

60. Pinellas Hope website, http://pinellashope.org/.

CHAPTER 4. THE CRIMINALIZATION OF SURVIVAL

1. National Alliance to End Homelessness, *State of Homelessness in America*, 9. This report is quite deceptive since it relies exclusively on state-level data, which inevitably leads to minimizing the scope of the problem at the urban level. The best proof of this assertion is in the report itself, since it contains data for Washington, D.C., America's only city-state. The national rate of official point-in-time homelessness in 2016 was 17.5 persons per 100,000, but in D.C. it was 110.8. If D.C. were amalgamated with Maryland (14.0) and Virginia (8.4), then the rate would appear considerably lower. This sheds light on New York State's official rate of homelessness (44.7), which is well above the national level but likely well below the rate in New York City. Similarly, California's (29.8), Oregon's (33.3), and Colorado's (18.6) rates all underplay just how urban a phenomenon homelessness is. Methodologically, these numbers are problematic as well, since point-in-time counts are usually limited in coverage (they are not spatially uniform across cities, much less whole states—there are no counts in most towns—and yet the baseline population is the state population as a whole). When the National Alliance to End Homelessness writes (10) that "point-in-time counts result in the most reliable estimate of people experiencing homelessness in the United States from which progress can be measured," we should add, "on a particular night in midwinter (counts are conducted in the last week of January), and not when arrayed at the scale of the state." That the picture painted by the National Alliance to End Homelessness obscures more than it reveals is amply shown in the city-level analysis in the United States Conference of Mayors, *The U.S. Conference of Mayors' Report on Hunger and Homelessness: A Status Report on Homelessness and Hunger in America's Cities, December 2016*, https://endhomelessness.atavist.com/mayorsreport2016.

2. Eric Holder, "Foreword," in National Law Center on Homelessness and Poverty, *Housing Not Handcuffs*, 7.

3. Ibid., 18–19; see also NLCHP, "Homelessness in America: Overview of Data and Causes," www.nlchp.org/documents/Homeless_Stats_Fact_Sheet.

4. See www.worldhunger.org/hunger-in-america-2016-united-states-hunger-poverty-facts/. The World Hunger Education Service updates these figures regularly; see www.worldhunger.org/hunger-news/united-states/.

5. Retrieved in 2008 from www.centeronhunger.org/pdf/Oct2005Bulletin.pdf.

6. Retrieved in 2008 from http://news.bbc.ci.uk/2/hi/americas/7106726.stm.

7. P. Rucker, "Cupboards Are Bare at Food Banks: Drops in Donations and Farm Surplus Cause Charities to Run Short," *Washington Post*, December 8, 2007, A1, http://nyccah.org/files/Queensfinal2007.doc.

8. The best work on the shifting geography of service provision remains the foundational work of Michael Dear and Jennifer Wolch and the Los Angeles

Homelessness Project. Dear and Wolch, *Landscapes of Despair*; Wolch and Dear, *Malign Neglect*.

9. The by-now classic language of "roll back" and "roll out" neoliberalism is from Peck and Tickell, "Neoliberalizing Space."

10. For just three examinations of these dynamics, see Staeheli and Mitchell, *People's Property?*, esp. chap. 3; Wells, "Policyfailing"; Lyon-Callo, "Making Sense of NIMBY." This last article reveals how NIMBYism often operates under quite progressive pretexts and is important for that reason.

11. Again, the foundational work of the Los Angeles Homelessness Project is always worth returning to. See Rowe and Wolch, "Social Networks in Space and Time"; Rahimian, Wolch, and Koegel, "Model of Homeless Migration"; Wolch and Rowe, "On the Street"; Wolch, Rahimian, and Koegel, "Daily and Periodic Mobility Patterns."

12. See Food Not Bomb's Facebook page, www.facebook.com/FoodNotBombsGlobal/; and the Right to the City website, http://righttothecity.org/.

13. Duncan, "Men without Property."

14. Quoted in K. Giles, "A Back Alley Approach to Fighting Crime in Minneapolis: The City Council Is Reviewing a Proposal to Keep Strangers Out of Its 455 Miles of Back Alleys," *Minneapolis Star Tribune*, May 31, 2006, 1A.

15. Ferrell, *Empire of Scrounge*.

16. See, e.g., "How to Keep People from Using Your Business's Dumpster," Dumpsters. com, www.dumpsters.com/articles/how-to-prevent-illegal-dumping; "Restaurant Waste Management," Katom Restaurant Supply, www.katom.com/learning-center/restaurant -dumpster-dangers.html; Pednault, *Preventing and Detecting Employee Theft and Embezzlement*.

17. The literature on CCTV is vast, and grew almost as fast as the use of cameras themselves in the 1990s. For two key accounts, see Norris, Moran, and Armstrong, *Surveillance*; Norris and Armstrong, *Maximum Surveillance Society*.

18. For the Vancouver example, in which it is utterly clear that homeless people were being targeted by the proposed law, see C. Pablo, "Dumpster Issue Divides City," *Straight. com*, March 1, 2007.

19. Koskela, "Webcams, TV Shows"; Koskela, "Other Side of Surveillance."

20. C. Savage, "U.S. Doles Out Millions for Street Cameras: Local Efforts Raise Privacy Alarms," *Boston Globe*, August 12, 2007.

21. Sloboggin, "Public Privacy." The issue of the "right to be left alone" is taken up more fully in part 2.

22. All definitions are from the *Shorter Oxford English Dictionary*.

23. J. Gosner, "Suit Challenges Trespass Law," *Honolulu Advertiser*, September 8, 2004. All the information in this paragraph is from that article.

24. For an outstanding and important analysis of such laws and policies, based on a deep, careful case study of banishment practices in Seattle, see Beckett and Herbert, *Banished*.

25. B. Begin, "Newsome Announces Plan to Increase Federal Housing Foot Patrols: Goal to Rid Area of Trespassing Loiterers," *FogCityJournal.com*, May 6, 2007.

26. Beckett and Herbert, *Banished*; K. Mitchell, "Trespass Law Targets the Homeless,"

Seattle Post-Intelligencer, June 27, 2007; C. McNerthney, "Solutions Sought at Crime-Plagued Steinbrueck Park," *Seattle Post-Intelligencer*, June 13, 2007.

27. E. Forbes, "Legislative Analyst Report: San Francisco's 'Quality of Life' Laws and Seattle's 'Civility Laws'" (File No. 011704), https://sfbos.org/legislative-analyst-report-san-franciscos-quality-life-laws-and-seattles-civility-laws-file-no.

28. Retrieved in 2008 from www.nom-tlcbd.org/id74.html. While this sign was easily available in 2008, by a decade later it no longer featured on the North of Market-Tenderloin CBD website. Such signs are still visible on business doors, however.

29. National Coalition for the Homeless, *Illegal to Be Homeless: 2004 Report* (Washington, D.C.: NCH, 2004); NLCHP, *Housing Not Handcuffs*, 31.

30. See http://homelessnation.org/en/node/5834.

31. NLCHP, *Housing Not Handcuffs*, 31–32.

32. Retrieved in 2008 from www.indybay.org.newsitems/2007/03/29/18385669.php.

33. Quotations from D. Schwartz, "'Soup Kitchens' Targeted," *Las Vegas Review-Journal*, July 13, 2006, 8B and Schwartz, "Feeding Homeless Outlawed," *Las Vegas Review-Journal*, July 20, 2006, 11A.

34. D. Schwartz, "Law Used to Thwart Homeless Helpers Targeted," *Las Vegas Review-Journal*, March 21, 2006, 1B.

35. Quotations from D. Schwartz, "Mayor Plans to Clear Homeless Out of City Parks," *Las Vegas Review-Journal*, June 22, 2006, 1B; and Schwartz, "Team Starts Parks Sweep," *Las Vegas Review-Journal*, July 11, 2006, 1B.

36. D. Schwartz, "Ordinance Does Not Deter Volunteers," *Las Vegas Review-Journal*, July 28, 2006, 5B; and Schwartz, "Media Cited for Feeding Homeless," *Las Vegas Review-Journal*, August 1, 2006, 1A

37. Schwartz, "Ordinance Does Not Deter Volunteers."

38. K. Ritter, "Las Vegas Marshals Ticket 7, Arrest 3 Amid Homeless Protests," Associated Press State and Local Wire, July 31, 2006; Schwartz, "Media Cited for Feeding Homeless."

39. L. Curtis, "Fed Up with Protests," *Las Vegas Review-Journal*, August 11, 1B.

40. Much to the chagrin of the *Las Vegas Review-Journal*: see Editorial, "Feeding the Homeless in Parks," August 27, 2007.

41. National Law Center on Homelessness and Poverty, *Feeding Intolerance*.

42. NLCHP, *Housing Not Handcuffs*.

43. C. Crass, "San Francisco Urban Politics and Food Not Bombs," *Practical Anarchy Online* (2000), www.practicalanarchyonline.org; Ziman, "Criminalizing the Charitable"; S. Schwartz, "S.F. Police, ADL Sued Again Over Political Spying Charges," *San Francisco Chronicle*, January 25, 1994; Ehrenreich, "Eye for Anarchy."

44. Both quotations from *East Bay Food Not Bombs*, pamphlet, no publisher. On People's Park, see Mitchell, *Right to the City*; and Mitchell, "People's Park Again."

45. Mitchell, "End of Public Space?"; Mitchell, *Right to the City*.

46. The first quotation is from J. Franklin, "Two Churches Back Group Feeding the Poor in Copley Square," *Boston Globe*, May 4, 1993, 24: the remaining quotations are from Editorial, "Feeding People in the Parks," *Boston Globe*, April 10, 1993, 10.

47. Zinn, "Introduction," ix–x.

48. Iveson, *Publics and the City*.

INTERLUDE

1. Outside in America Team, "Bussed Out."
2. Ibid.
3. Ibid.
4. Ibid.
5. Smith, *New Urban Frontier*.
6. Harvey, *Enigma of Capital* and *Seventeen Contradictions*.
7. Harvey, *Seventeen Contradictions*.
8. See Camp and Heatherton, *Policing the Planet*.
9. Smith, *Uneven Development*; see also the afterword to Harvey, *Limits to Capital*. It is just these processes that Naomi Klein describes in *The Shock Doctrine*.
10. Smith, "Toward a Theory of Gentrification"; and "Gentrification and Uneven Development."
11. Gilmore, "Forgotten Places."
12. See Pendras, "Confronting Capital Mobility."
13. Marcuse, "Neutralizing Homelessness."
14. Lefebvre, *Production of Space*.
15. Ibid., 285.
16. Ibid., 307.
17. Ibid., 357.
18. Ibid., 55.
19. See esp. Blomley, *Rights of Passage*.
20. Mitchell and Staeheli, "Turning Social Relations into Space"; Staeheli and Mitchell, *People's Property?*
21. Lefebvre, *Survival of Capitalism*.

CHAPTER 5. THE SUV MODEL OF CITIZENSHIP

1. Marx, *Capital*, 1:317.
2. Reisman, Glazer, and Denney, *Lonely Crowd*; Attoh, "Public Transportation and the Idiocy." Attoh here develops Marx's argument about the idiocy of rural life for contemporary urban conditions by following Draper's argument that "idiocy" means "privatized isolation." Draper, *Adventures in the Communist Manifesto*.
3. Marx, *Grundrisse*, 163–164.
4. Williams, *Country and the City*.
5. Colo. Rev. Stat. § 18-9-122 (2, 3) (1999); *Hill v. Colorado*, 530 U.S. 703 (2000).
6. Chen, "Statutory Speech Bubbles."
7. Ibid., 33, original emphasis.
8. *Hill v. Colorado*, 725.
9. Ibid., 724; the court's language is a direct echo, as we will see, of a 1921 decision regulating labor pickets. *American Steel Foundries v. Tri-City Labor Council*, 257 U.S. 184 (1921); see Mitchell, "Political Violence."
10. *Hill v. Colorado*, Scalia dissent; see also Chen, "Statutory Speech Bubbles."
11. *Hill v. Colorado*, Kennedy dissent, 773.
12. Ibid., Scalia dissent, 748–754, Kennedy dissent, 771–772; Lee, "Unwilling Listener";

Maffett, "Balancing Freedom of Speech"; Nauman, "Captive Audience Doctrine"; Zylch, "*Hill v. Colorado.*"

13. See *Cohen v. California*, 403 U.S. 15 (1971); *Erznoznik v. City of Jacksonville*, 422 U.S. 205 (1975).

14. *F.C.C. v. Pacifica Foundation*, 438 U.S. 726 (1978); *Frisby v. Schultz*, 487 U.S. 474 (1988).

15. *Frisby*, 487, 485.

16. Nauman, "Captive Audience Doctrine," 807.

17. *Hill*, 718, quoting *Rowan v. Post Office Department*, 397 U.S. 728 (1970).

18. *Hill*, 718.

19. Ibid., 750.

20. Ibid., 741; *Madsen v. Women's Health Center*, 512 U.S. 753, Scalia dissenting in part.

21. *Hill*, 723.

22. *Madsen*, 774, original emphasis.

23. *Schenck v. Pro-Choice Networks of W. New York*, 519 U.S. 357 (1997), 377.

24. Ibid., 383, quoting *Boos v. Barry*, 485 U.S. 312 (1988), 322.

25. *Hill*, 727.

26. Colo. Rev. Stat., §18–9–122(3), emphasis added.

27. *Hill*, 727.

28. Lee, "Unwilling Listener," 394; M. Soraghan, "DeGette Celebrates Decision," *Denver Post*, June 29, 2000, A9.

29. *Hill*, 727.

30. Ibid., 730–731.

31. Nauman, "Captive Audience Doctrine," 806, 809.

32. Ibid., 811.

33. Ibid., 813, 819.

34. *American Steel Foundries*, 204, quoted in *Hill*, 717.

35. The literature on these issues is vast. For just a couple, specifically geographic, entry points, see Iveson, *Publics and the City*, and Staeheli and Mitchell, *People's Property?*

36. Young, *Justice and the Politics of Difference*, 240.

37. For a review, see Mitchell, "People's Park Again."

38. Crilley, "Megastructures and Urban Change," 153.

39. Smith, *New Urban Frontier*.

40. The best discussion in geography remains Blomley, *Unsettling the City.*

41. Staeheli and Mitchell, *People's Property?* See also Maniscalo, *Public Spaces, Marketplaces.*

42. An excellent discussion of rights in relation to geography is Attoh, "What Kind of Right?"

43. Waldron, *Right to Private Property*, 39.

44. Ibid., 41.

45. Ibid., 41.

46. *Hague v. CIO*, 307 U.S. 496 (1939), 515.

47. The language of property regimes comes from Blomley, *Unsettling the City*; see also Staeheli and Mitchell, *People's Property?*

48. Waldron, *Liberal Rights*, 310–311.

49. Waldron, *Right to Private Property*, 42.

50. Isen, *Being Political*.

51. Ryan, "Libertarianism," 401.

52. This view's most prominent propagandist is de Soto, *Mystery of Capital*.

53. Ryan, "Libertarianism," 401.

54. Waldron, *Liberal Rights*.

55. See, for example, Holton, "Multicultural Citizenship."

56. B. Cox, "Panhandling Law Passed in Evanston: City Hopes to Curb 'Aggressive' Begging," *Chicago Tribune*, January 23, 2001, 2.

57. Sennett, *Flesh and Stone*, 310.

58. Blomley, *Rights of Passage*.

59. This was stressed on CCI's now defunct website.

60. For more on the zoning of protest, see Staeheli and Mitchell, *People's Property?*, esp. chap. 1, and Mitchell, "Liberalization of Free Speech."

61. Marx, *Capital*, 1:96.

62. Williams, *Keywords*, 161, 163.

63. Waldron, *Right to Private Property*, 398.

CHAPTER 6. JUDICIAL ANTI-URBANISM

1. Except where otherwise cited, all details in the discussion that follows are drawn from *Hicks v. Commonwealth*, 36 Va. App 48 (2002), 51; *Virginia v. Hicks*, 123 S. Ct. 2191 (2003), 2195; see also Post and Guinier, "Supreme Court, 2002 Term."

2. For an outstanding analysis of the use of trespass-barment procedures more generally to govern public space and its users, see Beckett and Herbert, *Banished*.

3. Brief of the Council of Large Public Housing Authorities, Housing and Development Law Institute, Housing Risk Retention Group, National Association of Housing and Redevelopment Officials, National Organization of African-Americans in Housing, and Public Authorities Directors Associations, 4–5. All briefs are available through LexisNexis and catalogued under U.S. 371 (2002).

4. By 2002 some 85 percent of PHAs had adopted a trespass-barment policy of some sort; see ibid., 7n3.

5. Brief of the City of Richmond and Richmond Redevelopment and Housing Authority, 8.

6. Ibid., 13.

7. Testimony of J. Laino, *Joint Appendix*, 55–59.

8. Statement of K. Hicks, *Joint Appendix*, 67–68.

9. Sentencing statement of Judge Nance, *Joint Appendix*, 68–72.

10. See Commonwealth of Virginia, Brief, 4.

11. Virginia Code §36–19.

12. Commonwealth of Virginia, Brief, 9.

13. Ibid., 1.

14. United States, Brief, 1.

15. Commonwealth of Virginia, Brief, 15.

16. Council of Large Public Housing Authorities, Brief, 5.

17. Ibid., 4.

18. *Virginia v. Hicks*, 2196n2.

19. Respondent, Brief, 3.

20. *Virginia v. Hicks*, 2196.

21. Richmond Tenants Organization, Brief, 3.

22. See Blomley, "'Acts,' 'Deeds,' and the Violences"; Blomley, *Unsettling the City*; MacPherson, *Property*; Staeheli and Mitchell, *People's Property?*

23. The sharpest legal argument from a rights skeptic remains Tushnet, "Essay on Rights."

24. City of Richmond, Brief, 3.

25. *HUD v. Rucker*, 535 U.S. 125 (2002), cited in City of Richmond and RRHA, Brief, 17.

26. States Brief, 12.

27. On Guantanamo, see *Hamdi v. Rumsfeld*, 524 U.S. 507 (2004).

28. ACLU, Brief, 5.

29. Ibid., 7n5.

30. Ibid., 7.

31. *Commonwealth v. Green* (Cir. Ct Richmond) No. 00m-2225 (2000), quoted at length in ACLU, Brief, 7n5.

32. *Chicago v. Morales*, 527 U.S. 41 (1999).

33. ACLU, Brief, 19, quoting *Hague v. CIO*, 307 U.S. 496 (1939). The key cases examining the ability of people to be on the streets and sidewalks, which always managed to be decided on other grounds (like vagueness), are *Kolender v. Lawson*, 461 U.S. 171 (1983) and *Papachristou v. City of Jacksonville*, 405 U.S. 156 (1972).

34. *Joint Appendix*, 13.

35. Ibid., 44.

36. *Hicks v. Commonwealth*, 33 Va. App. 561 (2000).

37. Motion to Dismiss (1999), in *Joint Appendix*, 4–7.

38. *Hicks v. Commonwealth* (2000), in *Joint Appendix*, 111.

39. Ibid.

40. Ibid.

41. *Hicks v. Commonwealth*, 36 Va. App. 48 (2002).

42. *Hague v. CIO*, 515–516, emphasis added.

43. *United States v. Grace*, 461 U.S. 171 (1983).

44. *Hicks v. Commonwealth* (2002), in *Joint Appendix*, 131.

45. *Hicks v. Commonwealth* (2002), in *Joint Appendix*, 134.

46. Ibid., 136.

47. *Broadwick v. Oklahoma*, 413 U.S. 601 (1973), 610.

48. *Gooding v. Wilson*, 405 U.S. 518 (1975), 530–521.

49. *Virginia v. Hicks*, 2197.

50. Ibid., 2197–2198.

51. Ibid., 2198, original emphasis.

52. Ibid., 2198.

53. Editorial, *New York Times*, June 17, 2003.

54. Cf. Low, *Behind the Gates*.

55. Post and Guinier, "Supreme Court, 2002 Term"

56. "Civic Innovation: Padres Writing Rules for Public/Private Park," *San Diego Union-Tribune*, January 11, 2004, G-2.

CHAPTER 7. DOING ANTISOCIAL THINGS

1. Forsythe is quoted in K. Giles, "A Back Alley Approach to Fighting Crime in Minneapolis: The City Council Is Reviewing a Proposal to Keep Strangers Out of Its 455 Miles of Back Alleys," *Minneapolis Star Tribune*, May 31, 2006, A1. See also Staeheli and Mitchell, "Don't Talk with Strangers."

2. Giles, "Back Alley Approach"; N. Coleman, "Let's Get Real: Alleys, Strangers Aren't a Problem," *Minneapolis Star-Tribune*, June 2, 2006.

3. See the City Council Staff Report, www.ci.minneapolis.mn.us/council/2006 -meetings/200660901/Docs/Alley-Q-and-As.pdf.

4. Ibid. See also Loukaitou-Sideris and Ehrenfreucht, *Sidewalks* and Rannila and Mitchell, "Syracuse, Sidewalks, and Snow."

5. City Council Staff Report.

6. T. Collins, "City Considered Closing Alleys to Outsiders: Minneapolis Could Be the First Big U.S. City to Restrict Pedestrian Traffic in All Its Alleys," *Minneapolis Star-Tribune*, September 1, 2006, B1; Giles, "Back Alley Approach."

7. Quoted in Collins, "City Considered Closing Alleys"; see also T. Collins, "Minneapolis Alleys Remain Open to All: Before the 10–3 Vote, the City Council Debates Civil Liberties, Ridicule, and Fighting Crime," *Minneapolis Star-Tribune*, September 2, 2006, 2A.

8. Coleman, "Let's Get Real."

9. Muñiz, *Police, Power, and the Production of Racial Boundaries*. In general, see Camp and Heatherton, *Policing the Planet*.

10. Collins, "Minneapolis Alleys Remain Open to All."

11. "Arguments in Favor of Measure S," www.ci.berkeley.ca.us/Clerk/Elections /Election_2012_Ballot_Measure_Page.aspx.

12. "An Ordinance of the City of Berkeley Adopting a New Section 13.36.025 of the Berkeley Municipal Code to Prohibit Sitting on Sidewalks in Commercial Districts," www.ci.berkeley.ca.us/Clerk/Elections/Election_2012_Ballot_Measure_Page.aspx.

13. "Arguments in Favor."

14. "Rebuttal to Argument in Favor of Measure S," www.ci.berkeley.ca.us/Clerk /Elections/Election_2012_Ballot_Measure_Page.aspx.

15. For ballot documents, see http://ballotpedia.org/San_Francisco_City_and_ County,_California_ballot_measures#2016; see also Kevin Fagan, "Voters Opposing SF Tents, Backing Housing for Homeless," *San Francisco Chronicle*, November 8, 2016. The title of this article is misleading; voters voted not for any new funds for affordable housing or homelessness services, merely for the reclassification of General Fund allocations.

16. Thomas Fuller, "San Francisco's Homeless Crisis Test Mayoral Candidates' Liberal Ideals," *New York Times*, May 30, 2018.

17. Longstreth, "Washington and the Landscape of Fear."

18. See, e.g., Katz, "State Goes Home."

19. Longstreth, "Washington and the Landscape of Fear." I focus more on the weird

ways in which fear of terrorism has transmogrified into paranoia in the book chapter on which some of my arguments here are based: Mitchell, "Pretexts, Paranoia, and Public Space."

20. Bauman, *Liquid Fear*, 3. See also Atkinson and Blandy, *Domestic Fortress*.

21. I am adapting the notion of a (willing) surrender to authority from Clayton Rosati, who developed it in, among other places, "Image Factory" and "Spectacle and the Singularity."

22. For a prominent example that long predates the attacks of 9/11 but perfectly anticipates the authoritarian reaction as well as the increasingly punitive politics of homelessness in West Coast cities, see MacDonald, "San Francisco's Matrix Program."

23. Quoted in Bauman, *Liquid Fear*, 5.

24. Parenti, *Tropic of Chaos*.

25. Emphasis added.

26. See the perceptive comments about "real community" and its link to the rise of unions (and against the forces of dispossessing capital) by Williams in *Country and the City*, 104.

27. Beckett and Herbert, *Banished*.

AFTERWORD

1. Mitchell, "Relational Approach to Landscape."

2. Staeheli and Mitchell, *People's Property?*, chap. 3.

3. Mitchell, "History of Homelessness."

4. Mitchell, *Lie of the Land*.

5. This is one of the key messages of the important new book by Vitale, *End of Policing*.

6. Which is why I refer to it mostly as a "so-called crisis" in this book. Mitchell, "Homelessness, American Style."

7. Hall, "Great Moving Right Show."

8. See Guillem Fernàndez and Jones, *Mean Streets*.

9. Gilmore, *Golden Gulag*, 54.

BIBLIOGRAPHY

This bibliography features works that have been published in journals and magazines or as books or that are easily accessible and frequently cited. Most newspaper, government, and archival sources and reports, as well as most websites, appear solely in the notes.

American Social History Project. *Who Built America?* Vol. 1. New York: Pantheon, 1989.
———. *Who Built America?* Vol. 2. New York: Pantheon, 1992.
Anderson, Nels. *The Hobo: The Sociology of the Homeless Man.* Chicago: University of Chicago Press, 1923.
Andrews, Thomas G. *Killing for Coal: America's Deadliest Labor War.* Cambridge, Mass.: Harvard University Press, 2010.
Anonymous. "Recent Court Filing: Criminal Law—Eighth Amendment Prohibition on Cruel and Unusual Punishment—Department of Justice Submits Statement Interest Arguing That City Ordinances Prohibiting Camping and Sleeping Outdoors Violate the Eighth Amendment." *Harvard Law Review* 129 (2016): 1476–1483.
Ashleigh, Charles. "The Floater." *International Socialist Review* 15 (1914): 34–39. Reprinted in Kornblugh, *Rebel Voices*, 80–83.
Atkinson, Rowland, and Sarah Blandy. *Domestic Fortress: Fear and the New Home Front.* Manchester: Manchester University Press, 2017.
Attoh, Kafui. "Public Transportation and the Idiocy of Urban Life." *Urban Studies* 54 (2017): 196–213.
———. "What Kind of Right in the Right to the City?" *Progress in Human Geography* 35 (2011): 669–685.
Bahr, Howard. *Skid Row: An Introduction to Disaffiliation.* New York: Oxford University Press, 1973.
Bahr, Howard, and Theodore Caplow. *Old Men, Drunk and Sober.* New York: New York University Press.
Baum, Alice, and Donald Burnes. *A Nation in Denial: The Truth about Homelessness.* Boulder, Colo.: Westview, 1993.
Bauman, Zygmunt. *Legislators and Interpreters.* London: Polity, 1989.
———. *Liquid Fear.* Cambridge: Polity, 2006.
Beckett, Katherine, and Steve Herbert. *Banished: The New Social Contract in Urban America.* Oxford: Oxford University Press, 2010.

Beier, A. L. *Masterless Men: The Vagrancy Problem in England, 1560–1640*. New York: Methuen, 1986.

Bittner, Egon. "The Police on Skid Row: A Study in Peace Keeping." *American Sociological Review* 32 (1967): 699–715

Blackmar, Elizabeth. "Appropriating 'the Commons': The Tragedy of Property Rights Discourse." In *The Politics of Public Space*, edited by Setha Low and Neil Smith, 49–80. New York: Routledge, 2006.

Blomley, Nicholas. "'Acts,' 'Deeds,' and the Violences of Property." *Historical Geography* 28 (2000): 86–107.

———. "Civil Rights Meets Civil Engineering: Urban Public Space and Traffic Logic." *Canadian Journal of Law and Society* 22 (2007): 55–72.

———. "Homelessness, Rights, and the Delusions of Property." *Urban Geography* 20 (2009): 557–590.

———. "How to Turn a Beggar into a Bus Stop: Law, Traffic, and the 'Function of Place.'" *Urban Studies* 44 (2007): 1697–1712.

———. *Rights of Passage: Sidewalks and the Regulation of Public Flow*. New York: Routledge, 2011.

———. *Unsettling the City: Space, Property, and Urban Land*. New York: Routledge, 2004.

Brissenden, Paul. *The IWW: A Study of American Syndicalism*. New York: Russell and Russell, 1919.

Brundage, David. *The Making of Western Labor Radicalism: Denver's Organized Workers, 1878–1905*. Urbana: University of Illinois Press, 1992.

Camp, Jordan T. *Incarcerating the Crisis: Freedom Struggles and the Rise of the Neoliberal State*. Berkeley: University of California Press.

Camp, Jordan T., and Christine Heatherton. "Asset Stripping and Broken Window's Policing on LA's Skid Row: An Interview with Becky Dennison and Pete White." In Camp and Heatherton, *Policing the Planet*, 141–149.

———, eds. *Policing the Planet: Why the Policing Crisis Led to Black Lives Matter*. London: Verso, 2016.

Cayo Sexton, Patricia. "The Life of the Homeless." *Dissent* 30 (1986): 79–84.

Chen, Alan K. "Statutory Speech Bubbles, First Amendment Overbreadth, and Improper Legislative Purpose." *Harvard Civil Rights–Civil Liberties Law Review* 38 (2003): 31–90.

Christophers, Brett, Andrew Leyshon, and Geoff Mann. "Money and Finance after the Crisis: Taking Critical Stock." In *Money and Finance after the Crisis*, edited by B. Christophers, A. Leyshon, and G. Mann, 1–40. Oxford: Wiley-Blackwell, 2017.

Cloke, Paul, Jon May, and Sarah Johnsen. *Swept Up Lives? Re-envisioning the Homeless City*. Oxford: Wiley-Blackwell, 2010.

Creel, George. *Rebel at Large: Recollections of Fifty Crowded Years*. New York: Putnam and Sons, 1947.

Cresswell, Tim. "Embodiment, Power and the Politics of Mobility: The Case of Female Tramps and Hobos." *Transactions of the Institute of British Geographers* 24 (1999): 175–192.

———. *The Tramp in America*. London: Reaktion Books, 2001.

———. "The Vagrant/Vagabond: The Curious Career of a Mobile Subject." In *Geographies of Mobilities: Practices, Spaces, Subjects*, edited by Peter Merriman and Tim Cresswell, 239–255. Aldershot: Ashgate, 2012.

Crilley, Darrell. "Megastructures and Urban Change: Aesthetics, Ideology, and Design." In *The Restless Urban Landscape*, edited by P. Knox, 126–164. Englewood Cliffs, N.J.: Prentice Hall, 1993.

Cronon, William. *Nature's Metropolis: Chicago and the Great West*. New York. Norton, 1991.

Crouse, Joan. *The Homeless Transient during the Great Depression: New York State*. Albany: State University of New York Press, 1986.

Crump, Jeffrey, and Christopher Merrett. "Scales of Struggle: Economic Restructuring in the U.S. Midwest." *Annals of the Association of American Geographers* 88 (1998): 496–515.

Culhane, Dennis. "The Cost of Homelessness: A Perspective from the United States." *European Journal of Homelessness* 2 (2008): 97–114.

Culhane, Dennis P., Wayne D. Parker, Barbara Poppe, Kennen S. Gross, and Ezra Sykes. *Accountability, Cost-Effectiveness, and Program Performance: Progress since 1998*. Washington, D.C.: Department of Health and Human Services and U.S. Department of Housing and Urban Development, 2008.

Daniel, Cletus. *Bitter Harvest: A History of California Farmworkers, 1870–1941*. Ithaca, N.Y.: Cornell University Press, 1982.

Davis, Mike. *City of Quartz: Excavating the Future in Los Angeles*. London: Verso, 1990.

Dear, Michael, and Jennifer Wolch. *Landscapes of Despair*. Princeton, N.J.: Princeton University Press, 1987.

DePastino, Todd. *Citizen Hobo: How a Century of Homelessness Shaped America*. Chicago: University of Chicago Press, 2003.

de Soto, Hernando. *The Mystery of Capital: Why Capitalism Triumphs in the West and Fails Everywhere Else*. New York: Basic Books.

Dixon, Paul, and Thomas Allen. *The Bonus Army: An American Epic*. New York: Walker and Company, 2004.

Draper, Hal. *Adventures in the Communist Manifesto*. Alameda, Calif.: Center for Socialist History, 2004.

Dubofsky, Melvyn. *We Shall Be All: A History of the Industrial Workers of the World*. 2nd ed. Urbana: University of Illinois Press, 1988.

Duncan, James. "Men without Property: The Tramp's Classification and Use of Urban Space." *Antipode* 10, no. 1 (1978): 24–34.

Ehrenreich, Barbara. "An Eye for Anarchy." *LA Weekly*, June 7, 2002.

Ehrenreich, Ben. "Tales of Tent City." *Nation*, June 3, 2009.

Ellickson, Robert. "Controlling Chronic Misconduct in City Spaces: Of Panhandlers, Skid Rows, and Public Space Zoning." *Yale Law Journal* 105 (1996): 1165–1248.

Engels, Frederick. *The Housing Question*. 1872. New York: International Publishers, 1935.

Ferrell, Jeff. *Empire of Scrounge: Inside the Urban Underground of Dumpster Diving, Trashpicking, and Street Scavenging*. New York: New York University Press, 2005.

Fields, Gary. *Enclosure: Palestinian Landscapes in a Historical Mirror*. Berkeley: University of California Press, 2017.

Flusty, Steve. "The Banality of Interdiction: Surveillance, Control, and the Displacement of Diversity." *International Journal of Urban and Regional Research* 25 (2001): 658–664.

Foner, Philip. *Fellow Workers and Friends: Free Speech Fights as Told by Participants.* Westport, Conn.: Greenwood, 1981.

———. *The Industrial Workers of the World, 1905–1917.* Vol. 4 of *The History of the Labor Movement in the United States.* New York: International Publishers, 1965.

Foote, Caleb. "Vagrancy-Type Law and Its Administration." *Yale Law Review* 104 (1963): 603–650.

Foscarinis, Maria. "The Federal Response: The Stewart B. McKinney Homeless Assistance Act." In *Homelessness in America*, edited by J. Baumohl, 160–171. Phoenix: Oryx Press, 1996.

Galarza, Ernesto. *Farm Workers and Agri-Business in California, 1947–1960.* Notre Dame: Notre Dame University Press, 1977.

Gilmore, Ruth Wilson. "Forgotten Places and the Seeds of Grassroots Planning." In *Engaging Contradictions: Theory, Politics, and Method of Activist Scholarship*, edited by C. Hale, 31–61. Berkeley, Calif.: Global Area and International Archive, 2008.

———. *Golden Gulag: Prisons, Surplus, Crisis, and Opposition in Globalizing California.* Berkeley: University of California Press, 2007.

Gladwell, Malcolm. "Million-Dollar Murray: Why Problems Like Homelessness Might Be Easier to Solve Than Manage." *New Yorker*, February 13, 2016.

Gowan, Teresa. *Hobos, Hustlers, and Backsliders: Homeless in San Francisco.* Minneapolis: University of Minnesota Press, 2010.

Gragg, Randy. "Guerilla City: A Homeless Settlement in Portland Has Its Own Government, Urban Plan, and Skyline." *Architecture* 91 (2002): 47–51.

Graves, Florence, and Hadar Sayfan. "First Things First: 'Housing First,' a Radical New Approach to Ending Homelessness, Is Gaining Ground in Boston." *Boston Globe*, June 24, 2007.

Gregory, James. *American Exodus: The Dust Bowl Migration and Okie Culture in California.* New York: Oxford University Press, 1989.

Groth, Paul. *Living Downtown: The History of Residential Hotels in the United States.* Berkeley: University of California Press, 1994.

Guillem Fernàndez, Evangelista, and Samara Jones, eds. *Mean Streets: A Report on the Criminalization of Homelessness in Europe.* Brussels: FEANTSA, 2013.

Gumpert, Robert, and Rebecca Solnit. "Division Street." *Harper's*, October 2016, 42–53.

Hackworth, Jason. *The Neoliberal City: Governance, Ideology, and Development in American Urbanism.* Ithaca, N.Y.: Cornell University Press, 2007.

Hall, Stuart. "The Great Moving Right Show." *Marxism Today*, January 1979, 14–20.

Hamill, Pete. "How to Save the Homeless—and Ourselves." *New York* 26 (September 1993): 34–39.

Hansson, Erik, and Don Mitchell. "The Exceptional State of 'Roma Beggars' in Sweden." *European Journal of Homelessness* 12, no. 1 (2018): 15–40.

Harvey, David. *A Brief History of Neoliberalism.* Oxford: Oxford University Press, 2005.

———. *The Condition of Postmodernity.* Oxford: Blackwell, 1989.

———. *The Enigma of Capital and the Crises of Capitalism.* New York: Oxford University Press, 2014.

———. "Labor, Capital, and Class Struggle around the Built Environment in Advanced Capitalist Societies." In *Urbanization and Conflict in Advanced Market Societies*, edited by Kevin Cox, 9–37. Chicago: University of Chicago Press, 1978.

———. *The Limits to Capital*. Chicago: University of Chicago Press, 1982.

———. *Seventeen Contradictions and the End of Capitalism*. New York: Oxford University Press, 2014.

———. *The Urban Experience*. Baltimore: Johns Hopkins University Press, 1989.

Hedges, Chris, and Joe Sacco. "City of Ruins: Camden, New Jersey, Stands as a Warning of What Huge Pockets of American Could Turn Into." *Nation*, November 22, 2010, 15–20.

Henderson, George. *California and the Fictions of Capital*. New York: Oxford University Press, 1999.

Hennigan, Brian. "From Madonna to Marx: Towards a Re-theorization of Homelessness." *Antipode* 51 (2019): 148–168.

———. "House Broken: Homelessness, Housing First, and Neoliberal Poverty Governance." *Urban Geography* 38 (2017): 1418–1440.

Herod, Andrew. "Labor's Spatial Praxis and the Geography of Contract Bargaining in the U.S. East Coast Longshoring Industry, 1953–1989." *Political Geography* 16 (1997): 145–169.

———. "The Production of Scale in United States Labor Relations." *Area* 23 (1991): 82–88.

Herring, Christopher. "The New Logics of Homeless Seclusion: Homeless Encampments in America's West Coast Cities." *City & Community* 13 (2014): 285–309.

Herring, Christopher, and Manuel Lutz. "The Roots and Implications of the USA's Homeless Tent Cities." *City* 19 (2015): 689–701.

Higbie, Frank Tobias. *Indispensable Outcasts: Hobo Workers and Community in the American Midwest, 1880–1930*. Urbana: University of Illinois Press, 2003.

Holton, Gerald. "Multicultural Citizenship: The Politics and Poetics of Public Space." In *Democracy, Citizenship, and the Global City*, edited by E. Isen, 189–202. New York: Routledge, 2000.

Hopper, Kim. *Reckoning with Homelessness*. Ithaca, N.Y.: Cornell University Press, 2003.

Hopper, Kim, Esra Susser, and Sarah Conover. "Economies of Makeshift: Deindustrialization and Homelessness in New York City." *Urban Anthropology* 14 (1985): 183–286.

Igler, David. *Industrial Cowboys: Miller & Lux and the Transformation of the Far West, 1850–1920*. Berkeley: University of California Press.

Ingler, D., and J. Perry. "Denver Free Speech Fight, February 2nd to May 1st, 1913, Letters, etc. Addressed to Vincent St. John, Commission on Industrial Relations File, National Archives." In *Fellow Workers and Friends: Free Speech Fights as Told by Participants*, edited by Philip Foner, 152–156. Westport, Conn.: Greenwood, 1981.

Isen, Engin. *Being Political: Genealogies of Citizenship*. Minneapolis: University of Minnesota Press, 2002.

Iveson, Kurt. *Publics and the City*. Malden, Mass.: Wiley-Blackwell, 2007.

Jones, D. "The Strolling Poor: Transience in Eighteenth-Century Massachusetts." *Journal of Social History* 8 (1975): 28–54.

Katz, Cindi. "The State Goes Home: Local Hypervigilance of Children and the Global Retreat from Social Reproduction." In *Surveillance and Security: Technological Poli-*

tics and Power in Everyday Life, edited by T. Monahan, 27–36. New York: CRC Press, 2006.

———. "Vagabond Capitalism and the Necessity of Social Reproduction." *Antipode* 33 (2001): 709–728.

Kawash, Samira. "The Homeless Body." *Public Culture* 10 (1998): 319–339.

Kelley, Robin D. G. "Thug Nation." In Camp and Heatherton, *Policing the Planet*, 15–33.

Klein, Naomi. *The Shock Doctrine: The Rise of Disaster Capitalism*. Toronto: Random House, 2007.

Kornblugh, Joyce. *Rebel Voices: An I.W.W. Anthology*. Ann Arbor: University of Michigan Press, 1964.

Koskela, Hille. "The Other Side of Surveillance: Webcams, Power, and Agency." In *Theorizing Surveillance: The Panopticon and Beyond*, edited by D. Lyon. Cullompton, UK: Willan, 2006.

———. "Webcams, TV Shows and Mobile Phones: Empowering Exhibitionism." *Surveillance and Society* 2 (2004): 195–215.

Kusmer, Kenneth. *Down and Out, On the Road: The Homeless in American History*. New York: Oxford University Press, 2002.

———. "The Underclass in Historical Perspective: Tramps and Vagrants in Urban America, 1970–1930." In *On Being Homeless: Historical Perspectives*, edited by Rick Beard, 21–31. New York: Museum of the City of New York, 1987.

La Ganga, Maria. "In Sacramento's Tent City: A Torn Economic Fabric." *Los Angeles Times*, March 20, 2009.

Lamb, H. Richard. "Deinstitutionalization and the Homeless Mentally Ill." In *Housing the Homeless*, edited by Jon Erickson and Charles Wilhelm, 262–278. New Brunswick, N.J.: Center for Urban Policy Research, 1986.

Laska, Shirley, and Daphne Spain, eds. *Back to the City: Issues in Neighborhood Revitalization*. New York: Pergamon Press, 1989.

Lee, William. "The Unwilling Listener: *Hill v. Colorado*'s Chilling Effect on Unorthodox Speech." *U.C. Davis Law Review* 35 (2000): 387–426.

Lees, Loretta, Tom Slater, and Elvin Wyly. *Gentrification*. London: Routledge, 2007.

Lefebvre, Henri. *The Production of Space*. Translated by Donald Nicholson-Smith. Oxford: Blackwell, 1991.

———. *The Survival of Capitalism*. New York: St. Martin's, 1976.

Leonard, Steven, and Thomas Noel. *Denver: From Mining Camp to Metropolis*. Boulder: University Press of Colorado, 1990.

Liebman, Ellen. *California Farmland: A History of Large Agricultural Holdings*. Totowa, N.J.: Rowman & Littlefield, 1983.

Limerick, Patricia Nelson. *The Legacy of Conquest: The Unbroken Past of the American West*. New York: Norton, 1987.

Lippert, Randy, and Keven Walby, eds. *Policing Cities: Urban Securitization and Regulation in a Twenty-First Century World*. New York: Routledge, 2013.

Lipsitz, George. "Policing Place and Taxing Time on Skid Row." In Camp and Heatherton, *Policing the Planet*, 123–139.

Longstreth, Richard. "Washington and the Landscape of Fear." *City and Society* 18 (2006): 7–30.

Loukaitou-Sideris, Anastasia, and Renia Ehrenfreucht. *Sidewalks: Conflict and Negotiation over Public Space*. Cambridge, Mass.: MIT Press, 2009.

Low, Setha. *Behind the Gates: Life, Security, and the Pursuit of Happiness in Fortress America*. New York. Routledge, 2003.

Lukas, Anthony. *Big Trouble*. New York: Simon & Schuster, 1997.

Lyon-Callo, Vincent. "Making Sense of NIMBY: Poverty, Power and Community Opposition to Homeless Shelters." *City and Society* 13 (2001): 183–209.

MacDonald, Heather. "San Francisco's Matrix Program for the Homeless." *Criminal Justice Ethics* 14, no. 2 (1995): 2–80.

MacPherson, C. B. *Property: Mainstream and Critical Positions*. Toronto: University of Toronto Press, 1978.

Maffett, Jennifer. "Balancing Freedom of Speech Against the Rights of Unwilling Listeners: The Attack on the First Amendment in *Hill v. Colorado*." *Dayton Law Review* 26 (2001): 327–364.

Maharidge, Dale, and Michael Williamson. *The Journey to Nowhere: The Saga of the Underclass*. New York: Hyperion Books, 1996.

Maniscalo, Anthony. *Public Spaces, Marketplaces, and the Constitution: Shopping Malls and the First Amendment*. Albany: State University of New York Press, 2015.

Marcuse, Peter. "Neutralizing Homelessness." *Socialist Review* 18, no. 1 (1988): 69–97.

Marston, Sallie. "The Social Construction of Scale." *Progress in Human Geography* 24 (2000): 219–242.

Marston, Sallie, John Paul Jones III, and Keith Woodward. "Human Geography without Scale." *Transactions of the Institute of British Geographers* 30 (2005): 416–432.

Marx, Karl. *Capital*. Vol. 1. New York: International Publishers, 1967.

———. *Grundrisse*. London: Penguin, 1973.

McMurray, D. "The Industrial Armies and the Commonweal." *Mississippi Valley Historical Review* 10, no. 3 (1923): 215–252.

McWilliams, Carey. *Factories in the Field: The Story of Migratory Farm Labor in California*. Boston: Little, Brown, 1939.

Merrifield, Andy. *The Politics of the Encounter: Urban Theory and Protest under Planetary Urbanism*. Athens: University of Georgia Press, 2013.

Mitchell, Don. "Anti-homeless Laws and Public Space II: Further Constitutional Issues." *Urban Geography* 19 (1998): 98–104.

———. "Controlling Space, Controlling Scale: Migrant Labor, Free Speech, and Regional Development in the American West in the Early 20th Century." *Journal of Historical Geography* 28 (2002): 63–84.

———. "The End of Public Space? People's Park, Definitions of the Public, and Democracy." *Annals of the Association of American Geographers* 85 (1995): 108–133.

———. "From Boise to Budapest: Capital Circulation, Compound Capitalist Destruction, and the Persistence of Homelessness." In *Gentrification and Global Strategy: Neil Smith and Beyond*, edited by Abel Albet and Núria Benach, 99–111. London: Routledge, 2017.

———. "A History of Homelessness—A Geography of Control: The Production of Spaces of Marginality and Order in Johnstown, Pennsylvania." Master's thesis, Department of Geography, Pennsylvania State University, 1989.

———. "Homelessness, American Style." *Urban Geography* 32 (2011): 933–955.

———. "Land and Labor: Worker Resistance and the Production of Landscape in Agricultural California before World War II." Doctoral dissertation, Department of Geography, Rutgers University, 1992.

———. "The Liberalization of Free Speech: or, How Protest in Public Space Is Silenced." In *Spaces of Contention: Spatialities and Social Movements,* edited by W. Nichols, B. Miller, and J. Baumont, 47–68. Farnham, UK: Ashgate, 2013.

———. *The Lie of the Land: Migrant Workers and the California Landscape.* Minneapolis: University of Minnesota Press, 1996.

———. "People's Park Again: On the End and Ends of Public Space." *Environment and Planning A* 49 (2017): 503–518.

———. "Political Violence, Order, and the Legal Construction of Public Space: Power and the Public Forum Doctrine." *Urban Geography* 17 (1996): 158–178.

———. "Pretexts, Paranoia, and Public Space: Rethinking the Right to the City after 9/11." In *Urban Spaces: Planning and Struggles for Land and Community,* edited by James Jennings and Julia Hordan-Zachary, 19–37. Lanham, Md.: Lexington Books, 2010.

———. "Property Rights, the First Amendment, and Judicial Anti-urbanism: The Strange Case of *Hicks v. Virginia.*" *Urban Geography* 26 (2005): 565–586.

———. "A Relational Approach to Landscape and Urbanism: The View from an Exclusive Suburb." *Landscape Research* 42 (2017): 277–290.

———. *The Right to the City: Social Justice and the Fight for Public Space.* 2003. New York: Guilford, 2014.

———. "The Scales of Justice: Localist Ideology, Large Scale Production, and Agricultural Labor's Geography of Resistance in 1930s California." In *Organizing the Landscape: Geographical Perspectives on Labor Unionism,* edited by Andrew Herod, 159–194. Minneapolis: University of Minnesota Press, 1998.

———. "The S.U.V. Model of Citizenship: Floating Bubbles, Buffer Zones, and the Rise of 'Purely Atomic' Individual." *Political Geography* 25 (2005): 77–100.

———. *They Saved the Crops: Labor, Landscape, and the Struggle over Industrial Farming in Bracero-Era California.* Athens: University of Georgia Press, 2012.

———. "Work, Struggle, Death, and Geographies of Justice: The Transformation of Landscape in and beyond California's Imperial Valley." *Landscape Research* 32 (2007): 559–577.

———. "Writing the Western: New Western History's Encounter with Landscape." *Ecumene* 5 (1998): 7–29.

Mitchell, Don, Kafui Attoh, and Lynn Staeheli. "Whose City? What Politics? Contentious and Non-contentious Spaces on Colorado's Front Range." *Urban Studies* 52 (2015): 2633–2648.

Mitchell, Don, and Nik Heynen. "The Geography of Survival and the Right to the City: Speculations on Surveillance, Legal Innovation, and the Criminalization of Intervention." *Urban Geography* 30 (2009): 611–632.

Mitchell, Don, and Lynn Staeheli. "Turning Social Relations into Space: Property, Law, and the Plaza of Santa Fe, New Mexico." *Landscape Research* 30 (2005): 325–432.

Monkkonen, Eric. "Introduction." In Monkkonen, *Walking to Work,* 1–17.

———. *Police in Urban America.* Cambridge: Cambridge University Press, 2004.

———, ed. *Walking to Work: Tramps in America, 1790–1935*. Lincoln: University of Nebraska Press, 1984.

Morin, Monte, Gale Holland, and Sarah Parvini. "Skid Row Shooting: On Skid Row, Sweeping Changes Adds to Distrust." *Los Angeles Times*, March 3, 2015.

Muñiz, Ana. *Police, Power, and the Production of Racial Boundaries*. New Brunswick, N.J.: Rutgers University Press, 2015.

National Alliance to End Homelessness. *The State of Homelessness in America, 2016*. Washington, D.C.: National Alliance to End Homelessness, 2016.

National Law Center on Homelessness and Poverty. *Feeding Intolerance: Prohibitions on Sharing Food with People Experiencing Homelessness*. Washington, D.C.: NLCHP, November 2007.

———. *Housing Not Handcuffs: Ending the Criminalization of Homelessness in U.S. Cities*. Washington, D.C.: NLCHP, 2016.

———. *No Safe Place: The Criminalization of Homelessness in U.S. Cities*. Washington, D.C.: NLCHP, 2014. www.nlchp.org.

Nauman, Robert. "The Captive Audience Doctrine and Floating Bubbles: An Analysis of *Hill v. Colorado*." *Capital University Law Review* 30 (2002): 769–821.

Newman, Kathe, and Elvin Wyly. "The Right to Stay Put, Revisited: Gentrification and Resistance to Displacement in New York City." *Urban Geography* 43 (2006): 23–47.

Noel, Thomas J. *Denver's Larimer Street: Main Street, Skid Row, and Urban Renaissance*. Denver: Historic Denver, Inc., 1981.

Norris, Clive, and Gary Armstrong. *The Maximum Surveillance Society: The Rise of CCTV*. Oxford: Berg, 1999.

Norris, Clive, Jade Moran, and Gary Armstrong, eds. *Surveillance, Closed Circuit Television, and Social Control*. Burlington, Vt.: Ashgate, 1998.

Outside in America Team. "Bussed Out: How America Moves Its Homeless." *Guardian*, December 20, 2017. www.theguardian.com/us-news/ng-interactive/2017/dec/20/bussed-out-america.moves-homeless-people-country-study.

Page, Brian. "Charting the Middle Ground: History, Geography, and City-Hinterland Relations in the Great West." *Ecumene* 5 (1998): 81–104.

Paisner, Steven. "Compassion, Politics, and the Problem Lying on Our Sidewalks: A Legislative Approach for Cities to Address Homelessness." *Temple Law Review* 67 (1994): 1259–1305.

Parenti, Christian. *Tropic of Chaos: Climate Change and the New Geography of Violence*. New York: Nation Books, 2012.

Parker, Carleton. *The Casual Laborer and Other Essays*. New York: Harcourt, Brace, and Howe, 1919.

———. "The I.W.W." *Atlantic Monthly*, November 1917, 651–652.

Peck, Jamie. *Work-Place: The Social Regulation of Labor Markets*. New York: Guilford, 1996.

Peck, Jamie, and Adam Tickell. "Neoliberalizing Space." *Antipode* 34 (2002): 380–404.

Pednault, Steven. *Preventing and Detecting Employee Theft and Embezzlement: A Practical Guide*. London: John Wiley, 2010.

Pendras, Mark. "Confronting Capital Mobility." *Urban Geography* 31 (2010): 479–497.

Post, Robert C., and Lani Guinier. "The Supreme Court 2002 Term: Leading Cases: I. Constitutional Law: 3. Trespass Policies." *Harvard Law Review* 117 (2003): 359–369.

Pred, Allan. "Industrialization, Initial Advantage, and American Metropolitan Growth." *Geographical Review* 55 (1965): 158–185.

Presthold, K. "How We Solved It at Oklahoma City." *Nation*, October 7, 1931, 7.

Rahimian, A., J. Wolch, and P. Koegel. "A Model of Homeless Migration: Homeless Men in Skid Row, Los Angeles." *Environment and Planning A* 24 (1992): 1317–1336.

Rannila, Päivi, and Don Mitchell. "Syracuse, Sidewalks, and Snow: On the Slippery Realities of Public Space." *Urban Geography* 37 (2016): 1070–1090.

Reisman, David, Nathan Glazer, and Reuel Denney. *The Lonely Crowd*. New Haven, Conn.: Yale University Press, 2001.

Ribton-Turner, Charles. *A History of Vagrants and Vagrancy and Beggars and Begging*. London: Chapman Hall, 1887.

Robbins, William. *Colony and Empire: Transformation of the American West*. Lawrence: University Press of Kansas, 1994.

Rosati, Clayton. "The Image Factory: MTV, Geography, and the Industrial Production of Culture." Doctoral dissertation, Department of Geography, Syracuse University, 2005.

——. "Spectacle and the Singularity: Debord and the 'Autonomous Movement of Non-life' in Digital Capitalism." In *The Spectacle 2.0: Reading Debord in the Context of Digital Capitalism*, edited by M. Briziarelli and E. Armano, 95–117. London: University of Westminster Press, 2017.

Rothman, David. "The First Shelters: The Contemporary Relevance of the Almshouse." In *On Being Homeless: Historical Perspectives*, edited by Rick Beard, 10–19. New York: Museum of the City of New York, 1987.

Rowe, Stacey, and Jennifer Wolch. "Social Networks in Space and Time: Homeless Women in Skid Row, Los Angeles." *Annals of the Association of American Geographers* 80 (1990): 184–204.

Ryan, Alan. "Libertarianism." In *A Companion to American Thought*, edited by R. Wrightman Fox and J. Kloppenberg, 400–402. Oxford: Blackwell, 1995.

Said, Edward. *Culture and Imperialism*. New York: Vintage, 1993.

Schneider, John. "Skid Row as an Urban Neighborhood, 1880–1960." *Urbanism Past and Present* 9 (1984): 10–19.

——. "Tramping Workers: A Subcultural View." In Monkkonen, *Walking to Work*, 212–234.

Schwantes, Carlos. *Coxey's Army: An American Odyssey*. Lincoln: University of Nebraska Press, 1985.

Schweik, Susan. *The Ugly Laws: Disability in Perspective*. New York: New York University Press, 2009.

Sennett, Richard. *Flesh and Stone*. New York: Norton, 1994.

Sharlet, Jeff. "The Invisible Man: The End of a Black Life That Mattered." *GQ*, July 7, 2015. www.gq.com/story/skif-row-police-shooting-charly-keunang.

Shell, Jacob. *Transportation and Revolt: Pigeons, Mules, Canals, and the Vanishing Geographies of Subversive Mobility*. Cambridge: Cambridge University Press, 2015.

Shogan, Robert. *The Battle of Blair Mountain: The Story of America's Largest Labor Uprising*. New York: Basic Books, 2006.

Simon, Harry. "Towns without Pity: A Constitutional and Historical Analysis of Efforts to Drive Homeless People from American Cities." *Tulane Law Review* 66 (1992): 631–676.

Sjoblom, R. "Case Note: Enforcing the Public Forum Doctrine on Private Property: *First Unitarian Church of Salt Lake City v. Salt Lake City Corporation.*" *San Diego Law Review* 41 (2004): 447–448.

Sloboggin, Christopher. "Public Privacy: Camera Surveillance of Public Places and the Right to Anonymity." *Mississippi Law Journal* 72 (2002): 213–315.

Smith, Neil. "Contours of a Spatialized Politics: Homeless Vehicles and the Production of Geographical Scale." *Social Text* 33 (1992): 55–81.

———. "Gentrification and Uneven Development." *Economic Geography* 58 (1982): 139–155.

———. "Homeless/Global: Scaling Places." In *Mapping the Futures: Local Cultures, Global Change*, edited by J. Bird, B. Cutis, T. Putnam, G. Robertson, and L. Tickner, 87–119. London: Routledge, 1993.

———. *The New Urban Frontier: Gentrification and the Revanchist City.* New York: Routledge, 1996.

———. "Toward a Theory of Gentrification: A Back to the City Movement by Capital Not People." *Journal of the American Planning Association* 45 (1979): 538–548.

———. *Uneven Development: Nature, Capital, and the Production of Space.* 2nd ed. Oxford: Blackwell.

Snow, David, and Leon Anderson. *Down on Their Luck: A Study of Homeless Street People.* Berkeley: University of California Press, 1993.

Solenberger, Alice. *One Thousand Homeless Men: A Study of Original Records.* New York: Russell Sage Foundation, 1911.

Sparks, Tony. "Neutralizing Homelessness, 2015: Tent Cities and Ten Year Plans." *Urban Geography* 38 (2017): 348–356.

Speer, Jessie. "'It's Not Like Your Home': Homeless Encampments, Housing Projects, and the Struggle over Domestic Space." *Antipode* 49 (2017): 517–535.

———. "Losing Home: Housing, Displacement, and the American Dream." Doctoral dissertation, Department of Geography, Syracuse University, 2018.

———. "Right to Infrastructure: The Struggle for Sanitation in Fresno, California Homeless Encampments." *Urban Geography* 37 (2016): 1049–1069.

Staeheli, Lynn, and Don Mitchell. "'Don't Talk with Strangers': Regulating Property, Purifying the Public." *Griffith Law Review* 17 (2008): 531–545.

———. *The People's Property? Power, Politics, and the Public.* New York: Routledge, 2008.

Starr, Kevin. *Endangered Dreams: The Great Depression in California.* New York: Oxford University Press, 1996.

Stein, Walter. *California and the Dust Bowl Migration.* Westport, Conn.: Greenwood, 1973.

Steinbeck, John. *The Grapes of Wrath.* New York: Viking, 1939.

Sugrue, Thomas. *Origins of the Urban Crisis.* Princeton, N.J.: Princeton University Press, 1996.

Takahashi, Lois. *Homelessness, AIDS and Stigmatization: The* NIMBY *Syndrome in the*

United States Near the End of the Twentieth Century. Oxford: Oxford University Press, 1984.

Tank, R. "Mobility and Occupational Structure in the Late Nineteenth-Century Frontier: The Case of Denver, Colorado." *Pacific Historical Review* 47 (1978): 211–214.

Taylor, Steven J. *Acts of Conscience: World War II, Mental Institutions, and Religious Objectors.* Syracuse, N.Y.: Syracuse University Press, 2009.

Thompson, E. P. *The Poverty of Theory and Other Essays.* New York: Monthly Review Press, 1978.

Timmons, Heather. "A Fatal Shooting Shows How 'Safer Cities' Initiative in Los Angeles Failed Skid Row." *Quartz*, March 2, 2015.

Tsemberis, Sam, Leyla Gulcur, and Maria Nakae. "Housing First, Consumer Choice, and Harm Reduction for Individuals with a Dual Diagnosis." *American Journal of Public Health* 94 (2004): 651–656.

Tushnet, Mark. "An Essay on Rights." *Texas Law Review* 62 (1984): 1363–1412.

Vitale, Alex. *The End of Policing.* London: Verso, 2017.

Vollmann, William T. "Homeless in Sacramento: Welcome to the Tent Cities." *Harpers*, March 2011, 29–46.

Waldron, Jeremy. "Homelessness and the Issue of Freedom." *UCLA Law Review* 39 (1991): 295–324.

——. *Liberal Rights: Collected Papers, 1981–1991.* Cambridge: Cambridge University Press, 1993.

——. *The Right to Private Property.* Oxford: Clarendon, 1990.

Watters, Stephen. "Homelessness in Sacramento: Searching for Safe Ground." Master's thesis, California State University, Sacramento, 2012.

Wells, Katie. "Policyfailing: The Case of Public Property Disposal in Washington, D.C." *ACME* 13 (2004): 474–494.

White, Richard. *Railroaded: The Transcontinentals and the Making of Modern America.* New York: Norton, 2011.

White, Richard, and Patricia Nelson Limerick, eds. *The Frontier in American Culture.* Berkeley: University of California Press, 1994.

White, William Allen. "A Tenderfoot on Thunder Mountain." *Saturday Evening Post*, November 8, 1902, 1–2, 14–15.

Williams, Raymond. *The Country and the City.* Oxford: Oxford University Press, 1973.

——. *Keywords.* London: Fontana, 1976.

——. *Marxism and Literature.* Oxford: Oxford University Press, 1977.

Woirol, Gregory. "Observing the IWW in California, May–July 1914." *Labor History* 25 (1984): 437–447.

Wolch, Jennifer, and Michael Dear. *Malign Neglect: Homelessness in an American City.* San Francisco: Jossey-Bass, 1993.

Wolch, Jennifer, Afsaneh Rahimian, and Paul Koegel. "Daily and Periodic Mobility Patterns of the Urban Homeless." *Professional Geographer* 45 (1993): 159–169.

Wolch, Jennifer, and Stacey Rowe. "On the Street: Mobility Paths of the Urban Homeless." *City and Society* 6 (1992): 115–140.

Worster, Donald. *Rivers of Empire: Water, Aridity, and the Growth of the American West.* New York: Pantheon, 1985.

Wright, Talmadge. *Out of Place: Homeless Mobilizations, Subcities, and Contested Land-scapes*. Albany: State University of New York Press, 1997

Wyckoff, William. *Creating Colorado: The Making of a Western American Landscape, 1860–1940*. New Haven, Conn.: Yale University Press, 1999.

Young, Iris Marion. *Justice and the Politics of Difference*. Princeton, N.J.: Princeton University Press, 1990.

Ziman, L. "Criminalizing the Charitable." *Z Magazine*, June 1997. www.zmad.org.

Zinn, Howard. "Introduction." In *Food Not Bombs: How to Feed the Hungry and Build Community* edited by C. T. Lawrence and K. McHenry, ix–x. Tucson, Ariz.: See Sharp Press, 2000.

Zylch, J. J. "*Hill v. Colorado* and the Evolving Rights of the Unwilling Listener." *St. Louis University Law Review* 45 (2001): 1281–1307.

INDEX

GEOGRAPHIES OF JUSTICE AND SOCIAL TRANSFORMATION